The Health

and

Management

of the

MASTIFF

Elizabeth J. Baxter
and
Patricia Bennett Hoffman

The History and Management of the Mastiff, 2nd edition
Elizabeth J. Baxter and Patricia B. Hoffman

Published by Dogwise Publishing
403 S. Mission St
Wenatchee WA 98801
1-800-776-2665
www.dogwisepublishing.com
email: info@dogwisepublishing.com

Photos and pedigrees from the authors' collection.

Limits of Liability and Disclaimer of Warranty:
The authors and publisher shall not be liable in the event of incidental or consequential damages in connection with, or arising out of, the furnishing, performance, or use of the information and suggestions contained in this book.

Cataloging-in-Publication Data is available upon request from the Library of Congress

ISBN 1-929242-16-6

Printed in the U.S.A

Acknowledgments

The United Kingdom
Elizabeth J. Baxter

1984 Edition: My sincere and heartfelt thanks to the following for their help:

Mr. David Blaxter, Miss B. Blackstone, Mrs. M. Hector, Mr. Bob Burn, Mrs. H. Mellish, Mr. Merle Campbell, Mrs. H. Taylor, Mrs. M. Reardon, Dr. A. Mayne, Mr. Raymond Boatwright, Mrs. L. Pratt (for her invaluable assistance with old Bull Mastiff pedigrees), Oxford University Press, the staff of the Kennel Club Reference Library, and Mr. Denis Baxter.

2004 Edition: I would like to thank Mr. Douglas Oliff for his assistance with this revision and the following people who have so kindly given me information about the state of the breed in various countries. Without their help, the chapter on "Mastiffs World Wide" would be very skimpy and uninteresting. Their help is hereby most gratefully acknowledged:

Austria - Dr. Hermann Werner Hager, Belgium - Marcel Wynants, Finland - Satu Leitinen, Germany - Ursula Ungerer, Isolde Schmidt and Mr. J. Feldmann, Denmark - Lise Hjerrild, France - David Blaxter and Anne Marie Class; Holland - Ginie Mortens, Italy - Dr. Lando Barberio, Netherlands - G. Martens, Norway - Finn Harald Roed and Thor Hundstad, Spain - Jose Castillo, Switzerland - Ursula Mueller - Naegli, Sweden - Kristina Lundberg, Russia - Alex Goley

I am bound to have omitted some names, for which I apologize in advance.

The United States of America
Patricia Bennett Hoffman

1984 Edition: I would like to thank the following for their generous help: Schuyler Baldwin, Robert B. Burn, Miss Barbara Blackstone, Merle Campbell, David and Carol Cole, Zita Deviny, Eve Olsen Fisher, Edward and Belva Funk, Vickie Head, John Ingle, Steven Oifer, Marie Moore, Ginette Patch, Charlotte Strong, Mike Gensburger, Jean Greco, Elizabeth Kessler, and Lynn Urban.

I am particularly grateful to Roberta Vesley, of the American Kennel Club Library, and her assistants Marie Fabrizzi and Aida Ferrer. Their contributions, help, and enthusiasm have been of inestimable value.

2004 Edition: I would like to thank the many people who gave information and photographs for this publication: Damara Bolté, Nicki Camerra, Gloria and Charles Cuthbert, Joan Hahn, Deborah Jones, Jo Kromhout, Mary-Louise Owens, Kimberley Wall.

Also, the following people who so kindly submitted information about the state of the breed in Australia and Canada: Danielle Belfield, Ann Briglia, Amasha Caffyn, Jan Morrfew, Clyde Owen, Sarah Reid, Bev Malloy

My apologies to anyone whose name I have inadvertently omitted.

Both authors wish to thank our editor, Charlene Woodward, for her patient and painstaking help with our book. Special thanks to Dr. Bennett Dyke for his assistance with the illustrations.

Publisher's Note

The History and Management of the Mastiff is an impartial and unbiased study of the Mastiff from its early days to the present. For anyone seriously interested in the breed, this is an unexcelled resource. This revised edition has additional information on history, added sections on activities, an overview of Mastiffs worldwide, and many new illustrations and pedigrees.

The authors bring almost 80 years of experience to the project, each having been deeply involved with Mastiffs since the early 1960's. They were personally acquainted with many of the major Mastiff breeders and fanciers of the past century, now long since gone and can be said to have "learned from the best". Because of their long association with the breed, they had unexcelled access to valuable historical documents and materials in conducting their research. Indeed they are themselves experts on the breed in their own countries and have sought to preserve the best of this magnificent breed by bringing this information to the public.

The portion of the book dealing with raising, training and other practical aspects, is based on the authors' experience and is designed to inform both novice and expert on issues specific to this increasingly popular breed. It is not meant to be an exhaustive discussion of those subjects and the reader needs to read widely to keep informed of the best information available.

THE ENGLISH MASTIFF

I had one myself once, which would not suffer anie man to bring in his weapon further than my gate: neigher those that were of my house to be touched in his presence. Or if I had beaten anie of my children, he would gentlie have assaied to catch the rod in his teeth and take it out of my hand, or else pluck downe their cloths to save them from the stripes: - which in my opinion is not unworthy to be notied.

HARRISON, Description of England, C. 1577

Given to Mrs. Baxter by Miss Blackstone – March 1984

Contents

Chapter 1

Pre-1800

Elizabeth J. Baxter

In the writing of a history of the Mastiff, it is necessary to apologise in advance for plagiarising much that has already been published. With so little concrete information available and with articles having been printed since the middle of the last two centuries on the breed, it is impossible to find completely fresh sources and therefore necessary to repeat much of what has already been written.

It seems likely that Mastiffs originated in the Middle East, and dogs of similar appearance are still to be found in Turkey, Russia and Poland. Bas-reliefs in the British Museum, from Babylon, show dogs very similar to the Mastiff as we know it today, with short broad muzzles and heavy bodies. The suggestion that they were brought to this country from Phoenicia seems unlikely, however.

Dogs of this type were native to this country when the Romans invaded (H.D. Kingdon 1871 was emphatic that the Mastiff was a specific breed "as much indigenous to Britain as the elm tree") and were prized for their size and courage. What must be realised is that up until the last century, the word "Mastiff" meant a type, and nobody knows whether the dogs found by the invading Romans were similar to today's Mastiffs or not.

Indeed, some historians claim that the British dogs were not of the molossian type, but were "Pugnaces" or fighting dogs. The name Molossus simply means a large dog, not a specific breed. Many of the big dogs today, of the Mastiff type are called Molossian—probably incorrectly. There may indeed have been animals of this type in Britain then, but other historians think that the native breed was probably lighter, shaggier and longer headed, being used for fighting and hunting. Nobody can say which definition is correct and in any case, cross-breeding would certainly have occurred. Whatever the truth of these opposing views the fact remains that these dogs were big, fierce and courageous. In fact, one Roman writer commenting on them held that they were "of such courage and ferocity that they are unmatched by any other breed." He goes on to say that they almost made a trip to Britain worthwhile! So whatever they are to be called does not seem to me to be of great importance — they were here, they were fierce, and they were prized for their bravery.

A point that should be mentioned here is the statement that they were exported to Rome to fight in the arenas, a Roman official being appointed to oversee this trade. The fact is that there was no such official, and this mistake arose because of an error in spelling and translation, from confusion over the words Cynegii and Gyneggi. An official certainly ran the weaving and printing works, but not the export of dogs. Having said this, I feel that given the love that the Romans had for cruel spectacles, it is not beyond the bounds of possibility that some found their way to Rome. There has always been controversy over this point, Mr. M. B. Wynn and Mr. Kingdon maintaining that there was an official put in charge of their breeding and export, with Mr. E.G. Oliver (who calls Wynn presumptuous, self satisfied and inaccurate) and James Watson (1906) holding the opposite view.

Be that as it may, Strabo, who lived before the conquest of Britain, writes that English Mastiffs were sometimes "bought by the Gauls to serve in the front of their battles".

W. K. Taunton (1903) and H. Kingdon, both agree that "the Mastiff" has been in this country "from time immemorial", perhaps originally as a war dog, but certainly as a housedog and guardian of property and stock. In Saxon times in its role as a watchdog it was known as a Bandog, or tied dog.

It is thought that their name derives from the old French, "Mastin" and Oliver says that it comes from the Latin "Mastinus" meaning housedog. It would appear that although such a big, heavy animal could be used for hunting (see descriptions given in *The Middle English Dictionary*) they were kept primarily for guarding stock against wolves, bears and other predators, especially in the period following the withdrawal of the Roman forces from this country.

The Mastiff is mentioned in the Forest Laws of King Canute (1017-1035) and continued to be kept as guards. In medieval times they were required to be "lawed" when kept near the king's deer forests; this meant that three toes of a front foot had to be cut off "at one blow" and this prevented them from hunting or chasing the deer. Chaucer also mentions Mastiffs.

The early history of the Mastiff is quite fully recorded in *The Middle English Dictionary* and contains some fascinating descriptions:

> Mastiff also maistif, masti, mastives, mastewys. (Blend of mastin & mestif also cp ML mastivus) A large and powerful dog used for hunting, Mastiff (masti) hound, one of the kinds of alaunt (quot: York MGame 65) Watchdog; large dog kept by butchers (al 1387) Trev. Higd. 8.187 Hounds and masteves bee-in alle the forestes of Englelond. Mastif is maner of hounds-byn of cherlich nature and of foul shape. Also of maystiffs and of alauntis ben manygood for the wilde boor. c1475 Bk. Noblesse 16: Every man kepyng the scout wache had a masty hound at a lyes to berke and warne yff ony adverse partye were comyng to the dykes. a1500 (c1440) Lydg. HGS 600-It wer a monstre a-geyn natur. that a gret Mastyff shud a Leoun bynde.

The story of Piers Legh II is well known—how he fell, mortally wounded, and his faithful Mastiff bitch guarded his body that was later brought back Britain for burial. From this bitch descended the Lyme Hall strain of Mastiffs, which were kept "pure" at Lyme Hall until the beginning of the 20th century.

This bitch must, because of the time involved, have been mated in France so the sire of these puppies is most unlikely to have been an English Mastiff. The Lyme Hall Mastiffs from pictures still extant were very different from today's animals. Their muzzles were longer and more tapering, and they look more like a Flat Coated Retriever, and as for colour, they could be piebald or brown and white. They did, however, look very like the Mastiff painted by Van Dyke in his famous portrait of King Charles I's children. The best-known Lyme Hall Mastiff, because it is the only picture available of a comparatively "modern" member of this strain, is Wamba, who seems to have been the last of the line.

The following is a description taken from the *Foure Bookes of Husbandrei* by Conrad Heresbatch, published in 1586. Probably you are familiar with it, but I feel it is worth repeating:

> In choosing a Mastie that keepeth the house you must provide such a one as hath a large, mightie bodie, a great shrill voice that both with his barking he may discover and with his sight dismay the thief-yea being not seen, with the horror of his voice put him to flight. His stature must be neither long nor short but well set; his head great; his eyes sharp and fierce; either brown or grey; his lips blackish neither turning up nor hanging too much down. His mouth blacke and wide his nether jaw far and coming out of it on either side a

fang appearing more outward than his other teeth; his upper teeth even with his neather, not hanging too much over, sharp and hidden with his lips. His countenance like a lion's, his breast great and shag haired; his shoulders broad; his legs big; his tail short; his feet very great. His disposition must be neither too gentle nor too curst that he neither fawn upon a thief nor fly upon his friends. Very waking, no gadder about, nor lavish with his mouth barking without cause. It maketh no matter that he be not swift for he is but to fight at home and to give warning of the enemy. A black dog is best because of the hurt that he may do to the thief by night by reason of not being seen.

The following, taken from an anonymous German Natural History of 1650, may also be of interest:

This kind of dog called a Mastiff or bandog is vast, huge, stubborn, ugly and eager, of a heavie and bourthenous body and therefore but of little swiftness, terrible and frightful to behold and more fierce and fell than any Arcadian cur. They are appointed to watch and keep farm places and country cottages, sequestered from common resourse and not abutting upon other houses, when there is any fear of thieves, robbers or night wanderers. They are serviceable against fox or badger, to drive wild and tame swine, to bait and take the bull by the ear, one dog or two at most is sufficient for that purpose be the bull never so monstrous and fierce. It is a kind of dog capable of courage, violent and valiant, striking cold fear into the hearts of men but standing in fear of no man, no weapons will make him shrink nor abridge his boldness. The fast hold which they take with their teeth exceedeth all credit, three against a bear four against a lion.

During Elizabethan times, Mastiffs were used for bear, bull and lion baiting, and prior to that it is said that Henry VIII once presented 400 Mastiffs to Charles V to be used as fighting dogs in his wars.

In the *British Sportsman's Dictionary* (1792) they are referred to as bandogs, or bond dogs, as they are kept on a chain. The word "Mastiff" seems here to mean guarding dog and was used for both Mastiffs and Bulldogs, simply to indicate a watch dog (Hutchinson's *Encyclopaedia*).

By the late eighteenth century, with the decline in bull and bear baiting, Mastiffs had become extremely scarce and had deteriorated; in fact in 1800 Sydenham Edwards wrote that the breed was nearly extinct and had been "bastardised by crosses" although purebred animals could still be found at a few places, namely at Lyme Hall in Cheshire, at Chatsworth (the Duke of Devonshire's estate), at the Earls of Harrington at Elvaston Castle, at Bold Hall in Lancashire and at the kennels of Mr. (or Commissioner) Thompson of Halifax in Yorkshire. Even so, Stonehenge writing much later in 1872, quotes from a letter said to have been written by Lt. Col. Garnier, a breeder of Mastiffs from 1850 onwards, claiming that the Chatsworth dogs were in fact "Alpine Mastiffs".

About 1800 Mr. Thompson (who is not to be confused with J. W. Thompson, his grandson, and the owner of Dorah in the 1820's) bred one of his three bitches, Rose, to Robinson's Bold, to produce Holdsworth's Lion. From this line come the dogs of the nineteenth century and the revival of the breed, with its accompanying arguments and dissensions as to type, purity of breed, and outcrossing.

1.1 Mastiff, A Brindle Dog. Oil painting by James Ward, 1815. (Collection unknown). U.K.

1.2 The Mastiff, Wood engraving by Thomas Bewick. (From *History of the Quadrupeds,* 1790). U.K.

The History and Management of the Mastiff

Chapter 2

1800-1900

The United Kingdom   *Elizabeth J. Baxter*

Before going into the revival of the breed in the nineteenth century, it may be as well here to give a few words as to the author's own feelings regarding the Mastiff, as a breed and a type.

I think that I must agree with Dalziel, writing in 1889, when he says that "I do not for a moment think that wolfhounds, bulldogs or Mastiffs such as the names now cover, were represented at the Roman time except in a rough, typical way. The description handed down to us is too meagre to admit any degree of accuracy". Stonehenge in 1882 says "The bulldog and the old English Mastiff have been bred in this country since earliest times but whether they have always been separate is something that cannot be settled."

It is my own feeling that the word "Mastiff" in the past covered many slightly different types of dog; and it is my personal view that large dogs were called "Mastiffs" just as today working dogs are called "collies" and inside this group of Mastiffs there were some strains that kept pure, others that were crossed with Talbots, Alaunts and other hounds. Dogs were not bred, until the 20th century, for looks alone but for working ability, so pedigrees as we know them would have been immaterial. If the "pure" type did all that was required of it, then it would stay pure; if not, other blood would be brought in.

Reading the violent arguments between Wynn, Kingdon and, later, James Watson, as to type, dogs used, and purity of stock, causes a wry smile. Accusations of breeding with Bull Mastiffs, Alpine Mastiffs and Bulldogs are made; but with the scarcity of stock at the turn of the eighteenth century it would have been difficult to revitalise the breed without recourse to such outcrossing.

Before proceeding to the dogs of the latter half of the nineteenth century and later, let us try to ascertain how the breed was re-established and stabilised and what animals were used. As we have seen, there were the dogs from Lyme Hall—the original Lyme Hall Mastiffs who, according to their pictures, did not look like the Mastiffs of today—the Chatsworth strain, the Elvastons and the Bold Halls.

The foundation stones, if such they can be called, of the revival were Commissioner Thompson of Halifax, circa 1800, already mentioned; followed closely by his grandson Mr. J. W. Thompson; Mr. T. H. Lukey; Mr. George White; the Holdsworths, and Mr. John Crabtree a game-keeper employed by Sir George Armitage of Kirkless Hall, Yorkshire. Of these, perhaps the most prominent were Mr. T. H. Lukey—called by Mr. M. B. Wynn "the father of the modern Mastiff" and Mr. Thompson Jr., who continued his breeding activities into the 1870's and, again quoting from Wynn, was "one of our oldest breeders".

John Crabtree, who was a contemporary of the elder Thompson, found a brindle bitch caught in a trap set for foxes (pedigree obviously unknown) and named her Duchess. She was mated to Holdsworth's Lion the son of Thompson's Rose and Robinson's Bold, becoming the double great-grandmother and great-great-grandmother of J. W. Thompson's foundation bitch, Dorah, born 1825. Dorah's breeder is put as Sir George Armitage, Crabtree's employer.

Mr. T. H. Lukey's first bitch was a cropped, docked brindle which he got from the well known dealer George White. She was called Old Bob Tailed Countess and was said by Wynn (and James Watson, in his *Book of the Dog*, 1906) to be an "Alpine" although Lukey himself said that she was of the Chatsworth strain. She was mated to a dog called Pluto belonging to the Marquis of Hertford and one of the progeny, Wallace, died in 1840. This means that Lukey was operating slightly after Crabtree and Thompson the first, probably about the same time as J. W. Thompson Jr. Pluto, again according to James Watson was a "black, rough coated Tibetan Mastiff". As to the ancestry of Old Bob Tailed Countess, whether she was in fact an Alpine or not, cannot now be proved one way or another. It cannot be deniedk, however, that in those days, long before rabies regulations and quarantine, St. Bernards—or Alpine Mastiffs—which were often smooth-coated, were brought into the country by English gentlemen who had been traveling abroad and such outcrossing is more than likely. One of Countess's pups, named Yarrow, was mated to the famous Couchez, a true Alpine Mastiff and this was the foundation of Lukey's kennel.

It is difficult to trace the dogs of the early part of the century with any degree of certainty because the same names are used over and over again and the only way to differentiate is to put the name of the owner before the name of each dog. Thus we get Salt's Lion; Thompson's Duchess; Lukey's Governor; Hanbury's Countess; and the names are used in subsequent generations. One reads that Lukey mated Countess with Col. Garnier's Lion and produced Governor, a very famous Mastiff; but this Countess was not his original Old Bob Tailed Countess but her great-granddaughter. The names Countess, Duchess, Duke, King, Tiger, are bandied about and interspersed with such names as White's Dog; a daughter of Duchess; a daughter of the Duke of Devonshire's bitch; so it is difficult at this stage to keep track. What we do know however is that from the dogs bred by Mr. Lukey and Mr. Thompson Jr. many of the best of the nineteenth century Mastiffs are descended. Other famous breeders in the century were the Marquis of Hertford (owner of the "black" Pluto), Lord Waldegrave—who owned Couchez the Alpine Mastiff—the Duke of Sutherland, Messrs Brewer, Beaufoy, Nichols and Cook; Capt. Piddocke, Col. Garnier, Miss Aglionby, Miss Hales and Mrs. Rawlinson.

Mr. J. W. Thompson in the 1850's bred Tiger from who are descended more famous Mastiffs of the 1870's and 1880's such as Ch. Beau, Ch. Cambrian Princess, Ch. Beaufort and Ch. Minting, the last two being exported to America.

Another very famous dog bred by Thompson Jr. was Quaker, known as Cautley's Quaker because of the name of his owner and to distinguish him from another dog of the same name. He was born in 1859 by Thompson's Saladin out of Thompson's Duchess and a look at his pedigree will show that he is descended from Lukey's Yarrow (Pluto/Old Bob Tail Countess) and, through Thompson's Dorah, to the elder Thompson's two original bitches, Rose and Trusty.

I will here refer to James Watson, a gentleman discussed more fully later in this chapter, but the comments in his book concerning both Thompson's Dorah and Cautley's Quaker deserve to be included here in the interests of clarity.

Watson took great delight in trying to prove that Mastiff pedigrees were, on the whole, very suspect as far as purity was concerned and I would like to quote from a paragraph in his *The Dog Book* where he is writing about these two animals. He says: "Dorah was bred to Fenton's Tiger and from this mating came Athrington Hall Lion. To this dog Mr. Thompson bred a bitch called Cymba—a smooth fawn 26 inches in height. From this mating came Thornton's Juno. Dorah was also mated with a dog of Sir Wilmott's called Lion. There is some doubt as to Bess in this litter. In the Turk pedigree Bess is put down as the dam of Dr. Ellis's Lion, whereas Wynn says Bess went to Crabtree as a puppy and that this Lion was out of Thompson's Juno. It is not a material point, as all we desire to show is where the "back numbers" came from—one bitch, one quarter Great Dane bred to dogs not one of which had a known pedigree.

Mr. Watson tends to belabour this point of purity ad infinitum but the part in his book which I find puzzling is that according to him, Wilmott's Dora and Thompson's Dorah (see the Cautley pedigree in Appendix 1) were one and the same animal. If this is so, Thornton's Juno mated back to her own father, and Dorah was indeed the dam of both Lion and Thompson's Bess.

Let us leave the complicated ancestry of Quaker and turn our attention to another well-known Mastiff born in 1867: this was Turk, one of Miss Hilda Aglionby's famous litter of five which included Wolf, Knight Templar, Emperor and Prince. The sire was King and the dam was Hilda, litter sister to Ch. Lion.

Cautley's Quaker lies some four generations behind Turk and thus once again one can trace the line back through Turk, Cautley's Quaker and Dorah to Thompson's Rose. But before going into more detail of the dogs of the latter part of the century, let us continue to examine the differences of opinion that were voiced as to the "purity" of the Mastiff. Admittedly, these opinions were published in the 1880's, 1890's and early 1900's, but they concerned animals of the early period of the eighteen hundreds.

One has to remember, trying to unravel the writings concerned, that over seventy years is being covered, the first half of which, even to the writers themselves, must have seemed almost like another age. This did not, however, stop them from voicing their opinions most strongly.

As far as these deep disagreements as to purity are concerned, it is probably easier to quote verbatim from articles written by the principal protagonists and we will start with Mr. H. D. Kingdon, writing in 1871, who was the champion of the Lyme Hall strain and who owned one of the Lyme Hall dogs. Prior to 1871, the time when Kingdon was writing, it was being claimed by Idstone, a contributor to the *Field* magazine, that the Mastiff breed had recently been resuscitated by crossing the bulldog with the boarhound. This claim drove Kingdon to a frenzy. He maintained that this "new breed" of which Miss Aglionby's (1867) five famous dogs were early examples, were all different in type and were descended from Lord Darnley's Nell, alleged to be a bull terrier bitch. In his article on "Non Sporting Dogs, Chapter 10", edited by Henry Webb,

Kingdon writes:

> I write to uphold the ancient and not the modern Mastiff ... to refute the fallacy of his originating in the talbot and the bulldog, a doctrine convenient to breeders who insist no Mastiff has a pedigree of 40 years standing and who have "manufactured" for our shows a big cross bred dog that has been exhibited under the name of Mastiff. How can descendants of Lord Darnley's Nell be true old English Mastiffs? What bone or bulk have they? Are not their limbs small or relatively so? Has not the rage for height incorporated staghound and resulted in the tall leggy dog with little bone, light limbs, houndy in barrel, weak in loin, flat flank and cow hocks?

The main plank of Kingdon's argument was that the only true, pure strains of Mastiffs left in the country at that time were those emanating from Lyme Hall (the fact that he had been lucky enough to obtain some of these animals may well have had something to do with it) and from Elvaston Castle. He admits that the Duke of Devonshire's Chatsworth strain was also pure but thinks that his is now extinct, leaving only Lyme Hall and Elvaston Castle as homes for the old original breed of Mastiff. Again, quoting from Kingdon:

> It behoves every Englishman to endeavour to restore this dog to its pristine purity by judicious breeding from the best ascertained pedigrees. To do this if purity is to be recovered we must breed from something less equivocal than many of the late prize winners, the cross bred specimens or we shall not get a Mastiff but a compound bulldog and wolfhound.

One reads these fierce and passionate arguments for and against certain breeders with a certain amount of compassion; does it not sound all too familiar today?

The other protagonist in this running battle was M. B. Wynn, well known as the author of *The Mastiff 1886*, who replied to Kingdon in another edition of Webb's *Dogs: Their Points, Whims, Instincts and Peculiarities* printed in 1873. He was concerned chiefly with pedigrees, and with proving that there were pure strains other than Lyme Hall, but also maintaining that was not necessarily a bad thing. In one rather biting paragraph Wynn comments:

> Nor do I enter into the vexed question of the origin of the Mastiff; I have my own theory; and will only say that I cannot suppose the Mastiff was the original type from which all others came. Climate, breeding, domestication will, we all know, change the leading

characteristics of any breed. . . . Permit me to observe, that I am neither writing down nor pointing my arguments against the pure Lyme Hall breed, i.e., the strain possessed by Mr. Legh, but in any remarks which I as a fancier hazard, I do so entirely against the *so called strain* of Mr. Kingdon's. If I were asked, I must say that Mr. Kingdon's dogs fall immeasurably short and are far different from those of Mr. Legh's and many of the leading characteristics are totally at variance.

He then goes on to say that he and other leading breeders find that the best results were obtained from a cross of the eldest and highest bred stock, with Lord Darnley's Nell's strain and he holds that the truest type of Mastiff head is found in the descendants of this bitch and the grand head of Ch. King is attributable to her—"the best blood without taint of bull is to be found in Mr. Hanbury's kennels".

Other old and leading Mastiff breeders listed by Wynn, apart from those which I have already mentioned, were King, Pemberton and Hanbury. Pedigrees that he lists are fascinating and he says that he has letters affirming Mr. Cautley's Quaker's pedigree goes back to at least 1815 "and some of us can keep clean of any bull cross *were we so inclined*" (my italics).

Without first-hand knowledge of the in-fighting that was obviously going on and the dogs concerned, names bandied about by Wynn are often misleading and I think it might be more enlightening if I quoted part of his article:

...Mr. Wm. Thompson, one of our oldest breeders; since it is known that he bred Bill George's Tiger, Cautley's Quaker, Saladin and many other good dogs, and that even that "father of modern Mastiffs", Mr. Lukey, crossed with Mr. Thompson's strain in the height of his palmy days...

At the present hour I own Brenda, a brindled bitch, by Druid out of his own sister June (1st Birmingham, 1868). Also Fan the Third, a fawn bitch, a true descendant of Cautley's Quaker's sister, crossed with Lyme Hall Mastiff. But though her blood is perfect, I by no means consider her my best specimen. I own also Bell, a grand brindled bitch, standing 27 inches, and 119 lbs. weight, with immense bone, good loin, and skull equally full as any bitch descended from Darnley's Nell. Bell is by Hanbury's Prince, and through him goes back to Saladin, and Bill G.'s old Tiger, whose pedigree goes back to 1815. Bell is first cousin to Hanbury's Phyllis . . . Now this is what I call pedigree and as I happen to be a very interested party, I should rejoice if I could obtain reliable proof that my well known bitch Empress (a granddaughter of Alp), could trace, her pedigree to anything as good as Wamba [the Lyme Hall dog] or any of Mr. Legh's strain. May I ask Mr. K. for the proof that Alp ever came from Lyme Hall? And if so what was the name of either sire and dam? what relation is she to Wamba?

Mr. Wynn's whole argument seems to be that Lyme Hall animals are not necessarily as good as those of Messrs. Lukey, Thompson, Hanbury, etc., who bred ones just as good but very often using an outcross for improvement.

The other writer talking about the early and mid-nineteenth century (whose book, known as either *The Book of the Dog*, or *The Dog Book*, was published in 1906) was James Watson whom I have already quoted on the subject of the ancestry of Thompson's Dorah and Cautley's Quaker.

Watson contradicted almost every other Mastiff writer, breeder and enthusiast. He maintained, probably correctly, that the "Mastiff of earliest writings" was not the Mastiff of "today". He held that the evidence of paintings regarding the dog called the Mastiff before 1800 did not show any great dissimilarity between Mastiff and Bulldog in either size or type. Watson thought that Wynn and others were so anxious to believe Mastiffs were a separate and pure breed that they twisted the facts; and there may well have been more than a grain of truth in this. In fact, what he says is so much at variance with all others that I feel I must quote him verbatim. "The Mastiff was the common dog, bred anyhow, and not recognised as a fit companion for the higher classes." "We owe our Mastiff to a few obscurely picked up dogs of unknown origin and from others that were either halfbred Great Danes or dogs known as Alpine Mastiffs." "The Lyme Hall strain was undoubtedly of alaunt descent."

He castigates the foundation stock of Thompson the first, and Crabtree, as well as Lukey and Thompson Jr., although admitting that all dogs of the latter part of the nineteenth century go back to those bred by them. "It will be seen what very slight support there is for the claim that the Mastiff is descended in all its purity from a magnificent lot of dogs of the highest breeding for many generations and through several centuries. The patent facts are that from a number of dogs of various types of English watchdogs and baiting dogs, running from 26 inches to 29 or perhaps 30 inches in height, crossed with continental dogs of Great Dane and of old fashioned St. Bernard type, the Mastiff has been elevated through the efforts of English breeders to the dog he became about twenty years ago."

One despairs at this distance of saying who was right and who was wrong. Probably as is so often the case, they both were wrong in part. But were Mastiffs in the early 1800's crossed with other breeds? I should say almost certainly. Were they as good or better than the original strain? Who can say? It is almost certain that over the centuries dogs were bred for working ability, stamina and temperament, not merely for looks, so keeping a strain "pure" would not be all that important in pre-registration and pre-Kennel Club days. About the time of Wynn, Kingdon and the others, showing and looks were coming more to the fore and breeding as such and the keeping of pedigrees more important. Before that, although pedigrees can indeed be traced back to circa 1800, it is nearly all hearsay and guesswork with few written records. One can only say that there was obviously just as much dissension in the 1800's as there as ever been. Whether the Mastiff as it found itself at the turn of the century was the same or very different from those dogs called Mastiffs at the start of the same century, is only speculation. The blood is there, even though perhaps diluted, and the breed is an old and honourable one, even if not as pure as some breeders would like to believe.

Let us now proceed to the other bone of contention—type. As the breeding of pedigree dogs gained popularity over the latter part of the 1800's, controversy also raged over the true appearance of the Mastiff as well as of its origin. Any large guard dog had come to be known as a "Mastiff" and all heavily built animals were being called Mastiffs. Of the Lyme Hall dogs, it was claimed that they had pure lineage back to 1415 and writers of the nineteenth century argued for and against this. This Lyme Hall claim was impossible to prove but it is it fact that there was a kennel of large dogs claiming to be the original old type of Mastiff at Lyme Hall until 1903 when they died out. They were never shown competitively and their use in "outside" breeding was almost unknown. Kingdon owned several and showed them with some success, but they were of a different type than the more easily available dogs of the accepted norm. They had longer, tapering muzzles and were of a different colour.

Compton, writing in 1904, comments on the likeness of the Lyme Hall dogs, especially Wamba, to the dog depicted by Van Dyke and thinks that they differ substantially from:

> . . . the type accepted today, which favours the short muzzle as distinct from the long.

. . . In three engravings, which I have before me, of Mastiffs depicted in the first quarter of the last century, two are distinctly "hound-headed" dogs, —the stop being situated in the approximate position of the Great Dane, —and the third so nearly a counterpart of the bulldog type, that it is difficult to distinguish it at a glance from the bulldog of the period. . . From this it is clear that if there is a divergence of opinion on the point, it is not one of purely modern date. And there certainly is a small modern minority which holds to the hound like muzzle, provided it is accompanied with breadth and depth.

This argument as to type, long muzzled or short being correct, would appear to have been going on since the mid-nineteenth century and continues today. Of the Bulldog type of Mastiff, accepted as correct in the latter part of the century, Leadbetter asserts:

I would mention that in 1866 my late father had a dog whose head was a facsimile of Ch. Holland's Black Boy today. *A longheaded mastiff is an abomination.* . . The long heads are so easy to breed in comparison to the right type.

J. Sydney Turner, in an article published in 1908, preferred the right type:

At the present time there is on the part of Mastiff exhibitors a craze for abnormally short muzzles which to the minds of many of those who knew the breed in its palmiest days is a kind of obsession.

It was to Crown Prince (whelped 1880) that the shorter head in Mastiffs is due. There is no nobler looking dog and but few nobler looking animals than a well proportioned and active Mastiff, but there are few more pitiable sights than a crippled giant. Why should the head of a dog atone for all other defects in structure? Mastiffs of the present day do not hold the high place in the mind of the public that they did in the 80's because of the absurd craze for shorter and shorter heads so that the dog has degenerated into a monstrosity.

Sydney Turner goes on to say "the short square head which most of our judges admire is not likely to be found associated with great length of body and well let down hocks because the head is a sort of fifth limb—as in most things the happy mediums seem to promise the best success, and this should be the keynote of our theme".

Taunton, writing in 1903, but again writing of actual animals living in the last two decades of the previous century, says:

That the Mastiff is not so popular at the present time as it was some years ago is a fact that cannot be denied. . . Possibly this lack of interest in the breed is to some extent attributable to these dogs having of late years been bred with abnormally short muzzles, the result being that many of the characteristics of the breed have been changed. . . The Mastiff of recent years has approached far too near to the Bulldog to please the general public. . . . That the Mastiff is a short-muzzled dog every one will admit, but there is a medium in everything; breadth and depth of muzzle are, in the writer's opinion, of more consequence than extreme shortness and, at the same time, more difficult to obtain.

There you have the differences of opinion ranging from Leadbetter's "a long headed Mastiff is an abomination" through to Sydney Turner's "absurd craze for shorter and shorter heads", while Taunton's "a medium in everything" should strike a responsive note in today's breeders.

Having discussed pedigrees and purity and touched on type, let us look briefly at the more mundane events of the latter part of the 19th century, at the breeders, the dogs, the show results and the registration figures.

Although the kennel club was not formed until 1873, dog shows as such began in 1859 and six Mastiffs were benched at Birmingham show in 1860. Mr. Hanbury's Empress won first prize. After 1870 progress was rapid and the decade 1870-1880 was the zenith of the Mastiff in that century. In 1871 there were 64 Mastiffs at the Crystal Palace show and in 1872 there were 81. In 1871 at Birmingham there were 29 entries in the open dog class.

Breeders of this era were John Wigglesworth, Edgar Hanbury, Loftus Leigh, J. K. Field, and Edwin Nichols. By 1885 a great number of Mastiffs were, as previously mentioned, descended from Lukey's Governor or Bill George's Tiger, Cautley's Quaker, etc. Miss Aglionby's Turk, born 1867, had a profound influence on the breed as did a dog born 13 years later in 1880, Ch. Crown Prince.

This famous, or infamous, dog was said to be by Young Prince (although doubt was thrown on this) out of Merlin. He had a superb head and with the craze for head type, he was used extensively at stud. However, he had straight stifles, cow hocks, a very weak back and, according to contemporary writers, he was a cripple. He also had a Dudley nose, which did not, strangely enough, seem to come through to his offspring but his unsoundness made W. K. Taunton, writing 25 years later, say: "We are still suffering for this today."

Dogs which were a good influence on the breed however, were Mr. Beaufoy's Beau, sire of Beaufort "the best all round Mastiff that has been seen for many years"; Cambrian Princess, the dam of Ch. Minting; the famous brindle Cardinal; Maximilian, son of The Emperor; Monarch; Rajah, his son Wolsey, another brindle; and Brampton Beauty, bred by Capt. Piddocke and owned by my grandfather, Mr. W. Norman Higgs.

In 1883, the Old English Mastiff Club was formed, thereby achieving the honour of being one of the oldest breed clubs in existence; but after 1880 the numbers of Mastiffs declined, as registration figures show. In 1880 there were 40 registrations; in 1881, 63 (it must be remembered that the figures for the most part reflect births in the previous year) and in 1893 only 26 animals were registered.

In 1890 however, on Friday 22nd August, the Old English Mastiff Club proudly held its "First Exhibition of Mastiffs" at the Crystal Palace with an entry of 51 animals. Amongst these were Ch. Hotspur, son of Ch. Crown Prince, and owned by Mr. W. K. Taunton, and Ch. The Lady Isabel owned by Dr. J. Sydney Turner. Mr. Taunton had ten Mastiffs entered at this show and Mr. Sydney Turner had nine including three puppies. Mr. Court Rice entered six and Mr. Norman Higgs five. It would seem that then, as in the 1960's, a handful of breeders supported the club's show with multiple entries.

One of the well-known winners of this time, was a dog called Ch. Ilford Caution who was subsequently exported to America. It may be of interest to list some of his "vital statistics" which are shown as follows: Length from tip of nose to stop 3 ¼ inches; length from stop to occiput 7 inches; girth of muzzle 17½ inches; girth of skull 28 inches; girth of neck 26 inches; girth of body from shoulders behind forearm 40 inches; girth round loins 35 inches; girth round stifle joint 21 inches; girth of forearm 11½ inches; girth of elbow 11 inches; girth of pastern 7 inches; and height at shoulder 32 inches. His weight "in fair condition" was given as 175 lb. Not a big dog by today's standards, perhaps, but one of the leading stud dogs of his day. He was advertised at stud as being the most likely sire to add head and muzzle to snipey bitches, and was described in show reports as "a dog of great size and bone, with a grandly massive head. From muzzle to end of tail he is every inch a Mastiff".

At Crufts Show in 1896 a contest took place between two famous Mastiffs, Ch. Peter Piper (born 1893) owned by Mr. Royle, a beautiful brindle, and Beaufort's Black Prince, called the best Mastiff in America, who had been imported into this country by Mr. Norman Higgs. The judge was Mr. H. G. Woolmore, Peter Piper's breeder, who adjudged this dog the winner. I can remember my mother talking about Black Prince, whom she had seen as a very young girl, and I only wish that I had taken more notice of my mother's recollections of the Mastiffs with which she was brought up.

By 1900 there were only three Challenge Certificate winners noted in the *Stud Book*, Elgiva, Holland's Black Boy and Marksman.

To conclude this discussion, let us look briefly at some of the sizes and weights of dogs registered. It will be seen that, as with Ilford Caution, the dogs of today are far bigger and heavier than those of 100 years ago.

Nero, February 1875; fawn by Monarch x Grace - 175 lbs.

His Lordship 1877 - 155 lbs.

Cardinal (brindle) 1880 - 155 lbs.

Crown Prince 1880 - 180 lbs.

Lady Gladys 29.5.1881 (Ch. Crown Prince x Lady Rowena)-126 lbs.

Finally a few show critiques published in the *Kennel Gazette* of that era which may prove amusing and interesting:

Critique of a show in 1880, by E. Hanbury: "I do not consider it any detriment to a Mastiff to possess a long muzzle provided it is broad in proportion. This is the view as confirmed by our oldest breeder, Mr. Lukey."

A critique on Ilford Cromwell a blue brindle, printed in the July 1882 *Kennel Gazette*; "sour headed with badly set ears and sly suspicious looking eye".

"Nero, coarse and head not the right shape."

"Emperor has quantity without quality; he is goggle eyed, slack in limbs and deficient in hock."

Perhaps we, now bemoaning the fact that show critiques are so seldom written, should read the above carefully and be grateful that judges are not quite so outspoken today.

The United States of America   *Patricia B. Hoffman*
The idea of a noble Mastiff accompanying the Pilgrims to the New World may be a pleasing one, but there appears to be no positive evidence that the breed came with the early settlers. It is possible, of course, that large dogs were passengers on the overcrowded *Mayflower*, but in the absence of any documentation, we will note it as an interesting

theory. The same may be said of the reputed Mastiffs in the South, who supposedly protected the colonists and caused the Indians to flee in terror at the sight of the strange beasts.

There are occasional references to Mastiffs in early books (James Fenimore Cooper mentions the breed), but, again, lacking pictures or accurate descriptions, we cannot be sure of the relationship of these presumably large dogs to the animals we know of in the latter part of the 19th century.

Since the background and early history of the Mastiff have been traced in the previous chapter, and since all the American stock came from the British Isles, this chapter will consider the breed from the time it made its first documented appearance in the United States.

Among the earliest imports about which we have any information were a pair brought in by E. Delafield Smith in 1871. According to W. Wade, who wrote in the American Kennel Register of February 1888, the dog was Pluto, bred by Frank Robinson. He was by old Ch. Turk (E. 2349) out of Countess. The bitch, Venus, was also sired by Turk, but out of Quakeress, bred by F. Heinzeman. Wade noted: "The pedigrees given Mr. Smith were singularly accurate and careful."

One of the first American-bred Mastiffs we can be specific about was a fawn dog named Jack. His dam, Juno, was imported by Arthur Austin of Massachusetts in 1871, and was bred to another import named Dash, from Wales. Jack was whelped in 1872, and was chosen to represent the breed in a portfolio of prints of dogs by Alexander Pope, a noted animal artist of the time. The colored print, dated 1880, has the following information on its accompanying sheet:

Jack was born Aug. 2, 1872, being the choicest of Juno's (called Brenda in England) pups. The father of Jack is Dash, an English Mastiff imported from Cardiff, Wales, by D. D. Kelley, Esq.

Juno was the mother of Jack, and imported by Hon. Arthur W. Austin, Nov. 1, 1871. She was of the oldest strain of Mastiffs in the kingdom, when there were but few Mastiffs in England. She was bred by Mr. Webb of Calcot, near Reading, Berkshire, and was sister to Empress that sold for £100 in England.

Jack is the father of many famous Mastiffs in New England. He was never shown but once—Boston, 1878 when he received first prize; also special for the best Mastiff in the show.

The print shows Jack looking very much like our dogs of today, with perhaps a slightly longer muzzle than we prefer. His back is level, angulation good, and he appears generally well balanced. Size is hard to determine, as he is shown on a terrace in front of a railing, but he seems quite large.

The Boston show where Jack won his prizes was held on 26th, 27th, 28th and 29th March 1878. It was the "First Annual Exhibition Bench Show of Dogs by the Massachusetts Kennel Club". (The first dog show in America had been held only a few years before, in 1874.)

There were 21 other Mastiffs entered, a very respectable number by any standard. Several were sired by Jack—at least seven can be identified as his progeny. As the show took place before dogs had registration numbers most of the pedigrees, if given, were less than informative. For example, it was stated that an entry was "sired by Hunnewell's dog". Another stated the Mastiff was by "One-Eyed Turk x Jessie". Furthermore many dogs had the same name; there were innumerable Turks of the period.

The Westminster Kennel Club's "First Annual New York Bench Show" was held in May 1877. Its catalogue was reprinted on the Club's 100th anniversary and the following information was taken from it.

There were 25 Mastiffs entered, and one Dido had her puppy (age not given) with her. The judge was the Rev. J. Cumming Macdona, an English breeder of St. Bernards, who also judged that breed, plus Gordon Setters and Pointers. According to Stonehenge, in the 1887 edition of *The Dogs of Great Britain, America, and Other Countries*, who listed show winners at New York from 1877 through 1886, prizes went to Vandal and Norma, who each won $10 for their owner, A. A. Brown of England. Norma's entry, a typical one, read: "NORMA, two years; by Rajah, No. 2,333, out of Nellie; full pedigree. 200 guineas."

Pedigrees were skimpy, to put it mildly. The most detailed was that of Mr. G. H. Andrews' entry, Young Ivan, listed as:

Fawn, with black points, four years; by Ivan, Ivan by Broadwood's Captain, out of Broadwood's Brenda. Young Ivan winner of 2nd prize at Crystal Palace, England; his sire, Ivan winner of 1st prize. Not for sale.

Other dogs were offered in a wide price range, from King Olaf "formerly Young Sultan" at $1000, down to $50 for a young "brown" dog named Lion.

The History and Management of the Mastiff

At these early shows there were frequently dogs with the same name, and as in the case of Young Sultan, names changed. Warwick shown in 1880, later became Duke. Further confusion occurred, as in 1882, when in Mastiff Class 4 at New York, Mastiff bitches, "John Fox's puppies by Askhim" were transferred from Class 12, which was Smooth Coated St. Bernards!

Early records were most confusing. The first "official" stud book was issued in 1878 as the *National American Kennel Club Stud Book*, but it listed only sporting breeds. Volume II did not appear until 1885, at which time all breeds were entered.

Prior to this, Mastiffs, if registered at all, were entered in the *American Kennel Register*, which was published from 1883 to 1888, when it was combined with the *American Kennel Club Stud Book*. This meant that for the years 1885 to 1888 there were actually two registers. A dog could have had an "A" number, indicating listing with the American Kennel Club; or "AKR" for the *Register*; or "E" denoting English Kennel Club.

The *Register* first appeared weekly, later monthly, and carried information on all breeds. The fee for entering a dog in their "Pedigree Register" was 25 cents and a penny stamped envelope. Later the price was raised, and in January 1885, the editor wrote: "... it was not without some misgiving that we decided upon fifty cents, fearing a marked falling off in the number of entries." Apparently the doubled cost had no ill effect, as the editor noted that in the previous month over two hundred dogs had been listed.

In addition to registering, owners could also "claim" a kennel name (cost, if any, not given). Sales, changes of ownership, stud service and deaths were noted. The pages of the magazine make fascinating reading, as there is much material on Mastiffs.

Much of this information was contributed by William Wade, an enthusiastic breeder and promoter in the 1880's of very decided opinions. He was a wealthy philanthropist from Philadelphia, who was particularly interested in the handicapped. This led to his friendship with Helen Keller, and he presented her with one of his Mastiffs. Miss Keller, then nine years old, wrote to him in 1889 that: "the beautiful Mastiff puppy you sent me has arrived ... I should like to call her Lioness, for your dog." Sadly, however, Lioness was killed the following year when she wandered into town and was shot by a zealous policeman. Wade gave the child another dog, and in 1892 she wrote to a friend: "And I have another beautiful Mastiff-the largest one I ever saw. . .His name, is Eumer." Wade, in addition to giving Miss Keller a pony and a donkey, helped her family financially and she was a frequent visitor at his home in Hulton.

To return to the *Register*. Articles by W. Wynn on Mastiffs were printed; visits to famous kennels; and very candid comments on shows and dogs. In 1887, Wade wrote tartly: "Peeress is shown. . .as rather longer headed than Old Champion Turk, and one of the most majestic faces I ever saw, totally free from the disgusting snub nosed, conceited looking beasts now dubbed Mastiffs." The controversy over head type raged throughout the entire period that the *Register* appeared.

Remarks on shows were equally blunt. On the New York show of 1883: "Nevison has a bad habit of knuckling over at times, and did so in the ring." He placed first, however, and won the "Champion Dog Class" in New York the following year. At other shows: "Creole could hardly walk across the ring." "Jumbo had bad ears." There was also "much grumbling about judging".

The Illinois Kennel Club's First Annual Bench Show of Dogs took place in Chicago in June 1885. There were 12 entries in three and a half classes, the half class being for puppies of both sexes. The last consisted of three littermates by Spartacus out of Beauty II, and were priced at $50 and $60. Class One "Champion Mastiffs—Dogs or Bitches" had but one entry, Homer, owned by Winlawn Kennels of New York. Of the five entries in the second class "Mastiffs - Dogs", two were from the same kennel, and the sire of the puppies was also entered. Winlawn had two of the three bitches, and only one of their entries was for sale: Hector (Nevison x Venus) for $200.

These early shows were quite different from those of today. All were benched, and lasted three or four days. Winnings at previous shows and sale price were given, but the sire, dam, and even the dog's name might be omitted. There were miscellaneous classes, which included crossbreds, and even a class for "Trick Dogs".

As noted earlier, the first volume of the *National American Kennel Club Stud Book* (1878) was devoted to sporting dogs only. The second volume, published in 1885, listed all breeds. The first roster of Mastiffs included five males and four females, all fawn color, all but one American bred. Dogs and bitches were listed separately, in order by registration number. A typical entry:

3274. Turk. Mr. W. H. Lee, Boston, Mass. Breeder, owner. Fawn; by Rayah, out of Brenda; Rayah by Prince, out of Venus; Brenda by Modoc, out of Nell. Bench Shows, 1st, Boston, 1882.

It should be remembered that all animals were entered in the early stud books, regardless of whether or not they had offspring. This practice was changed in 1952, when only breeding stock was listed. Also, in the earlier volumes of the *Stud Book* the sire, dam, and progeny might have been entered in the same year, and sometimes the parents were actually registered after their offspring.

The American Kennel Club was organized in 1884 at the instigation of a number of breeders, among whom was Dr. Frank Perry, of the Ashmont Kennels. More of Dr. Perry later. After a meeting the same year, the name of the club, originally "The National Bench Show Association", was changed to its present title, "The American Kennel Club". The first stud book under that name came out in 1886. Called *The American Kennel Stud Book, Vol. III*, it appeared in four parts, issued quarterly. Dogs and bitches were listed separately; names were in alphabetical order; and registration numbers were in sequence.

Forty-one Mastiffs were entered, 24 females and 17 males. Ten were imported from England. Dr. Perry's name appeared as breeder of seven, buyer of four, and owner of six imports. The most famous of the latter was Ilford Cromwell (4399), a brindle who later became one of the first American champions when the AKC officially awarded the title in 1889. Cromwell's entry gave a long list of his winnings, including those in England. His extended pedigree was also printed: his sire was Cardinal; his dam Cleopatra. Their English registration numbers were not given. A head study of Cromwell appeared in *Harper's New Monthly Magazine*, May 1887, and it would appear that he had what we would term a hound head, and also a large white blaze on the chest.

Another future champion, registered in 1886, was Ilford Caution (4398), imported and owned by E. H. Moore of Melrose, Mass. Caution, who was used extensively at stud, was bred by the then Secretary of the English Mastiff Club, R. Cook.

A highly entertaining book written by Charles H. Mason was published in 1888. Titled *Our Prize Dogs*, it consisted of extensive critiques on the winners in all breeds at eight major shows of 1887: Hartford, Buffalo, Newark, Providence, Boston, Pittsburgh, Philadelphia, and New York. In his preface, the author, who had judged at several of the shows, noted that if the book met with sufficient favor, a volume on the 1888 shows would be forthcoming. In view of the general tone of the 1887 comments, it is not surprising that no further issues appeared.

Mason gave a very detailed description of Ilford Caution. Apparently the dog was weak in the rear, as the critique mentioned that the hind legs were "very deficient in muscular development. Hocks too straight, rather weak and turning inward more than is desirable". However, Mason went on to state: "Notwithstanding this dog's light quarters and defective hocks, we are prepared to see him head the list of successful Mastiff sires in this country." He gave Caution's height as 31 inches at the shoulder, and the weight as 175 lbs. In the *Register* for September 1886, Wade wrote that Caution was "a no-loin, no quarters dog", in an acerbic exchange of letters on Mastiff type.

Only four brindles were listed in the 1886 book. Pedigrees were by no means precise: Ashmont Fawn (4402), for instance, had her sire Jumbo described as "out of a pair of Mastiffs, imported by Lord Dufferin of Canada". An entry typical of those showing more details was that of:

> 4417. VENU.S. II. Ashmont Kennels, Boston, Mass. Breeder, Wade Pittsburgh, Pa. Whelped November 5, 1882; fawn, with black points; by Lee's Turk out of Wade's Gipsey, by Curtis Marquis, out of a bitch, name and pedigree unknown, believed to have had Lyme Hall blood, Turk by Wright's Max, out of Bowditch's Tutu.

To add to the confusion, several prominent breeders such as Wade and Moore did not use kennel names, although Moore used the prefix Melrose at a later date. Wacouta and Ashmont used those prefixes from their beginnings. An interesting sidelight on 4397, Hero II, showed how dogs changed hands. Watson wrote of Hero, who was registered by Ashmont:

> [he was a dog] that we had picked up in a New York dealer's store and which turned out to be Mr. R. Exley's formerly of Bradford . . . Hero II was by Salisbury out of Venus by Green's Monarch, and had won second in the puppy class at the Crystal Palace. He was a tall, well-built dog, somewhat plain in face. We sold him to Mr. John Burgess, the collie exhibitor, and when Dr. Perry wanted a stud dog, we suggested Hero II, telling him he could win, which he did at New Haven immediately afterwards; and Dr. Perry then bought him and won wherever he showed him for two years. (*The Dog Book*, 1906, p. 566.)

At the New York show in 1886, there were so-called "Champion Classes" which were won by Homer and Prussian Princess, both later registered in Volume IV of the *Stud Book*. Mason's book illustrated Winlawn's Homer, and called him "undersized but massive . . . a rather nervous dog" and went on to say that he weighed 140 lbs.! In comments in the *Register*, Wade, never one to mince words, pronounced Homer "a dwarf".

The first listing of Mastiffs had breeders concentrated in the eastern part of the United States, but in Volume III, Ohio, Illinois, Michigan, Wisconsin and Minnesota were represented. Owners were to be found in such then remote spots as Kansas and Dakota—the latter still a territory, as it did not become a state until 1889.

It was about this time that the outspoken W. Wynn fulminated in the Register (August, 1886):

> "The American breeders are not able to produce a good looking dog" is the opinion of English critics. It is certain many second-rate, badly grown specimens, amounting almost to cripples, have been drafted from this country for America.

He then went on to discuss the true type of Mastiff, emphasizing that a large one wasn't necessarily a good one, and that an unsound, but typical dog was better than a sound, but robust one that didn't look like the breed.

Volume IV, 1887, became *The American Kennel Club Stud Book, Official*, with a total of 116 Mastiffs, 60 males and 56 females. More breeders' names appeared, some of which were to become famous. Winlawn Kennels (belonging to W. P. Stevenson) registered Homer (7455), mentioned previously, who became the first American-bred champion two years later. His sire was Cato (E.12 817) and the dam was Queen II (7485) listed in the same volume as her son. Under his entry came a list of his impressive winnings, including: "Winner of Am. Mastiff Club challenge cup, for the best American-bred Mastiff (present holder of same), New York, 1887." It must be remembered that prior to 1889, the term "champion" was used to indicate that a dog had won at a major show.

Winlawn also listed another future champion, the imported Prussian Princess (7484, E. 14 269), again with a long list of awards, beginning with puppy at Crystal Palace in 1883 and ending with "champion, New York, 1887". Mason called her "a bitch of fair size and nice quality" but said "bone should be heavier". She weighed 150 lbs.

The Lady Clare (6552) was imported by George and H. B. Cromwell of Staten Island, and later became a champion. She was described as "fawn, white star on chest" and had been extensively shown in England by her breeder, Dr. S. J. Turner. According to Mason, she weighed 118 lbs. and was 26 inches at the shoulder! He also noted that she had a good head "with lower incisors projecting". In fact, many of the dogs of the time were definitely very undershot. Clare's sire was the famous English Champion Beau, and her dam was The Lady Isabel who was stated to have weighed 135 at 27 inches. So much for the giants of the past.

A breeder who later came to America and was a prominent figure was Dr. C. A. Lougest, then living in Liverpool. He exported his fawn German Empress (7473, E. 14 739) to E. D. Hays of New York City. "Not of the type we want," said Mason.

Lougest also owned Imperial Chancellor, exported to Charles Marshall of New Jersey, to become number 7456. The breeder was given as R. Cook, sire Crown Prince; dam, Ilford Claudia. The dog was illustrated in the November 1887 *Register*. The accompanying notes said in part that he "Has been chosen to import a strain of new blood to the celebrated Lyme Hall bitches."

Then J. L. Winchell's name appeared; a name that became very well known. Among the seven Mastiffs bred or owned by him was Moses (6534), a "stone fawn" sired by Ilford Caution out of Bess. Although the dam's number was not given, she was, in fact, registered the following year in Volume V. Moses went on to become a champion in 1895, which, as he was whelped in 1887, made him quite a veteran.

Dogs of Wade's breeding were entered, as well as some bred by Perry and Moore. Fifteen Mastiffs were imported. Only six brindles were listed, and the rest were described in various ways: yellow, golden, silver, dark silver, greyish, as well as fawn. One bitch had "white partly up the forelegs" and Leo (7458) had "black ears and muzzle, some white on breast and tip of paws". The popularity of the breed was increasing rapidly, and by 1887 owners were located from Maine to California, including such unlikely cities as Cheyenne, Wyoming and Butte City, Montana, neither of which states had yet been admitted to the Union.

C. C. Marshall, who was a judge as well as a breeder, wrote the following in *Harper's New Monthly Magazine*, May 1887:

> The Mastiff, as it exists today, is an artificial breed, whose characteristics are maintained only by the most careful breeding. There is therefore opportunity for the greatest diversity of appearance, all depending as it does on the selection and crossing of various strains of blood. This diversity shows itself frequently in the matter of size. The minimum height allowed by the English Mastiff Club is twenty-seven inches. The maximum height of the breed is said to be thirty-four inches, but a height greater than thirty-one or thirty-two inches is seldom attained. . .great height, though desirable, is not an essential characteristic of the Mastiff.

Interesting comments, in view of the arguments still raging over a century later.

The background of some Mastiffs seems to have been somewhat murky. Writing in the *Register* of April 1887, an unsigned (and with reason) article on "Mastiff Pedigrees" read as follows:

> Many purporting to be English pedigrees are evident concoctions, a lot of names picked up at random, and stuck together, none of them being known in Mastiff pedigrees, except a few that are put in wrongly in the chain of descent.

Then came comments by the omniscient Wade:

> Those "New England" pedigrees are a nuisance and should be wiped out of every pedigree. Let the dogs, many of them good ones, simply go as with pedigrees of their American ancestors, the English part is one complicated series of blunders. . .The present state of confusion, imposture and rank flat-footed lying about these pedigrees is discreditable on the energy of the parties from whom the pedigrees come. Not on their honesty or honor, for they have undoubtedly been victims of some swindler. . . .

The pedigrees in question were of two imports. One, Corsair, was eventually registered in 1888 as 11,715, with breeder, whelping date and pedigree unknown. The other dog, named Basco, was never listed.

The first breed organization was said to have been established about this time, and was called the American Mastiff Club. It was active during the last years of the century, but apparently expired about 1900. *The American Field* of 3rd March 1888, gave an account of the "Second Annual Meeting of the American Mastiff Club". It was held in February, at Madison Square Garden, and officers were elected. Robert Lenox Belknap was president; secretary and treasurer was Richard H. Derby, M.D.; and there were three vice-presidents and an executive committee. The annual report showed that there were 44 members and six associate members. The Club had offered money prizes at various shows, and three challenge cups (no details given) at Westminster Kennel Club, as well as silver medals. The Club had become a member of the AKC in 1887. An interesting practice was that of photographing the winners of the challenge cups and sending copies to all club members, "an excellent method of recording the efforts of breeders to secure the true type of Mastiff".

In conclusion, Wade writes:

> It was a fortunate circumstance for the development of the American Mastiff Club, that already in the mother country the Old English Mastiff Club has for several years existed. The American club may be justly regarded as an offshoot of the older organization, and whatever success has attended its history during the past year should be attributed to the hearty good will shown by the parent club.

English members of the club were listed, among whom were W. K. Taunton, who judged at Westminster, Mark Beaufoy, and the OEMC secretary, Richard Cooke.

Ties with England were very close, and the following account appeared in the English *Kennel Gazette* in 1890 about a show of that year:

> The Old English Mastiff Club hit upon a novel and most interesting way of welcoming to our shores that well-known and enthusiastic breeder of Mastiffs, Dr. Derby, the Hon. Secretary of the American Mastiff Club. It was natural to suppose that Dr. Derby, whilst among us, would like to see the cream of the Mastiffs in this country, and the Old English Mastiff Club, therefore, arranged to hold a non-competitive members show at the Crystal Palace.

The account went on to tell of 51 dogs on show from 2 to 6 p.m.

There was also a short-lived branch of the OEMC in America, which caused a great deal of controversy. In 1886, Dr. Perry asked that an American affiliate be formed, and after some reluctance, one was formed the following year. Perry was Chairman and Wade was secretary. Then came an irate letter from the officers of the American Club, complaining that they hadn't been informed of the branch, and wanted to "enter our most earnest protest against the action of the Club", giving as reasons that several of the new group were "not deemed worthy of membership in the American Mastiff Club". From all of which it can be deduced that there was much friction among several breeders. At any rate, the outcome was that the American branch was discontinued in the same year, having existed for less than twelve months.

The English club presented two silver challenge cups to the American club. One, a replica of their "Forty Guinea Cup" was first offered in 1891. A year later, a copy of the "Twenty Guinea Cup" was sent over, and these trophies were awarded at various major shows until 1895. After that year there was no further mention of the cups, and both were eventually returned to England. The first cup was later renamed the "Thirty

Guinea Cup", and is still awarded. It is described as: "A silver claret jug with acanthus leaf decoration and applied band of flowers and grape vine ornamentation round neck; the cover surmounted by a Mastiff's head." The other trophy continued to be known as the Twenty Guinea, and is still awarded to the best Mastiff not over eighteen months of age of the opposite sex to the winner of the Forty Guinea.

The American club had its own challenge cup, called The Westminster, which was loaned to the U.K. Old English Mastiff Club (OEMC) for their 1890 show, then returned to America. What became of it, and the other trophies owned by the club, is not known.

Very little further information is known about the American Mastiff Club. A notice dated April 1891, stated that the Executive Committee had met in 1889, and dues were to be $5, or $25 for a life membership. Herbert Mead was secretary and treasurer at the time.

To return to the *Stud Book* for 1888, Volume V, and its listings: this was the last year that it appeared quarterly. In that year the AKC voted that all dogs that had been registered with the *American Kennel Register* prior to 1ˢᵗ January 1888, could be entered in their book without charge. This may have accounted in part for the very large entry of 239 dogs. Parts 2, 3, and 4 bore the notation "Examined by Committee of the American Mastiff Club". In a few cases "pedigree not authenticated" was noted but the animal was entered nevertheless.

Few pedigrees referred to the previous *Stud Books*, and there were four re-entries, as it was possible to relist if the dog's name or owner were changed. For example, Prince Karl was first given the number 8819, but later in the same volume became 9704, the only difference being a change of owner. English dogs could be registered, as 8795, Constable, was listed as being owned and bred by W. K. Taunton of London. There was also a rather baffling entry: "8793, Clement (formerly King of Ashmont)—bred by L. Crabtree, England." In the previous volume, Nydia (7482) was listed as being sired by King of Ashmont (late Clement, E. 18 976).

A few show wins were still given, mostly by larger breeders such its Winchell and Moore. The latter's name occurred as breeder of 23 of the entries. He acquired four from other breeders and imported four.

One of Moore's English dogs was the famous Minting (8815), bred by Mrs. Willins. He was described as "light fawn with black points" and was sired by the English Champion Maximilian, out of English champion Cambrian Princess. Whelped in May 1885, Minting became an American champion in 1889, along with the eight other Mastiffs to gain the title the first year it was officially awarded by the AKC. The dog's show career was spectacular—among his many wins was a triumph at Boston in 1887, where he was "Special for largest dog of any breed". He stood 31 inches and weighed 184 lbs., as Mason wrote in his *Prize Dogs*, and praised Minting to the skies. After discussing the many fine points, mentioning his "true character and exquisite quality", Mason went on to write:

> This is a fit place to express satisfaction over the steady improvement that has taken place in the Mastiff class since 1881. Never shall we forget the peculiar animals that were led into the ring to compete against our exhibits, Salisbury and Creole, in the New York Show of that year. The dogs were only eclipsed by the total ignorance of the breed displayed by the men who, at that time, were considered judges.

We might add here that Creole won at that show, but Salisbury was placed third, which might account for Mason's bitterness!

Wade, never easy to please, also approved of Minting. He wrote in the *Register*, August 1887:

> Neither the sire or dam of Minting are thoroughly sound. Both are bad behind, Cambrian Princess having bad, straight hocks; yet Minting has hocks to carry him over a church.

Registrations continued to be rather casual at times, as in the case of Captain James Sennett's Flora (10,750), who was: "Buff, black points. Breeder, date of birth and pedigree unknown." A more typical entry follows:

> 10,575. LEOTA V. T. J. Venard, Lodoga [*sic*], Ind. Breeder, Berkshire Kennels, Hinsdale, Mass. Whelped September 23, 1887; light fawn; by Berkshire Caution out of Daisy G. by Leon Turk, out of Maid of Athens by Major, out of Madia; Leon Turk, by Turk, out of Baby; Berkshire Caution, by Ilford Caution (4398, vol. III), out of Countess, by Turk out of Jule.

However, Berkshire Caution was registered the following year in Volume VI as 15,792. Countess was entered as 11,783 the same year as her offspring, being given the prefix Melrose, and listed as being whelped in 1882, bred by W. Lee.

Berkshire Kennels belonged to P. Amidon, a name that was to appear again, and Perry and Wade continued to register. Wyoming Kennels, owned by E. Sears, of Massachusetts, entered a future champion, Sear's Monarch (8827), bred by Eli Bellows. The dog was sired by Lord Raglan, of whom Shields wrote in *American Book of the Dog, 1891*:

Distrust a stud dog that is cooped up without free exercise . . . Lord Raglan was set down as impotent until his last owner put him on the road, following his buggy, then he got puppies with as much certainty as the average stud dog.

Lord Raglan was registered in the same Stud Book as his son, as 11,731, and as owned by Wacouta Kennels. He was a Crown Prince dog, out of The Lady Rowena. Wacouta also owned Wacouta Nap (10,562), one of their five imported dogs. Nap became a champion the following year. His birth date is given as both 1884 and 1885, his breeder as R. Morgan of Wales (by Lion out of Bess) and previously AKR 3435. Mason, who had judged the dog, described him as 30½ inches tall and weight as 165 lbs., remarking "a better body than is seen in a majority of the prize Mastiffs in this country".

The last Mastiff entered in the 1888 volume, later to become a champion was Winchell's Merlin (11,736). Whelped and registered that year, he did not gain his title until 1895. Rather confusingly, he had been entered in an early part of the volume as Argus, 10,538, but the name was changed when his first owner returned him to his breeder. Merlin's breeding was Ilford Caution out of Bess.

The New York show of 1888 must have been quite a spectacle. Entered in the "Champion Class" were Ilford Caution, Ilford Cromwell and Homer. Champion Bitch Class boasted The Lady Clare, Prussian Princess, and Bal Gal (the last never an official champion, however). Moses, Boss, Minting, and Imperial Chancellor were in the Open Dog class, and the total entry was 45.

The *Stud Book*, Volume VI, for 1889 was not issued in parts, and there was no pedigree examination. The grand total was the astonishing number of 373, due in part to the ruling that after 1888 unregistered dogs could not be shown at AKC events.

The famous Beaufort was registered as 15,130. His owner was given as W. K. Taunton and his agent was J. L. Winchell. The dog was whelped in 1884 and became an American champion in 1890. His sire was the English champion Beau, and his dam The Lady Isabel. Beaufort was stated to have weighed 165 lbs., and measured 29 ½ inches at the shoulder, again, not very large by present-day standards. He was quite a traveler in the happy days before travel restrictions and quarantine. He was sent to America about 1889, remained with Winchell long enough to win his title and be used extensively at stud, then returned to England. The exact date of his trip home is not known. Beaufort's entry lists his English wins: "6 firsts, 11 challenge prizes, 17 specials and OEMC Challenge Cup six times—barred from further competition for this cup."

Several pictures of Beaufort exist. *Harper's Weekly* for 28th February 1891, had a drawing by G. Muss Arnold. He was shown of excellent type, with a short muzzle. Other illustrations confirm this, and the battle over the long versus short muzzle continued then (as now). In the same year Wade wrote of Beaufort, in Shield's book, p. 583:

> . . . a dog with the extreme of short face and realising as near the ideal of the standard as a dog is likely ever to do, yet without a single deformity and not overdone in a single particular. His only fault, if fault it may be termed, is large dew claws, which impede his action behind, and which should have been removed when a puppy. . . . Beaufort's merits are in his excellent fore legs, straight and strong, his deep capacious chest, his admirable hind legs, with perfection in hocks, the very broad flat kind most desirable in Mastiffs, his vast skull, neat ears, and bulky loin. His head is fashionable today, but should the longer head of Turk, Colonel, etc., become the fashion in years to come, Beaufort will still be thoroughly the Mastiff in bodily properties.

If the "Colonel" referred to as being long headed was the dog illustrated in the *Register*, February 1884, it was indeed of houndy type. Whelped in 1875, Colonel weighed 168 lbs. and was 31 inches at shoulder. He belonged to R. Alston, of England, and the picture was drawn from a photograph owned by Wade. *The American Agriculturalist* for April 1886, showed Colonel, presumably the same dog, but the caption stated that he was owned by Mr. W. Wade of Hulton, Pennsylvania.

In 1889 Perry, Mead, and Moore had substantial entries. Moore led the way, with 24 from his own kennel, plus two imports, both of which became champions at later dates. Ilford Chancellor (15,619) obtained his title in 1895, which would have made him ten at the time, and although it seems unlikely, the records confirm this. His color was not given, but as both his parents, Ilford Caution and Brenda Secunda, were fawn, it may be assumed that he was also fawn. His breeder was given as R. Cook, but both parents were registered in the United States. In the spring of 1889, Moore's Ilford Caution, Countess, and Minting all died.

The other English import was Moore's The Lady Coleus (12,368) an 1893 champion. Her breeder was Albert Andrews and R. Cook later owned her. Her English registration was under the name Ilford Lady Coleus (formerly Lady Virginia), according to an article in the 1935 *English Kennel Gazette*, written by E. G. Oliver, with an illustration. Her sire was Beaufort, her dam, Vistula. Since Vistula was whelped on 12th April 1886 and her daughter 1ˢᵗ August 1887, her dam was far younger at the time of breeding than we prefer today. Wacouta Kennels had registered Vistula in 1888 (11,796), as bred by Andrews of England.

Many new kennels appeared, and with the Mastiff's tremendous popularity "puppy mills" seem to have sprung up. An instance of that kind of operation was "Beech Grove" of Indiana. Its owner registered 18, bought two from other breeders and acquired two imports. The nine litters were bred from 1885 to 1889. Four were from the same bitch, who was obviously bred on each heat, a not uncommon practice in those days (and in the same sort of operation today, unfortunately).

Breeders used a wide range of terms to describe their dogs: "black ears and muzzle, grey forehead"; "light fawn with brown points"; plus assorted shades of fawn, including lemon and cream. Only six brindles were entered, one of which, Duke of Connaught (12,861), was "blue brindle" whatever that may have indicated.

A number of entries were Canadian owned and bred. A popular name was Bismarck—there was Chancellor Bismarck, Count, Prince, and just plain Bismarck. Of Count Bismarck, Mason had written: "This puppy may win other prizes, but if he does, the company he is in will be poor." Several Harrisons were entered, with Ben, Ben II, and Benjamin H. Clumsy and Fresh the American were dogs; Don M. and Baby Bunting were bitches.

The breeder Charles C. Marshall, mentioned earlier, judged at Westminster in 1889, according to Volume I of the AKC *Gazette*. Minting won the Challenge Dog Class, and The Lady Clare took the Challenge Bitch. In the nine entries in the Dog Class, Moore's Alonzo placed first, while Lady Coleus won the Bitch Class. There were also Novice Dog, Novice Bitch, and Puppy classes. Several of the dogs were not registered with the AKC, so evidently the ruling was not strictly enforced that year. There was a total of 75 entries.

The year also marked the strengthening of the AKC, as the National Dog Club, headed by Perry, agreed to amalgamate, thus bringing all national groups together. Not much is known of NDC, nor whether it maintained a registry. The same year the tart comment was made of the winners at the Philadelphia show: "Neither are good ones and are too old to improve in their worst faults." At the Columbus, Ohio, show the *Gazette* reported that Moses beat a dog called Tiger Royal: "Former beats latter in skull, loin and bone, is also a bit better behind, and is a taller dog."

The year 1890 (Volume VII of the *Stud Book*) brought a slight drop in registrations, down to 219. Of these, three were imports, and only three brindles were included in the total number, although in a few cases color was not given.

Breeders were located in nearly two dozen states. Familiar kennel names continued to appear, but with fewer entries. Moore listed five, but according to Watson (*The Dog Book, 1906*), he stopped breeding after Minting's death. Perry listed two, Wade one, Winchell eight. Beech Grove continued on a large scale, with 11 of its own breeding plus two others from other kennels. James Day of Connecticut jumped into the fancy by buying no fewer than six dogs from various sources. One, Day's Tasso (16,893) had "chocolate muzzle and ears". Some of the large numbers entered by breeders were rather deceptive, as many owners would register an entire litter and never be heard of again.

The only entry from 1890 to become a champion was Elkson (18,966), who gained the title in 1895. His sire was Ilford Chancellor and his dam was Madge Minting. Elkson began his show career early, as his *Stud Book* entry stated: "1st puppy, and 1st open, Rockford, 1890. " Few show wins were given, and those chiefly by the more prominent breeders."

Another import had the delightful name of Goddess of Liberty (16,280), by Prince of Wales out of Queen Liberty. A fairly typical entry for the year read as follows:

ZULU (16,636) - Dr. W. S. Tremaine, Buffalo, N.Y. Breeders, Associated Fanciers, Philadelphia, Pa. Whelped Jan. 21, 1888; fawn; by Berlin Victor, out of Mattie, by Leo, out of Belle, by Hurd's Harold, out of Arthur's Dido; Leo by Sultan II, out of Nell II; Berlin Victor by Hero II (4397, Vol. III), out of Venus II (4417, Vol. III).

Volume VIII, 1891, had only a slight variation in numbers. There were 211 registered, two imported from England and five from Canada. Several Canadian-owned dogs were listed, and Wade sent a dog to Ontario.

There were many new breeders, but the old-timers continued on a lesser scale. Moore had dropped out, and Wacouta Kennels listed one male, but he had been whelped in 1888. A new name, James Whitney, of Rochester, New York, entered several Mastiffs. His kennel name was Flower (or Flour) City—both spellings were given in *Stud Book* and show results. He imported Cardinal Beaufort (22,942), an 1890 fawn grandson of Beaufort (Sir Stafford x Frigga).

A son of Beaufort was registered in 1891, the future champion Beaufort's Black Prince (19,366). He was whelped in 1890 out of an unlisted bitch named Gerda. In spite of his name, he was fawn colored. Bred and owned by Winchell, the dog had an interesting history. After winning his American championship in 1894, he went to England and was owned by W. Norman Higgs, my co-author's grandfather. At Crufts in 1896 (again according to the previously cited article by Oliver) "the two best dogs of the day" competed, as Mrs. Baxter related earlier. The judge, H. G. Woolmore, gave the prize to Peter Piper—perhaps not too surprising a decision, as he had bred the dog.

Many of the year's entries came from Richland Kennels in Milnor, North Dakota, 14 in all. The owner, W. B. Bradley, evidently registered every Mastiff he owned or bred. However, most of them do not seem to have appeared in later pedigrees.

Only one brindle was entered, whose listing is quite typical:

DUCHESS OF WARD (20,317). Chas. E. Cooper, Pullman, Ill. Breeder, Wm. Hood. Whelped March 1, 1886; brindle; by Dictator (7448, Vol. IV), out of Pride, by Duke, out of Juno, by Towser, out of Josie; Duke by Romeo, out of Juliet.

Another future champion, Prince Cola (32,060), was born in 1891, but not registered until 1894. He won his title in 1897. His sire was Ilford Chancellor, his dam Lulu Minting (17,890). The fawn dog had several owners during his career.

The "Third Annual Chicago Bench Show" of 8th-11th April 1891, had a substantial entry of 49, the final number being a litter of puppies. The only dog in the Challenge Class was Ilford Chancellor, at the time the property of Flower [sic] City Kennels. A list of his winnings included New York, Baltimore and Pittsburg [sic] for 1891. The same kennel had the only Challenge Bitch, Lady Coleus, and their Caution's Own Daughter won Open Bitches. Elkson, owned by Edwin Kimball, won Open Class for Dogs and also Puppies under 18 months.

Prices were given for most of the dogs, ranging from $ 5000 for a bitch named Mai (Minting x Breeze) to $ 50 for Moses Duke (Moses x Duchess of York). Elkson was a bargain at $ 500. Cash prizes were offered, as well as the American Mastiff Club's Challenge Cups for best dog and bitch, plus the English offering of the Forty Guinea Cup (these could be won only by members of the respective clubs).

For light relief at the lengthy show, one could have watched Prof. Parker's "Celebrated Troupe of Trained Dogs", which included, among other delights, Katie, who "creeps like a baby"; Nellie, who "balances on the back of a chair", presumably to be unseated by Cap, the Russian Poodle who "upsets chairs". There was also an exhibit of tumbling dogs, whatever that may have been, as well as the first show of whippet racing in this country.

Charles Marshall's report on the Westminster Kennel Club Show was reprinted in full in the *Gazette*. Evidently his selections had caused quite a commotion, as he explained his placings in great detail. He had given Beaufort a third! According to his comments, the dog was in poor condition, due to having been used at stud, or as his owner stated "was exhausted by service at the stud, giving me a statement of the extent to which he had been used within three days". It appears that his judging of bitches was also criticized. Caution's Own Daughter had been given fourth, "because of her white mask . . . I had never had before me one of these white or pink-faced Mastiffs". Three full columns were devoted to Marshall's critique indicating the importance of the breed in the Gay Nineties.

There were no dramatic changes in the 1892 Volume IX. Registrations continued to dwindle rather slowly, with a total of 194 entries. No brindles showed up, and only two imports, both females. The notation "Examined by Pedigree Committee of American Mastiff Club" appeared.

Winchell continued to enter, with nine from his own kennel plus two from other breeders. Charles Bunn of Peoria, Illinois, owned seven and imported Ilford Cameo (23,598), a fawn bitch bred by Cook. Bunn also registered a future champion, Sinaloa (23,525), a female sired by Ormonde out of Phaedra, who completed her title in 1895.

Exeter Dirce (26,737) was imported by Whitney's Flower City Kennels from James Hutchings (Beaumaris x Doris) but she does not seem to have produced any litters.

Breeders were scattered all over the country, in such unlikely spots as Deer Lodge, Montana, where Remus was bred by Chas. Laribee. His entry read as follows:

Whelped 1887; fawn, black points; by Romulus (6538, Vol. IV), out of Boss' Bess, by Boss (8788, Vol. V), out of Bess (8835, Vol. V).

This is a fairly typical entry, except more registry numbers were given. In many pedigrees the numbers on older dogs were not entered although they were in fact registered.

Apparently Mastiffs came in a rather wide range of colors. In addition to light tan and tawny, the following fawn shades were listed: stone, silver, golden, grey, seal, dark and light. One dog had "black nose and toe nails".

At the 1892 "Fourth Annual Chicago Bench Show", held on 9th-12th February, the American Mastiff Club again offered two cups for Best Dog and Best Bitch belonging to club members. Cash prizes and medals were also awarded. The total number of entries was 42, including absentees, and there was a litter of puppies with number unspecified.

The 101 Mastiffs of the year 1893, Volume X of the *Stud Book* were "Examined by Committee of the Mastiff Club of America" but no pedigrees were noted as "not authenticated" as had happened occasionally in the past. It appeared that it was still possible to enter a dog with a rather long pedigree and no AKC numbers. For example:

QUEEN SPEARO (28,143). T. P. Fitzgerald, Chicago, Ill. Breeder, owner. Whelped Feb. 13, 1892; fawn; by Duke of Bethlehem, out of Spearo, by Leo, out of Empress, by Dante, out of Victoria; Leo, by Jacob, out of Ruth; Duke of Bethlehem, by Lyon, out of Cleopatra, by Rob Roy, out of Myrfle [*sic*]; Lyon, by Pope, out of Duchess.

No future champions were listed for the year, and the only champion for 1893 was Lady Coleus, an 1888 entry as noted above. One breeder gave a few show wins, so it was still permissible but not usual. Occasionally the breeder was unknown but no instances of unknown pedigree.

Dr. Lougest had six entries of his own breeding. New breeders continued to show up, but Winchell and Berkshire had but one entry each. There were no imports, and only two brindles appeared. For the fawns, in addition to the usual descriptions, there were such notes as "fawn, black face and white markings", "white spots", "white forepaws", "fawn, black and white" which would seem to indicate a certain lack of uniformity in color and markings. One wonders just where the white spots occurred.

By 1894 (Volume XI), there was a drastic drop in entries to 70 Mastiffs for the year. Two of these were re-entered, making an actual total of 68. Doubtless the low number was caused in part by the financial panic of the previous year.

Winchell continued to breed, with six entries. One rather puzzling entry was that of Black Prince's Brampton (35,054), in which he was listed as owner and breeder. The sire was his Beaufort's Black Prince, and the dam was Brampton Beauty (31,952), who, however, was listed in the *Stud Book* as belonging to W. Norman Higgs of England, and bred by one Capt. Piddock [*sic*]. Some complicated transactions must have been going on, as it was about this time that Higgs took Beaufort's Black Prince back to England as noted above. Black Prince's Danger (34,507), the same breeding as Black Prince's Brampton, was listed as bred by Higgs; Black Prince's Patrol (35,019) as bred by Winchell, but out of Young Bess (35,020) who was listed in the same volume, Patrol sired by Beaufort's Black Prince, as was Young Bess!

One dog bred by Moore was entered, but as it had been whelped in 1887, it seems Moore had dropped out. The then Secretary of the American Mastiff Club, Herbert Mead, had five listings. A very large number of dogs were registered by midwesterners, with Illinois and Indiana in the lead, with Iowa and Texas following. There were two imported Mastiffs, and no brindles. White spots and markings continued to be noted.

During the hey-day of the Mastiff's popularity, many famous American names showed up as owners: Wrigley, McCormick, Studebaker, Roebuck, Mrs. Jefferson Davis and many others. These serve to indicate that the Mastiff was *the* dog to own in the 1880's and early 1890's.

In 1895 registrations had dropped to a mere 37. Volume XII of the *Stud Book* stated that the American Mastiff Club was still checking pedigrees, but the committee had very little work for the year. All the entries were fawn and only a few dogs were imported. Familiar names were those of Herbert Mead, with four dogs; Winchell with seven; Lougest with two imports and one of his own breeding.

The American Kennel Gazette, reporting the Mascoutah Kennel Club's "Sixth Annual Bench Show held at Chicago, Ill., March 5, 6, 7, and 8, 1895" did not give the number of Mastiffs entered, but the breed rated its own judge, Arthur Trickett. Challenge Dogs went to Elkson, owned at the time by A. Morse, and that in bitches to Charles Bunn's Sinaloa. Mr. Bunn, of Peoria, whose name had appeared for the first time the previous year as a breeder, swept the board. His Marquis won Open Dogs; Rowena, Open Bitches; Hegira, Puppy Bitches; and Leamington, Novice Dogs and Bitches.

An interesting little sidelight on transatlantic sales appeared in, the 11th October *Stock-Keeper and Fancier's Chronicle,* 1895:

Mastiff Dog, three years old, sire Beaufort's Beau, A.K.S.B. x Salva, A.K.S.B., imported from America, cost £25 as a pup, to be sold cheap. Apply Trevor Roberts, 1 Crosshall-street, Liverpool.

A bitch named Ethel became a champion in 1895, but no record of any sort can be found, so her breeding and owner remain a mystery.

But what was happening to the breed? Volume XIII, for 1896, had but 28 Mastiffs listed. Only a few years before, in 1891, Wade had written:

Certainly the Mastiff had come to stay. Other breeds of large dogs may temporarily overshadow him, in point of numbers or popular fancy, but the Mastiff has too firm a position in the canine interests of the country—he represents too much of the wealth of the canine world, and is too highly appreciated by dog-fanciers of all classes—to ever be neglected, either at home or on the show bench.

A few familiar names occurred as breeders, with Bunn leading the way with four. Lougest had but one entry, and Winchell had two dogs plus an imported bitch, who was the only brindle for the year. She was Miss Constable (39,324), bred by W. Norman Higgs, whelped in 1892. She was by Dick Constable out of Count Biddy, a littermate to Lougest's import Maggie Murphy of the previous year, where the dam was given as Coombe Biddy. Apparently neither bitch had progeny. The American Mastiff Club still offered the two English trophies as well as their own cups and medals at Westminster.

Volume XIV for 1897 registered 15, all fawn. Even this number is deceptive, as some of the entries had been whelped as early as 1892, and one was an 1891 bitch. Bunn registered Leamington, winner at Chicago the previous year, but N. G. Alexander owned him. Bunn had five other entries from various years.

The following year, 1898, showed a slight increase, as 24 were registered. Dr. Lougest imported two, and both were brindle—evidently the lack of that color had become a problem. One was from Holland, Black Peter (47,734), and the other, Tigress III (46,651) was English. Several offspring of Black Peter were entered at the same time: a brindle male named Iron Duke, and two bitches, Black Diamond and Black Thorn, both fawn. Lougest also bought a litter of five puppies from Robert Boyle, by Leamington out of Juno IV. One entry came from Winchell, who gave up his kennel about 1898. Of the 19 entries at Westminster, 10 came from Lougest. The American Mastiff Club was no longer a member of the AKC so it must have been about this time that the organization became defunct.

The last year of the century had an entry of 18 in the *Stud Book*, Volume XVI. Of these, only seven were females, a dangerously low figure for future breeding. One entry, California Cube (51,971), became a champion the following year. An 1897 dog, his pedigree was:

By Cube, out of Pedigree, by Turk, out of Sultana, by Ingleside Crown Prince, out of Lornita Hilda; Turk by Chino Lion, out of Chino Beauty; Cube by Edric (18,480, Vol. VII), out of Echo (14,711, Vol. VI).

The dog was the last to win a title for many years, as there were no champions listed until 1914.

F. J. Skinner imported a brindle male from A. W. Lucas, and named it Baltimore after his home town. Its birth year was given as 1899, so it must have been quite a small puppy when it was sent.

At the Mascoutah Kennel Club's "Ninth Annual Dog Show" in March 1899, the American Mastiff Club offered its Westminster Cup (value $300) plus three other silver cups and a gold medal. However, none could have been awarded as there was a stipulation that three Mastiffs had to be present for each class. There were only three dogs and two bitches, and two were absent. Interestingly enough, the first prize in the Open Class for bitches was withheld. The single entry was Maude D.

However, for entertainment there was a 16-act program which included a balancing act by an Italian Greyhound and a dog with a human brain, who performed "mathematical feats of addition, subtraction, etc.". And, "NOTICE: Before leaving the show, visit Clipper II, No. 366. The only Novelty in the Show. He is the DOG WITH SOLID GOLD CROWNS ON HIS TEETH. Dr. L. W. Young put them on. The same operation could add a deal of novelty to your dog, and is absolutely painless." Clipper was a Bull Terrier, third in Open Dogs, and was not for sale. Shows were indeed livelier in those days.

U.S. MASTIFF REGISTRATIONS BY YEAR, 1885-1899

1885 - 9	1893 - 101
1886 - 41	1894 - 70
1887 - 116	1895 - 37
1888 - 239	1896 - 28
1889 - 373	1897 - 15
1890 - 219	1898 - 24
1891 - 211	1899 - 18
1892 - 194	

2.1 Lyme Hall Kennels in the 19th Century. U.K.

2.2 Jack (Dash x Juno). Lithograph by Alexander Pope, 1880. USA

2.3a Champion Salisbury, imported 1881 (Watson). USA

2.3b Lady Beatrice circa 1880 (Watson). USA

2.3c Lady Coleus, 1889 (Watson). USA

2.3d Paula circa 1880 (Watson). USA

2.4 Colonel, 1884 *(American Kennel Register)*. USA

2.5 Mastiff types of the 1880's *(American Kennel Register)*. USA

The History and Management of the Mastiff

2.6 Beaufort, ca. 1885 (Eng. Ch. Beau x The Lady Isabel) (Ashmont). USA

2.7 Homer, 1889 (Cato x Queen II). The first American bred champion. Owned and bred by Winlawn Kennels. USA

2.8 Ilford Caution, 1886 Bred by R. Cook, owner E.H. Moore *(American Kennel Register)* USA

2.9 Imperial Chancellor, 1887 (Crown Prince x Ilford Claudia). Bred by R. Cook, owner C. Marshall. *(American Kennel Register)* USA

2.10 Ch. Minting, ca. 1889 (Eng. Ch. Maximilian x Eng. Ch. Cambrian Princess). Bred by Mrs. Miller, owner E.H. Moore (Ashmont). USA

Chapter 3

1900-1920

The United Kingdom   *Elizabeth J. Baxter*

If 1900 saw the Mastiff breed at a low ebb, the succeeding years saw a gradual recovery until disaster overtook it once again at the time of the First World War, 1914-1918. Registrations showed 48 for 1906, 35 for 1908, reached a peak of 60 in 1913 and thereafter declined: 54 in 1914, 34 in 1915 and in 1918 only three Mastiffs were actually registered; the war years had taken their toll.

However, the earlier years of the 1900's were full of hope, with good dogs being bred, among them Ch. Brompton Duke and Ch. Brompton Duchess, the Duke of Cleveland, Galazora, Ch. Ronald Widmere, Berenice, Survivor, and the two brindles Beowulf (21.5.1912) and Ruthless Defender (10.4.1914). A name that appeals to me enormously is that of a bitch registered in 1906—Alice Sit by the Fire.

The premier breeders of the day were Lt. Col. Z. Walker, Mr. W. K. Taunton, Mr. G. Cook and Mr. Robert Leadbetter. The latter bred and owned the Hazelmere Mastiffs and his was a large kennel which was advertised every month in the *Kennel Gazette*. Mr. George Cook owned the prefix Cleveland, but from registration information, seemed to register his stud dogs and not worry about the bitches—most of the dams of his litters appear as "unregistered" or "unknown"; but more of that later.

Mark Beaufoy, writing in the Mastiff notes of the *Kennel Gazette* in January 1905, says: "I think the present day Mastiff moves better and is more active than its progenitors . . .but Mastiffs will not show themselves well and a dog pulled across the ring by its chain may be the best or worst mover in the world for all the judge can tell." Things have not changed much down the years!

One thing that strikes the researcher into this era is the number of Mastiffs registered at the Kennel Club with information recorded as "unknown" and with parents as "unregistered". It was quite common for well known stud dogs to be used on bitches which were not registered and one can only assume that if a Mastiff looked like a Mastiff and its breeder vouched for it, then it was accepted as such and because it was not *registered* at the Kennel Club did not necessarily mean that it was not purebred. It is also likely that about this time, outcrosses were being made to St. Bernards, as of course they had in the last century, to try and increase breeding stock.

But quite apart from any St. Bernard outcrossing, which was probably winked at, at the same time (i.e. about 1910) there appears in the *Kennel Gazette* the heading, under registrations "Cross-Breed-Bull Mastiff" and the intertwining of the pure bred Mastiffs with this new Bull/Mastiff cross provides opportunities for absorbing detective work. This is not to say that even these outcrossings were a startling new development—obviously they had happened in the previous century—but here we have it logged and to a certain extent recorded; although it is quite impossible to follow all trails to a satisfactory conclusion.

In 1909 Amazon Queen was registered as a Bull and Mastiff; 1911 saw "Bull and Mastiff Cross Breed, Astle's Madge by Terrible Turk out of Vixen". One of the earliest Bull-Mastiff breeders was a Mr. J. Barrowcliffe whose name crops up time and time again with his prefix Stapleford. In 1912 he registered "Ideal Queen", as a Cross Breed—Bull Mastiff, by Stapleford Pedro out of Nance; she (Ideal Queen) was born on the 16th April 1911. Both Pedro and Nance are recorded as being "unregistered" so it is impossible to trace them back through Kennel Club records; only through old pedigrees and word of mouth.

Stapleford Pedro and his ancestors are important to interested Mastiff breeders because he is behind both the Withybush and the Havengore kennels of the 1920's and 1930's. An old pedigree I have in my possession actually names him as being by Salisbury (Mastiff) out of Pinxton Pride (Mastiff) but the fact remains that he was used on both pure bred Mastiffs and cross breed—Bull Mastiff bitches and sired puppies which were registered some as Mastiffs and some as Bull Mastiffs. By a Bull Mastiff bitch called Nance, already mentioned, he sired Stapleford Agrippa, brother to Ideal Queen. Mr. Barrowcliffe owned them all. The pedigrees of Ch. Woden, Ch. Master Beowulf and Shirebrook Lady are reproduced (see Appendix I) and these will show more clearly than I can write, the extent of the mixture of blood that occurred.

The registration system of these years was a little less than perfect. Marwood Pride, registered in April 1914 as a Mastiff, was by Pedro out of an unregistered bitch called Connie. But on old pedigrees, Connie is down as a Bull Mastiff and is the mother of Helen, a registered Bull Mastiff. The mystery deepens still further when elsewhere in the Gazette we find a Bull Mastiff registration of January 1915, printed as "by Stapleford

Pedro unregistered (Mastiff) out of Gyp Bull Mastiff". So he is described, this interesting dog, Pedro, respectively as unregistered, unknown, and a Mastiff, the sire of registered Mastiffs and registered Bull Mastiffs. I think myself, and this is only hearsay and going on old pedigrees, that he was in fact a Mastiff, although unregistered, but was owned by the dedicated Mr. Barrowcliffe and used to produce Bull Mastiffs—but when opportunity arose he was also used on Mastiff bitches.

In 1914 a Collyhurst Squire was born, although he was not registered until 1919, and then as a Mastiff. He is by Stapleford Pedro out of a pure Mastiff bitch, Minerva. He is described in the Gazette as a "rich apricot" and he appears in the pedigrees already mentioned. In 1920 another name appears, that of Parkhull or Penkhull, Lady, owned by a Mr. H. Beasley and sired by Stapleford Agrippa (by Pedro out of Nance) out of Helen, who is listed as "unregistered, Bull Mastiff". If I seem to be belabouring the point of these Bull Mastiff outcrosses, it is because they are a common denominator of nearly all post war breeding. Parkhull or Penkhull Lady was herself registered under the heading "Cross Breed-Bull Mastiff". Even under this new registration heading of Cross Breed-Bull Mastiff, dogs were appearing under the listing of "unregistered" and/or "unknown".

To add still further to the confusion of registrations in general, in April 1921, under the heading of "Cross Breed, Bull Mastiff, we get "Sir Roger, by Poor Joe, (Bull Mastiff) out of Peggy (Bull Mastiff, unregistered)". But in August of the same year we find a dog called Poor Jerry, registered as a Mastiff, but being by "Poor Joe, out of Peggy (unregistered)". It would appear from this that litter brothers could be registered as two separate breeds. Perhaps they went on looks alone and the wishes of their owners. We also have to bear in mind that Poor Joe is elsewhere down as being by Brompton Duke—Mastiff, out of Galazora—Mastiff, so why he should appear in one edition as a Bull Mastiff passes my comprehension. In addition, he was the sire of Miss Bell's Woden (see pedigrees). Another interesting Mastiff registration was "Tiger Lily, by Tiger of Holloway, Mastiff out of June, Great Dane/Mastiff cross".

It is easy to get completely confused by the contradictory information given in the Kennel Gazettes of this period and perhaps easy to give too much emphasis to it. I do feel, however, that this is an important era in the history of our breed and we have to try and understand how the two different types of animals were quite inextricably woven together, in order to appreciate the Mastiff as we have it today. The dearth of breeding stock at the end of the First World War, as at the end of the Second, intensified the use of animals that might not otherwise have been used so extensively.

The period 1900-1920 is not to be thought of as a low period in the history of the breed; in many ways it saw an upsurge and a revival. The registration of Bull Mastiffs would not of itself have been all that important; in fact, seen against the number of pure bred Mastiff registrations for those years, they were comparatively few. Three of these registrations which should perhaps be mentioned as being free from any taint of Bull Mastiff blood but recorded during the war years were Gathnell (6.9.1916) brindle by Priam of Wingfield out of Lady Brombess; Ch. King Baldur; and Ch. Weland, born 1919 by Adamite out of Gascoigne Queen. Of these three dogs, Weland was exported to Canada and his line lost; Gathnell does not seem to have been used much at stud (his father, Priam of Wingfield is in fact like Weland behind most of the 1920 Canadian pedigrees); and King Baldur, who was used at stud, is behind the first purebred male Bull Mastiff champion, Roger of the Fens.

The fact remains that the lines carrying the Bull Mastiff out-cross blood seem to have come together in the post First World War years, to form the basis on which so many of today's kennels are founded. I am not arguing about whether this is a good or a bad thing, only that it is a fact. There are no Mastiffs alive today that do not go back to the Bull Mastiff registrations of the first 20 years of the 20th century. That is why it is important to understand them.

The United States of America   *Patricia B. Hoffman*

The history of the Mastiff after 1900 makes painful reading. It is difficult to believe that from the hundreds of dogs that were registered but a few years earlier, a drop to a mere handful occurred, then they almost totally disappeared from the *Stud Book*. The 1893 financial panic may have had some bearing, but more likely was the change in fashion. It was no longer chic to own a Mastiff. The First World War also fell within the period, but the decline had begun long before that.

In 1900, Volume XVII of the *Stud Book*, there were only 13 entries. Only one was imported, a brindle bitch named Herodias (54,739), by Tom Bowling, out of Di Vernon, whose pedigree went back to Beaufort. Her importer was R. D. Winthrop of Long Island; her breeder A. W. Lucas, and she was whelped in 1897. If she was ever bred, her progeny were not registered.

Dr. Lougest registered two males by his Black Peter out of an unlisted Lady Rossington. From the New Orleans kennels of Septime Villere came three entries: two littermates from Fred Hyatt of Missouri, and the remainder from various other breeders.

What had become of all the older breeders, located in almost every state in the union? C. A. Lougest was almost the only "old-timer" to continue breeding. He ran the following advertisement in the *Gazette* for April 1900:

> Mastiffs at Stud, Black Peter, Celebrated Brindle Mastiff (47,734) Highest pedigree. Fee $ 50. Leon II (43,047) Fawn Colored Mastiff, by Ch. Emperor William-Empress. Fee $ 25. . . . The above-named dogs are all 1st prize winners at shows held under AKC Rules, and this offers a grand opportunity for breeders to introduce the best blood at a reasonable price. . .

Evidently there were few takers for the opportunity. The last dog ever listed as having been bred by Lougest was entered the next year (*Stud Book* Volume XVIII, 1901). This was a brindle puppy named Paul (by Black Peter out of Black Beauty) who was owned by F. J. Martin, of Bangor, Maine. However, Lougest did acquire an 1895 fawn bitch, Lady Elkson II (60,045), but nothing further seems to have been heard of her. Four other Mastiffs were registered—one each by Hyatt and Villere.

Pedigrees could still have been rather vague, such as that of Flora (64,347) bred and owned by T. P. Daniels of New York:

> By Rex, out of Schmox, by Terry, out of Fannie, by Carlo, out of Polly; Terry by Rover, out of Dolly; Rex by Jack B. out of Chelsea, by Dick out of Blaze; Jack B. by Terry, out of Brasius.

Again, 1902 had but six entries in Volume XIX of the *Stud Book*. Hyatt and Villere accounted for four of the entries, and Martin owned one.

A slight gain was shown in 1903, with four males and three females in Volume XX. All but one were bred by Villere, two litters by Rex, Jr. (58,585) x Lady Nell (51,009), from 1902 and 1903. The other entry was an imported brindle male, Young Marksman (77,304) from Ledbetter [*sic*] of England and owned by F. J. Martin.

The year 1904 had but two Mastiffs from the same litters entered the previous year; one male, one female, indicating the perilous drop in breeding stock.

However, 1905 was a bit more encouraging, as ten were registered. Half of these were imported from England. Three brindles went to Lougest, and Martin had two brindles. These two, Peter the Great (85,648) and Paula (88,986) were the parents of four of the remaining entries, all one litter. The last entry was a bitch called Julia (88,580), described as "tan body; black face and tail" bred by M. F. Walsh of New Orleans.

Very few Mastiffs seem to have been shown during the decade—six for 1905 and eight in 1906. Registrations for the latter year went down to two (Volume XXIII).

Lougest again imported a bitch, Mount Vernon Playful (93,897), a fawn, by Mellnote [*sic*] out of Ethel May. The other entry was also a bitch, sired by a dog named King James, out of the bitch Julia, registered the year before.

In 1907 Martin imported a brindle male called Hazelmere Black Prince (108,828) who sired two males that were listed in the same volume. They were out of Lady Helen (68,517). The remaining entry of the four for the year, Volume XXIV, was Duke V (105,742), owned by Louis Emmons of Indiana. Described simply as tan, his pedigree was "unknown". He was stated to have been "1st, Open, Indianapolis, 1907; 1st Open, Cincinnati, 1907" but as a grand total of four Mastiffs were shown during that year, these wins were less impressive than they appeared at first sight.

In 1906 James Watson had lamented:

> When things get so bad that they cannot be worse, the only movement is in the line of improvement, and there are signs of a revival of interest in the Mastiff in England as well as America. Mr. Cooke, of Bangor, Me., has lately become interested in the Mastiff and tells us he has had quite a large correspondence forced upon him by persons who have learned of his importations. What these gentlemen should do is to join the Mastiff Club, if there is anything left to join, get hold of the challenge cups and what is still left of the moribund organization and put money and vim into the resuscitation of the breed. (*The Dog Book*, p. 569.)

Mr. Watson spoke too soon, as no "resuscitation" took place, and what happened to the "Club" and its cups remains a mystery. The "Mr. Cooke" referred to was doubtless a mistake for Forest Martin.

There were but two entries in 1908. George Kretz, of New Jersey, who had previously bought a puppy in 1905 from Martin, imported both. He acquired two fawn females, both bred by Mrs. R. J. Burch.

Both were sired by Mellnotte [*sic*]. Priscilla (117,258) was out of a bitch named Queen Alexandra; Synthia (117,259) was also by Mellnotte. But, sad to report, the following year went down to one registration. Rex IV (132,992), a fawn, was out of Julia by James, so no new blood was appearing.

Another call for action came from R. A. Sturdevant, who wrote in *Country Life in America*, September 1910:

It is still possible to revive this noble breed, but steps must be taken at once, as the strain has nearly run out, and good breeding stock is even now difficult to find in this country. . . . It is earnestly to be hoped that some fancier will see his great opportunity in bringing the Mastiff back to his own.

Apparently, there was little, if any, response. That same year (1910), only one female was registered in Volume XXVII. Midget (137,507) was bred by W. T. Simpson of Zanesville, Ohio. Her parents were simply given as Wodan and Darkie.

Another bad year was 1911. The *Stud Book* (XXVIII) showed but one entry, and that an import. W. DeClow, of Cedar Rapids, Iowa, imported a dog named Bornel (146,319), and no Mastiffs were recorded as having been shown. In 1912, no entries appeared.

However, matters improved in 1913. Morris Kinney, of Kinnelon Kennels in New Jersey, registered seven imports. Three male puppies were littermates, sired by Brompton Duke out of Batchworth Beauty (Kinnelon Brompton, Defend, and Ruler (174,036-8). A female, Kinnelon Batchworth (171,219) came from the same litter, whelped in March 1913.

At the same time Kinney brought in the dam, who was a 1910 brindle (170,427) by Cleveland Leopold out of Felica. The remaining two imports were sisters, Countess of Britain (170,429) a 1911 fawn, and Bullwell Queen (170,428), from 1910. Their sire was Wolfram and the dam Nottingham Queenie.

The *English Illustrated Kennel News* of 12th December, published an article on "Messrs Morris and Warren Kinney's Dogs", signed by a gentleman calling himself Fulgur. Pictured are British Monarch, Bernice, and Marquis of Lidgett. Mr. Kenney, according to the article, went to Cruft's in 1913 "with the intention of acquiring a team of Mastiffs, hoping to bring the grand old variety back into favour". It then went on to discuss Ch. British Monarch (who, however, was not officially an American champion until 1914). "He is of immense size and substance, excels in type and quality, has wonderful legs and feet, and owns a really beautiful head and body." Indeed, judging by the photo, he was a fine specimen. Fulgur wrote of Bernice that she was "the equal of any dog in head, bone, and body proportions". Both these Mastiffs were fawn. Monarch was sired by Salisbury, out of Countess Soudersburg [sic] and was actually registered in 1914 as 178,974. Bernice became a champion in 1915, the year she was entered in Volume XXXII (189,643). She was sired by Ronald Widmere out of Buena Ventura.

There was one other entry for 1914, Merion Monarch, (185,694) who was imported by William Folwell, of Merion, Pa. (Pegasus x Jessie Marton). P. D. Folwell, of Philadelphia, acquired an imported bitch in 1915, Queen Bess II (192,746), a fawn puppy by Viscount of Lidgett out of Lightning. This Volume (XXXII) was divided for the first time, and Mastiffs appeared in "Non-Sporting Division". The other entry of the three for the year was a Scottish dog called, appropriately, Ben Lomond (207,987) who was by Bayardo out of Towards Pride, bred by A. W. Goldie and imported by A. M. Tupper of Massachusetts. It is of interest to note that apparently none of these dogs produced, or, if they did, none of their offspring were registered. Again, what happened to all of them?

No entries occurred in 1916 and 1917. However, Folwell's Queen Bess became a champion in the latter year.

By 1918, the *Stud Book* had become a part of the *Gazette* and was issued monthly. The only entry for that year was Beowulf (240,548), a dog bred in Canada by C. W. Dickinson, who was to supply virtually all the dogs to the United States for many years. Beowulf was sired by Priam of Wingfield out of Parkgate Duchess. A fawn owned by Mrs. A. E. Ingle, of Rochester, New York, he went on to become a champion in 1922.

Dickinson bred all the five entries for 1919. One pair, Ashburn Roland and Stella (255,192 and 255,193) were by Priam of Winkfield [sic] out of Helga of Winkfield. Two others, Tarzan (262,544) and Lady Juno (266,991) were by Prince of Wingfield out of Juno of Wingfield; the final entry was Rufus of Wingfield (266,835) by Conrad of Wingfield out of Boodrien of Wingfield—all of these had substantially the same bloodlines.

Writing some years later, in 1922, in *Kennel and Bench*, W. O. Ingle wrote about the early Mastiffs of the century. After commenting on the sad decline of the breed:

> In 1913, however, Morris Kinney of Butler, N.J., started a revival by importing "British Monarch," "Marquis of Midgett" [sic!], "Bernice," "Countess of Britain" and "Batchworth Beauty". . . . Unfortunately, however, Mr. Kinney gave them up in a few years, and it remained

up to my good friend, C. W. Dickinson, Toronto, Canada, to keep up the interest in this grand old breed . . . . My re-entry into the Mastiff fancy was in 1917 when I purchased "Beowulf" for a guard and companion for our country home, and he has certainly proved to be such in every way.

I could find no record of Marquis of Midgett, which was in any case a misprint for Lidgett. A photo of such a dog appears in the 1913 article mentioned above, but no information on the dog was given. Another of our Mastiff mysteries!

U.S. MASTIFF REGISTRATIONS 1900-1919

1900 - 13	1910 - 1
1901 - 6	1911 - 1
1902 - 6	1912 - none
1903 - 7	1913 - 7
1904 - 2	1914 - 2
1905 - 10	1915 - 3
1906 - 2	1916 - none
1907 - 4	1917 - none
1908 - 2	1918 - 1
1909 - 1	1919 - 5

Chapter 4

1920-1940

The United Kingdom   *Elizabeth J. Baxter*

This is a period which seems to have been mainly ignored by the majority of Mastiff writers, although Mr. E. G. Oliver writing about 1934 comments on the fact that:

> At the end of the war breed stock was scanty but it should have been possible, with care and good management, to revive the breed on pure lines; but all rules which should regulate careful breeding were disregarded by some fanciers, several outcrosses chiefly with Bull Mastiffs were introduced and the progeny were mated together indiscriminately without any attempt to eliminate the alien blood. Consequently many of the so-called Mastiffs lacked the benign and noble expression typical of pure bred stock and combine puggy faces with short bodies, light loins and straight hindquarters. This deterioration in the type unfortunately discounts the increase in numbers and improvement in competition which has taken place in the last few years.

Apart from this he ignores the dogs, the kennels, and the breeders of the between wars period as does Mrs. Norah Dickin in her book *The Mastiff* 1935, written at the same time but unfortunately withdrawn from publication because of a dispute over copyright. The only comprehensive book written since the Second World War, was *The Mastiff*, written by Marie Moore and published in 1978 by Denlinger, and this too only mentions this period briefly…

Mr. Oliver was not alone in voicing his disapproval of the use of the Bull Mastiff blood, and comments were made in the Old English Mastiff Club annual report for 1922 as follows.

> In the course of the year the attention of the Kennel Club was called to the registrations of Bull Mastiffs as Mastiffs with the result that the registrations have been cancelled and the dogs had to be reg-

istered as crossbreeds. The great importance of watching carefully the pedigrees of Mastiffs must be apparent to everyone interested in the breed and it is therefore with regret that your committee have noticed the singular apathy shown by members in forwarding to the Honorary Secretary the pedigrees of Mastiffs bred and owned by them, to be included in the club's record of Mastiff pedigrees.

This was followed by 1923 by:

In your committee's report for 1922 attention was directed to the registration at the Kennel Club of Bull Mastiffs as Mastiffs. Your committee earnestly hope that some method may be adopted by the Kennel Club whereby evidence of unregistered dogs being of the breed they purport to be may be secured. Certain dogs registered as Mastiffs should have been registered as crossbreeds. Bad results may follow such registrations and it is only reasonable to presume that the sale of these crossbred dogs as Mastiffs, which has been and is taking place, can hardly fail to have a prejudicial effect on the breed.

Finally, in their report for 1924, we read: "Your committee regret that during the past year registrations have appeared under the heading of Mastiffs which should, in their opinion, have appeared under that of Crossbreeds."

It will, therefore, be apparent that the whole question was a vexed one. Although there certainly were Mastiffs available who did not carry any outcross blood and these were used extensively, with their apparent vigour, the "new" lines were also used a great deal and two of the best known and most influential of our kennels, the Havengore and the Withybush, were, in part, founded upon them. I find it slightly amusing that by 1929 Miss Bell (Withybush), Mr. and Mrs. Scheerboom (Havengore) and the Olivers should all be on the Old English Mastiff Club Committee. The Olivers, and the club itself, were strongly opposed to the introduction of what they considered to be "alien blood", yet all of them ended up on the governing body of the OEMC. There must have been a considerable amount of disagreement!

Miss Ianthe Bell was the owner of one of the most renowned kennels, not only of this period but of any period. She did not use the prefix "Withybush" until after the Second World War and her early dogs were registered with simple names, such as Woden, Ursula, Helga, etc. Miss Bell's foundation bitch was Squire's Daughter of Westcroft, the mother of Woden. He was born on 12th January 1924 and his pedigree is given in Appendix I. Woden proved a great stud force and was much used.

Miss Bell was the breeder of such well known dogs as Ch. Ursula, 18th May 1926; by Woden out of Victoria Menai; Ch. Uther Penarvon, born 1st October 1929 by Rufus out of Bilichilde; Helga, by Woden out of Victoria Menai; Lady Hildur by Ch. Blaise of Westcroft out of Lady Byron; Son of Thunder by Adamas out of Vilna; and the lovely Ch. Lady Turk, 20th July 1929, by Ch. Bill of Havengore out of Nerica. She also owned Ch. Cleopatra of Westcroft, 26th October. 1920, by Ch. King Baldur out of Princess Lie a Bed. It is probably to Miss Bell that we owe the survival of the brindle colour, as it was then, as it was to become again in the 1950's, extremely rare and her Nerica, Ch. Lady Turk and the dog, Son of Thunder, were all brindles.

The Havengore Mastiffs do not appear to have done quite so much actual winning between the wars though they were always a force to be reckoned with. From Ch. Bill of Havengore, a son of their foundation bitch Crescent Rowena and Ch. Master Beowulf came the beautiful "typical" Mastiff heads which today we so admire. Bill's pedigree is shown in full (see Appendix I), and it is thought provoking to realise that this beautiful dog (see judge's critique in the next paragraph) carried not only the "new blood" but probably, through Cleveland Leopold, a strong dose of St. Bernard blood also.

In passing it may be of interest to quote some judges' comments about this dog. Writing in 1927, Mr. Norman Higgs says: "Bill of Havengore was suffering from the result of an accident so I will dismiss him with this remark, that I consider him the most perfect headed Mastiff exhibited at Richmond; his is the correct type." Mr. Hunter Johnston, in August 1926, says: "A dog that came nearer to my ideal of what a Mastiff should be than any other that was shown. A beautifully moulded head with small, well carried ears, and a good deep square muzzle, sound legs, plenty of bone and stands well. His one weak point is a curious twist in his tail which detracts somewhat from his appearance when viewed stern on. This dog carries me back to the breed's palmy days of the '80's for he reminded me very much of the late Mr. Mark Beaufoy's famous Beau."

Ch. Bill was used by Miss Bell on her bitches so it would appear that these two owners cooperated in their breeding plans and had the same views, aims and aspirations. Between them, they greatly influenced the evolution of the Mastiff both of that period and of today.

The third major kennel was the Hellinglys owned by Mr. and Mrs. E. G. Oliver. There appears to have been a fair amount of "needle" between the Olivers and the other two kennels as will be noted from Mr. Oliver's comments on the Bull Mastiff influence on the breed and the people who used it. Of the three kennels, it was the Hellinglys who kept strictly to the pre-war bloodlines and away from any lines which they considered could be tainted with an outcross. Their great force was Ch. Joseph of Hellingly (whose name had been changed from "Studland"). He was born 24th September 1925 and was by King Baldur of Wantley out of Tweedview Belle. He was for the Olivers what Bill was for the Scheerbooms and Woden for Miss Bell. The Hellingly kennel was probably larger than either of the others, and won consistently throughout the twenties and the thirties. Some famous dogs which they owned in the twenties were Hannibal of Hellingly, 6th June 1929 by Ch. Cleveland Premier out of Hecuba of Hellingly; Hecuba of Hellingly, winner of the OEMC breeders bowl; Ch. Joy of Wantley, 12th February 1925 by Ch. King Baldur out of Hecuba of Hellingly; Boadicea of Hellingly; Lumbering Sheila; Lady Here of Hellingly; Almost of Hellingly and Flavia of Westcroft.

There were other well known kennels in the period leading up to 1930, probably the best known for its quality being Haddon Hall, whose dogs were registered under the Menai suffix; the property of Messrs R. Humphrey Thomas and C. R. Oliver (not to be confused with E. G. Oliver). They bred Ch. Yosemite Menai, born 17th February 1924 by Ch. King Baldur out of Ch. Berenicea of Ashenhurst; her daughter Ch. Juno of Menai, born 20th September 1925 by Ch. Cedric of Ashenhurst; Anglesea Menai and his brother Comet Menai; and Victoria Menai (name changed from Lady Norah), born 12th September 1924 by Ch. King Baldur out of Pinxton Lady. This was another line, which was free from any of the new blood, but Mr. R. H. Thomas died in April 1932 and the kennel faded from view.

Ch. Yosemite Menai won the Challenge Certificate at Crufts in 1927 and her daughter, Ch. Juno, did the same in 1928. Of Anglesea Menai it is recorded that he is: "A typical Mastiff, fawn, lovely head, black mask ears and eyes. Stands 34 inches, weighs nearly 15 stone, girth 47 inches." And of Comet Menai: "Very similar to his brother Anglesea and the only dog able to get Ch. Yosemite Menai in whelp except the late Ch. Cedric of Ashenhurst, his sire—3 years, seven dogs having failed." This seems to have a familiar ring about it for the present day breeder, I feel!

The Cooks, father and son, owned the Cleveland kennels and their best-known dog of this time was Ch. Cleveland Premier, born 16th April 1925, by Adamas out of Vilna. It is of interest to note that Adamas was a brindle, one of the lines by which this colour was retained. Another of the Cooks' dogs were Cleveland Hugo, and they were, of course, breeders from pre-war days.

Mr. Guy Greenwood owned the "Hillcrest" Mastiffs, having Ch. Duke and Benvolio, his son. Benvolio was born on 20th February 1927, out of Bess of Bronygarth and won fifteen firsts, a Challenge Certificate and the Old English Mastiff Club's Beaufort, County and Thirty Guinea Cups.

The Benton Mastiff kennel was the property of Mr. H. C. Liddell, and Benton Adonis, born 2nd April 1926 by Ch. Blaise of Westcroft out of Sheila of Westcroft, looks to be a dog with a good head but slightly weak in the hindquarters. His litter brother, Benton Timothy, has a slightly longer muzzle but better hindquarters. Both were fawns.

The Saxondale kennels, whose owner, Mrs. Taylor, died in 1990, continued breeding Mastiffs up until the mid 1960's, commenced operations in the mid 1920's, choosing a Hellingly Mastiff, Hilda of Hellingly, as her main foundation bitch.

Mrs. Kennett bred two champion dogs, and two champion bitches, Blaise of Westcroft and Bulger; and Chloe and Cleopatra of Westcroft. Mr. N. Haigh bred Ch. Cedric of Ashenhurst and Ch. Bernicea of Ashenhurst; Mr. A. Baggaley bred Superbus, and Mrs. L. Woods bred the lovely fawn bitch Ch. Volo of Ileden (born 30th April 1929), who won the challenge certificate at Crufts in 1929, with Ch. Joseph of Hellingly taking the premier award in dogs.

Of the actual breeders, the old stalwarts from pre-war days, Mr. H. Cook and his father Mr. George Cook, and Mr. Guy Greenwood were still active. Mr. W. K. Taunton, the doyen of the breed, died in 1926 but others, like Mr. S. Crabtree and Mr. Norman Higgs although no longer actually breeding, remained on the Club's judging list. In fact, the Old English Mastiff Club's list of judges, printed in 1929, consists of Mr. Cleminson, Mr. Cook, Mr. Sam Crabtree, Mr. Hunter Johnson, Mr. Joice, Mr. Norman Higgs, Mr. Walker Hall, Mr. G. Greenwood and Mr. Croxton Smith. Some of the "newcomers" such as Mr. Illingworth, Mr. E. M. and Mr. H. C. Liddell, Mr. and Mrs. Oliver, Miss Bell and Mr. and Mrs. Scheerboom were on the Club's Judging list for open and members shows.

Let us now turn from the actual kennels and breeders to some background information and a few statistics. Registrations crept up, from three in 1918 to 99 in 1924. In 1929 Mr. Greenwood, the Chairman, reported at the Annual General Meeting of the OEMC that: "The number of Mastiffs registered last year is the largest for 21 years, consisting of 122; the average attendance of dogs at championship shows has again considerably increased, the average figure this year being 29 against 24 last year, an increase of over 20 per cent." Of these 199 registrations re-marked upon by Mr. Greenwood, nine were Havengore and 20 Hellingly. Membership of the Club itself for 1928 was 87, another increase on pre-vious years. The whole outlook was a healthy one.

During the 1920's comparatively few Mastiffs were exported to the United States, one being Caractacus of Hellingly, who was sent out in 1928 to Mr. E. Stillman. He was bred by Mr. H. Cook and was by Cleve-land Premier out of Princess Bunty. However, two were sent to Canada; Ch. Weland, born in 1919, and Thor of the Isles, exported in 1930. We-land was free of any outcross blood but Thor was almost entirely Bull Mastiff and, mated to the Canadian bitch Betty, ensured that the Bull Mastiff blood permeated the stock of Canada and America and was re-introduced to this country via Canadian stock sent to us after the war. This will be enlarged upon in a subsequent chapter. The 1920's were the first decade during which quarantine laws were really enforced, al-though they had been brought in at the end of the First World War. For the first time dogs could not be sent out of the country "on loan" to be returned freely at a later date. This must have had an effect on the breed-ing programmes of kennels in Canada, America and here.

The 1930-1940 decade saw the emergence of many new kennels and breeders and the disappearance of some others; the Menai kennel faded away and in its place we see the rise of the Tiddicar Mastiffs, belonging to Mr. L. Crook who, among others, owned Ch. Ajax of Hellingly and Black Prince of Tiddicar; Princess Bess of Tiddicar (by Ajax out of Break of Day) and Rex of Tiddicar (by Black Prince out of Beta) were both exported to the United States in 1936.

Mrs. Edgar owned the Deleval Mastiffs and these Mastiffs, like the Hellinglys, are behind all of today's British Mastiffs as they are in the pedigree of Sally of Coldblow, the sole surviving English bitch capable of breeding after the Second World War. Mrs. Edgar owned Sir Galahad of Deleval in the 1930's. Believed to be the largest dog of his day, he weighed 16 stone. She also bred and owned Ascelin, Wulfric, Torfrida, Joanne, Gydia, Boadicea and Urica of Deleval, among others.

Mrs. Dickin, writing in the mid 1930's, confirms that Mr. H. Cook was still active and says of him:

... Perhaps the best known prefix in the Mastiff world, the Cleve-land. The son of Mr. George Cook, himself a well known breeder, he has owned and bred Mastiffs all his life and most of the dogs of today can trace some of his strain in their pedigrees. Famous dogs he has bred are too numerous for mention but they include Ch. Cleveland Premier, Ch. Cleveland Ponorogo, Robert of Hellingly, and lately that wonderful litter by Cleveland Comedian ex. Arethusa of Hellingly, which includes three champions, Ch. Comedienne of Broomcourt, Ch. Cleveland Hugo and Ch. Blackmask of Broomcourt. (*The Mastiff*, pp. 80-81.)

The Broomcourt dogs, owned by Mr. B. Bennett, look from their pictures to be extremely handsome and typical Mastiffs.

Mrs. Dickin herself, the secretary of the Old English Mastiff Club, was the owner of the Goring Mastiffs and she was active up until her death in the early 1960's.

The Hellingly Mastiffs continued to make their presence felt and in 1932 we see our first male brindle champion, Ch. Marksman of Hellingly. Of the dogs which actually won their way into the *Kennel Club Stud Book*, 17 Hellinglys were recorded in 1937 and 12 in 1938, while they also made up Ch. Josephine and Ch. Cardinal.

The frontispiece of the Crufts catalogue for Mastiffs in 1934 shows a dog called the Mhor, born 26th October 1930, by Ch. Ajax of Hellingly out of Selene and the property of Miss S. Reid of Allendale, Northumberland. We read that he won over 30 prizes in breed and variety classes and the description of the Mastiff is printed below—slightly different from that given in today's Cruft's catalogue:

One of the oldest and noblest of British breeds, the Mastiff for some time has been under a cloud but it is satisfactory to know that the numbers are once again increasing. The Romans found these dogs in England and were so impressed with their size and power that many were sent to Rome to fight with wild beasts in the Amphitheatre. Presumably they were more active than those we know, as the Forest Laws forbade them being kept in the neighbourhood of forests unless some of the claws of the front feet were cut off with a chopper. In the reign of Queen Elizabeth they were used for baiting lions, bears and bulls, four of them being loosed against a lion and three against a bear. The modern dog is large, massive, powerful and symmetrical and, at his best, can move with unexpected freedom. The head is broad and looks almost square, the lips are deep and somewhat pendulous, and the ears are small and thin. The chest is broad, causing the forelegs to be set on wide apart, and the body is extremely powerful. Great size is desireable so long as there is quality as well. Their high intelligence and fidelity in alliance with their great strength make them ideal guards. They take their duties in this respect with a good deal of seriousness and some have been known to make a tour of the house at regular intervals during the night, just to assure themselves that all is well.

In 1934 another Havengore champion was born, "Christopher of Havengore, beautiful-headed dog who looks as good as anything we have in the ring today" according to a contemporary critique.

Before commenting on the registrations for the 1930's to 1940's, I would like to digress a little if I might, and mention the breed notes of this decade. There are interesting matters which they bring to light, many of them touched on in a previous chapter and which will no doubt be mentioned again many times. Mr. W. Norman Higgs, who had been one of the founder members of the OEMC and a Mastiff breeder since the 1880's was breed note writer for *Our Dogs*. Despite his age, he voiced his own opinions loudly and clearly. The Mastiff has, of course, during the length of its history been plagued by violent disagreements and arguments over type—chiefly head type, colour and ancestry. This decade was no exception. Added to which there were now two breed clubs, the Old English Mastiff Club and the Mastiff Breeders Association (founded by the Olivers) and the two clubs did not see eye to eye.

The breed notes for this period are extremely informative and I propose to quote from some of them. Mr. S. Crabtree, one of the very old and well-respected breeders, wrote suggesting that the modern breeders were producing Mastiffs with bigger skulls and shorter forefaces than the standard description and suggesting that it might be necessary to revise the standard. Mr. B. Bennett immediately burst into print saying:

We seem to have developed big, turnip headed skulls and muzzles to my mind are excessively long and more like a hatchet than a square box. . . . The main idea seems to be that nothing but size counts and dogs with a bad tail or undershot mouths have been damned whilst dogs with sound bodies and heads bearing a closer resemblance to an Alderney cow than a Mastiff have walked away with the prizes. I fail to see why sound dogs with appalling heads should be boosted. How many dogs today have a flat skull, square stop, width and depth of muzzle and a truncated muzzle?

Mr. Higgs then joined the fray suggesting that none of the present day animals conformed to the standard in that they were nearly all undershot whereas they should have level mouths. He held that a short muzzle produced a false impression of squareness and often was in fact narrow and produced a dish faced appearance. Quite vitriolic correspondence on type and head type raged throughout the autumn of 1932 and was only brought to an end when the editor closed the correspondence.

Another item of interest brought to light in the breed notes of that year was a letter from Mr. F. J. Hawkins, who wrote:

In the standard description of the Mastiff nothing is said about dew claws. These appendages appear on Mastiff puppies as they do on other breeds. In the writer's experience about half the puppies born have had dew claws on the hind legs. A perusal of old literature reveals that many Mastiffs 60 or 70 years ago which were at the top of the tree, exhibited this propensity of an extra toe, often not even a dew claw but an integral part of the foot .. these facts are doubtless reconcilable with the theory that the Mastiff and St. Bernard had a common origin.

The question of the St. Bernard and other outcrosses was the other matter which greatly engrossed the Mastiff enthusiasts of that period, chiefly because of the red colour which was becoming increasingly common at that time and which was put down to the St. Bernard crosses in the late nineteenth century and/or early twentieth century. On 29th September 1933 Mr. Crabtree wrote:

No one who has been in the breed any length of time will have any doubt about the fact that the St. Bernard blood has been introduced into the breed and there is no doubt in my mind that the primary reason for the cross was to introduce new blood into inbred stock and another reason may have been to get stronger and shorter muzzles. Whatever the reason, I think that the red and red brindle also emanated to a certain extent to that outcrossing. Also if we assume the registration of Penkhull Lady is correct, then the introduction of the bulldog would certainly have a great tendency to introduce the red brindle into the Mastiff—and to give the undershot mouths and turned up jaws as well as short faces, all very undesirable features.

Next month a reply came from a Mr. Baggalley:

My opinion is that the red colour in Mastiffs definitely comes from the St. Bernard even if in some cases it comes through the Bull-Mastiff. . . . the use of the St. Bernard is evidenced in the red colour, woolly coats and gay tails. I am firmly convinced that the reds in Mastiffs originally come from the St. Bernard even if later some came through the Bull Mastiff and I do not think Penkhull Lady is any more responsible for the red colour than the source Mr. Bennett mentions. It seems to me that any defect whatever in the Mastiff today . . . is put down to Penkhull Lady.

One more letter can be quoted, from John Edgar Allen, also writing in October 1933:

Sir, about the red colour in Mastiffs; I took up Mastiffs 34 years ago so know a fair amount. The bulk of the reds come from Cleveland Leopold and Cleveland Monarch (brothers) both red. Sire Caractacus, dam Princess Marton. The latter was by Duke of Cleveland x Lady Marton. Lady Marton was an orange tawny coloured smooth coated St. Bernard. I once challenged the late Mr. Price (Princess Marton's breeder) about resorting to a St. Bernard cross to produce the red colour and he admitted that as Lady Marton was in season he had tried his luck, with the above results.

It is interesting to note that the dog named here as specifically carrying a strong outcross of St. Bernard blood, Cleveland Leopold (1904), was used extensively at stud, being in the pedigrees of Ch. Woden and Ch. King Baldur to name but two; so lines carrying the St. Bernard outcross and the new Bull-Mastiff cross were inextricably mixed. It would appear likely that here we had the source of the shorter muzzles and broader skulls which were a bone of such contention then, and even now.

It seems from remarks made in correspondence in these breed notes and other letters of the early 1930's that there was quite widespread knowledge of an outcross again to a St. Bernard which had taken place shortly after the First World War but although hints are made no names are named and one is left to guess which kennel, if any, took this step; a guess which is still being made today.

To return to the more mundane question of registrations for the 1930's, these continued to be satisfactory, showing 164 in 1933 (of which 18 were Hellinglys), 101 in 1937 and 115 in 1938. In 1939 registrations, with the war looming, were down to 70 and the following years were disastrous.

Another event of importance for the breed occurred shortly before the war, when the sudden, tragic death of Mr. Oliver resulted in the Hellingly kennel was disbanded. The great majority of their dogs, such as Monarch, Kathleen, Katrina, Damon, Maud, Duke, Dagmar, Kate and King were sent to America between 1937 and 1939, mostly to the Altnacraig kennels of the Clarks. These animals are now behind the descendants of animals re-imported into this country after the Second World War and their bloodlinesare represented today, in this country, solely through the dogs sent to America in the 1930's.

Other Mastiffs, too, had been sent to America in the early part of this decade, among them Goldhawk Elsie, bred by Mrs. R. M. Langton; she was by Sioux Chief out of Tess of Woodbrook; Millfold Lass and Roxbury Boy were bred by J. Peters, by Ajax of Hellingly out of Sweet Memory; and Buzzard Pride bred by Mrs. Briscoe of Ireland, was by Comet Menai out of Judy of Hellingly. It is interesting to note that these dogs, between them, represented a mixture of "pure" pre-war blood and the outcross blood are the antecedents of Mastiffs bred by Mr. Merle Campbell and supplied by him as foundation stock to Mrs. H. Mellish who in turn supplied this country with pups which saved the breed, after the war.

We, therefore, have to come to the conclusion that Mastiffs, of any and every country, now contain an amalgam of all the bloodlines of the 1920's; the stock sent to America prior to the war, sent to avoid destruction here, ensured that even the Altnacraig dogs—pure Hellingly stock—were interbred with other lines to produce the Mastiff as we know it today.

The period 1920-1940 was a period of improvement, stabilisation and increase. Some people may think that the author is bemoaning the fact that there is so much Bull Mastiff blood behind present day Mastiffs, but this is not the case. The arguments of the early 1920's were echoed to a large extent by arguments in the previous century—outcrossing always provokes discussion. It was nothing new, but merely that better records were being kept; and given the shortage of breeding stock after the First World War it was understandable, however much the purists might deplore it. Personally I find it intriguing that the "typey" heads which are so sought after are found, in the 1920's, commonly in animals carrying the new blood—yet judges, judging the progeny of these animals, rave about "head type" and comment on how like the dogs of the 1880's they are. One could always say, with truth, that Bull Mastiffs evolved in part from Mastiffs so perhaps they were merely repaying a debt. It does go some way to explaining the difference in head types which we still see today, the shorter muzzled heavy head and the longer muzzled variety which would seem to be what the Hellinglys preferred. It also echoes the arguments for and against very short and longer muzzles, voiced by Sydney Turner and W. K. Taunton, and Taunton's plea for "a medium in everything" at the end of the 19th century. The most important thing is the breed itself, the Mastiff. Even if we do not all see eye to eye in our interpretation of the breed standard—which is after all the blueprint by which we must abide—let us give thanks that the breed has been saved on more than one occasion, to go from strength to strength.

The United States of America   *Patricia B. Hoffman*
The genetic pool of the Mastiff in the early part of the decade was very small, as virtually all the dogs were of the Wingfield line. Interest in the breed was on the increase, and a "Mastiff Club of America" was organized in Toronto Canada, in 1920. Its first president was C. W. Dickinson, of that city, and the secretary and treasurer was W. 0. Ingle, of Rochester, New York, who had imported Beowulf a few years earlier. The following year Mr. Ingle became president and the secretary was Miss Katherine McGuire of Ossining, New York. Unfortunately, we do not have any information on this earlier club, but it evidently was short-lived. Any records it had have disappeared.

All the four entries for 1920 in the thirty-seventh volume of the *Stud Book* were bred by Dickinson. Christine (279,912) was listed as having been bred by him with Beowulf as sire, so evidently the dog returned stud service to its breeder. The following year Miss McGuire acquired a littermate sister, Cleopatra (296,410). Rufus of Wingfield was entered as owned and bred by Dickinson, but in Volume XXXVI (1919) he had been owned by W. Smith, Jr. of Grand Rapids, Michigan.

In 1922 both Beowulf and Cleopatra became Champions, the last of the breed to gain the title until 1937. Mr. Ingle acquired Mary of Knollwood (325,600) from F. J. Montgomery of Canada. Prasagutus of Wingfield (326,472) had the same sire and dam, Wodin the Saxon and Princess Mary, but entered as bred by Dickinson. Also in Volume XXXIX for 1922, Ingle had three puppies listed by Beowulf out of Mary, one of which went back to Dickinson.

Volume XL, 1923, had but two entries. One was a brindle bitch, Beomarie, again the Beowulf-Mary breeding, who went to F. J. Beier of Buffalo, N.Y. The other was a Wingfield bitch.

By 1924 (Volume XLI) some of the Canadian imports began to show up as sires and dams. Five Mastiffs were listed. Three were littermates, sired by Ashburn Roland out of Cleopatra. F. J. Beier, who had previously bought Beomarie, acquired Hereward the Wake (399,158) from Dickinson, a brindle. The final entry was another Beowulf- Mary bitch called Rowena II (425,505).

In 1925, in addition to one Dickinson import, a fawn called Sad Face, Volume XLII at last showed some new blood. Robert the Devil (453,697) was imported but apparently had no offspring (Adamite x Penwortham Fanny).

About this time the *Gazette* and the *Stud Book* were published separately again. The magazine began to use pictures, as well as notes called "Where Fanciers Gather". However there were no notes on Mastiffs for several years. In 1926 breed club columns were first printed. That year, in Volume XLIII, only one Mastiff showed up, a Dickinson dog called Masked Marvel of New Jersey (554,970), by Orlando of Wingfield out of Eanfelda of Wingfield. And 1927 had not a single Mastiff registered!

In 1928, matters improved slightly as four entries came in. Only one, Sandy Girl (618,336) was of Dickinson's breeding. The other three were imported. Cleveland Dorothy (636,917) was a 1927 fawn, sired by Cleveland Chancellor out of Princess Bunty. The two fawn males were Parsifal (642,669) by Duke out of Fantine, and Caractacus of Hellingly (663,176), whose sire was Cleveland Premier, and his dam Princess Bunty. Only the latter sired puppies, according to the records.

The last year of the decade had but two Mastiffs, both registered by Beier. One was Betty (673,924), from Dickinson and the other was from his own Hereward the Wake out of Christine, named Burnetta (665,980).

Indicative of the greater interest in the sport of dogs was the appearance in 1928 of the magazine *Popular Dogs*. In 1929 it announced the formation of the present Mastiff Club of America. The article is given here in full, as it is the only record we have of the early years of the Club. It is of interest to note that of the dogs mentioned, Derek and Dauntless of Dervot, the Chapman imports, and Hawkeye Bruce were apparently never registered with the AKC. (Dauntless may have been Dantes, entered in 1933.)

"Mastiff Club to Meet" by C. R. Williams, *Popular Dogs Magazine*, 1929:

> The year 1929 has witnessed a fluttering among Mastiff fanciers which proves that this grand old breed is likely to begin the long climb back to the popularity it enjoyed forty years ago. It is strange how these changes in canine fashion occur. Over a year ago, without any of the principals knowing one another or of their plans, *simultaneously* the late Eliot Stillman imported the silver fawn dog puppy, Caractacus of Hellingly, from Mrs. E. G. Oliver; Miss Joanna Chapman imported a pair of apricots for breeding purposes; Stamford White, of Beloit, Wisconsin, imported one of the leading winners

of England in Mr. Guy Greenwood's Parsifal; Coy Burnett of Los Angeles, California, imported from Mr. Baggaley's famous kennels another pair, Derek of Dervot and Dauntless of Dervot; while, to return to New York once more, John W. Barnhart was importing another silver bitch for breeding purposes.

All this was taking place just as the Mastiff fancy lost one of its stanchest supporters in the death of H. H. Dickinson, of Toronto. Of the old guard there remained only F. J. A. Beier, of Williamsville, N. Y. He has been breeding and showing and importing Mastiffs for more than forty years and is the recognized authority in America today. Recently photographs and stories of his Mastiff kennels have appeared in the news-papers of some thirty cities throughout the country and he has been deluged with letters from people who wish to own a Mastiff. He imported the good silver stud dog, Hawkeye Bruce, last June.

As might be expected, the Westminster Kennel Club show in Madison Square Garden last February found a number of Mastiffs on the bench for the first time in several years. Mr. Barnhart's bitch won Best Mastiff. A month later, March 13th to be exact, several enthusiasts met to organize the Mastiff Club of America, Inc., which was chartered as a Membership Corporation under New York laws soon afterward.

The first meeting of members was held September 7th at Miss Elizabeth G. Stillman's Kenridge Farms, Cornwall-on-Hudson, N. Y., in connection with the show of the Storm King Kennel Club, where she is the guiding spirit. At that meeting by-laws and Standard were adopted, and from the incorporators the following officers were elected: F. J. A. Beier, president; John W. Barnhart, vice-president; Paul W. Chapman, Jr., vice-president and treasurer, and C. R. Williams, secretary. The other incorporators are Miss Elizabeth G. Stillman, Mrs. Grace E. Williams and Chauncey D. Stillman.

The first annual meeting will be held during the Westminster Kennel Club show, February 10th to 12th, in New York City, when officers and directors will be elected for the coming year. Hon. Justice Townsend Scudder, famous as a judge of his fellow-men as well as Spaniels, has been granted a special license to judge Mastiffs.

The club is ready to help anyone to import good specimens. Through its efforts Mr. and Mrs. G. A. Hedfors, of Baldwin, N.Y., have secured the imported silver fawn bitch, Lady Marjorie of Beamsley. She will probably be on the bench at Madison Square Garden. Mr. Barnhart's bitch will be prevented from repeating her triumph of last Westminster because she is expected to be heavy in whelp at the time.

Miss Stillman is looking forward to visiting England next summer and expects to bring back foundation breeding stock which will make her Kenridge Kennels famous for its Mastiffs. Other people prominent in the game are seriously considering taking up the Mastiff—"most fashionable of the big dogs."

Everyone interested in this ancient breed is cordially invited to join the club. Applications may be made to the secretary, Room 612, 225 W. 34th St., New York City. Dues are only $5 yearly and new members will pay $5 initiation fee.

The founding of the Mastiff Club of America in 1929 heralded an increase of interest in the breed. After the death of C. W. Dickinson in the late 1920's and the dispersal of his kennels, breeders turned back to England as a source of stock. Forty Mastiffs were imported during the decade, and a complete list is found at the end of this chapter.

The year 1930 had a rather slow start, with eleven entries in Volume XLVII of the *Stud Book*. F. J. Beier, a long-time fancier, imported four. The only Canadian dog was a bitch, Eanfelda of Wingfield (735,005), by then seven years old. The three English imports were: Thor of the Isles (735,952) by Prince, out of Jersey Queen, listed as "silver fawn"; Goldhawk Buster (735,006) was by Cleveland Chancellor out of Woodbrook Princess; and Warrior (759,967) was by, Blaise of Westcroft out of Cleopatra of Westcroft. All were fawn.

Several of the dogs mentioned in the article on the founding of the Mastiff Club were listed in 1930. Benardo of Pinetrees (739,223) and Mattesdon Tondelayo Goodbreed (739,224) were both "red fawn". The former was by Prince out of Nanette of Pinetrees; the latter by Duke out of Flavia of Westcroft. Both had much of the same ancestry, as their dams traced back to Jersey Lion and Penkhull Lady. Mrs. Hedfors brought in Lady Marjorie of Beamsley (739,167), a 1929 fawn, sired by Anglesea Menai x Mary of Beamsley. Miss Ianthe Bell, later to use the kennel name Withybush, sent a brindle male, Dagonturk (744,859) to George S. Amory. Out of Nerica, his sire was Bill of Havengore, thus introducing another famous kennel line into this country. Vagabond King of Ileden (754,204) was sired by Cleveland Premier out of Honor of Hellingly. From these assorted imports came a number of kennels and breedings, most of which died out in later years and cannot be found in pedigrees of today.

In 1931 (Volume XLVIII), the listings dropped to four, and three of these were from England. Wardwell Jones owned Prince Patrick of Penn (783,275), who was to be the sire of many litters. His sire was King Peter of Penn and his dam Lady Patricia of Penn. Jones also owned Vagabond King. Lady Dinah of Eastburn (776,333) and Stella Menai (763,284) added to the roster of bitches. The former was by Plutarch out of Queenie; the latter by Anglesea Menai out of Maida Menai. The only American-bred was Sherman's Kate (971,436) by Caractus of Hellingly out of Bayberry June.

Six entries were listed in 1932; two of these were imported. Benton Jasper (823,420) was by the famous Joseph of Hellingly out of Benton Elizabeth. The other was Revilow (837,341), a fawn dog with the same parentage as Lady Dinah of Eastburn.

Two entries by Wayne Alter: Lady St. Paul and St. Paul Mike (Caractacus of Hellingly x Bayberry June). Mike and Buddy were given as bred by John Cole, by Warrior out of Bayberry June, which gives an indication how dogs changed hands.

In 1933 (Volume L) the entry jumped to twelve. A litter by Buddy out of Lady Marjorie of Beamsley accounted for five. Also American-bred were Taurus of Silvermine (900,418) and Little John (898,355) entered by Estelle Davy, as sired by Prince Patrick of Penn out of Bayberry June, who seems to have moved around a lot and produced a large number of puppies.

Imports were Dudley Leland's Dantes of Dervot (895,154), by Cleveland Premier out of Bretwalda Maid of Wantley. Gem of Goring (877,427) was a fawn bitch by Thor x Wyndley Boadicea.

At this time Colonel P. Hobart Titus made his appearance. He was to become one of the principal breeders of the next decade. His three imports were to be the foundation of his kennel, known as Manthorne, and thus of many later breeders.

Roxbury Boy (854,778) was a fawn, by Ajax of Hellingly, out of Sweet Memory. Millfold Lass (854,779) was a littermate. Goldhawk Elsie (854,780) was by Sioux Chief out of Tess of Woodbrook. Her sire was reported to have been a very large dog, standing 33 inches and weighing 228 pounds.

An article in *Country Life*, September 1934, described a visit to Manthorne. Photos with it showed Millfold Lass and her litter sired by Prince Patrick of Penn. Her sire, Ajax of Hellingly, was also pictured. According to the author of the article, Charlotte Marsden, both Elsie and Lass traced their ancestry back to the Lyme Hall strain, but no evidence was advanced. Lass is described as silver fawn, Elsie "that most rare and beautiful Mastiff coloring, the true apricot".

The only champion of the decade was Titus's Manthorne June (A31469), whelped in 1935 and gaining her title in 1937. Her parentage was Buddy x Millfold Lass.

Manthorne listed its first puppies in Volume LI, 1934: three males from the litter of nine mentioned above. Wayne Alter entered two, Duke Legh of Lyme (939,435) (St. Paul Mike x Gem of Goring), and Dorothy W. (958,200), same sire, out of Mazie of St. Paul. These accounted for the total of five entries.

Eighteen of the twenty seven Mastiffs registered in 1935 (Volume LII) were from Titus breeding. Three were from the Patrick-Lass litter; five from a Roxbury Boy and Elsie breeding; and a very large number (A3461-70) from Buddy and Millfold Lass-including the future champion Manthorne June. Additional entries were by Wayne Alter who listed four more out of his Mazie of St. Paul and three from Gem of Goring, all sired by St. Paul Mike. Imports were Buzzard Pride (979,365) from Ireland, (Comet Menai Judy of Hellingly), and Brutus of Saxondale (933,445), by Arolite out of Hilda of Hellingly.

Mr. and Mrs. John Brill's Peach Farm Kennels entered the Mastiff scene in 1935, with the acquisition of Manthorne Peach Farm Matilda (999,250), a Roxbury Boy x Goldhawk Elsie puppy. They also bought Manthorne Mogul (A31,461). The first litter from this pair came in 1937, and the Brills kept Peach Farm Clothilda, who was subsequently bred to Baron of Altnacraig. From the Clarks of Altnacraig came Austin of Chaseway.

From 1935, Peach Farm Kennels figured prominently in many American and English pedigrees, for reasons that will be discussed later. It was the only kennel in this country to breed continuously until 1982 when Mrs. Brill died, at which time the dogs were dispersed.

Volume LIII (1936) had five of the thirteen Mastiffs as imported. A brindle male, Samson of Lympne (A91,127) was sired by Piers of Deleval out of Morwena of Trelyon. Princess Bess of Tiddicar (A73,812) was imported by Mrs. Byron Rogers (Ajax of Hellingly x Break of Day). This bitch apparently went almost immediately into the ownership of the Clarks of Altnacraig, according to an article written several years later.

Edward Griffin imported Black Mask of Broomcourt (A67,724), a male sired by Cleveland Comedian out of Arethusa of Hellingly, and Broomcourt Nell (A67,723) (Brigadier x Veldicea). Rex of Tiddicar (A87,260) by Black Prince of Tiddicar x Beta belonged to 0. E. Bache and completed the list of imports. The remaining entries were all bred by Titus and Alter.

Probably the best-known breeders of the 1930's were Mr. and Mrs. James Foster Clark, whose elaborate kennel and breeding program were well documented. A *Gazette* (January 1942) article described Altnacraig, as the establishment was called, with many illustrations. The Clarks founded their bloodlines almost exclusively on the Olivers' Hellingly line.

Among the 26 registrations in the 1937 *Stud Book* (Volume LIV), there were four dogs, all with the suffix "of Hellingly" imported by Altnacraig. They were: Kathleen and Katrina (King Baldur of Hellingly out of Elaine of Hellingly); Damon (Duke of Hellingly x Berenice of Hellingly); and Maud, whose sire was Marksman of Hellingly out of Girl of Trelyon. Another Hellingly dog, Monarch, littermate to Maud, was listed as owned by Mrs. Byron Rogers, but apparently he went to the Clarks shortly afterwards.

The Clarks had an interesting plan, called "adoption", by which the Mastiff was placed in a home as a pet. They did not believe that the breed would develop to its full potential in a kennel situation. Later, if the animal proved suitable, it would be used as breeding stock. Rights of the Clarks and of the custodian of the dog were carefully arranged to prevent any difficulty as time went on. Apparently the scheme was not in effect long enough to have much impact on the breed. Very few descendants of the Altnacraig line can be traced.

Two males completed the roster of imports for 1937. Stanley Rinehart, Jr., owned a dog called Roger of Ancramdale (A161,317), by Sir Timothy out of Sarah of Frearn. Crusader of Goring (Robert of Goring x Deidre of Deleval) was imported by Anna Hoyt and listed as A174,361.

Most of the remaining entries for the year were litters bred by Titus, Alter, and Griffin, showing how few fanciers were active at the time. However, Peach Farm listed its first litter, whelped in April 1937. There were two males and two females, sired by Manthorne Mogul out of Manthorne Peach Farm Matilda.

Volume LV of the *Stud Book* showed an increase to thirty entries, mostly American bred. Edward Griffin was listed as breeder of fourteen. What must have been a complete litter went to Dr. Harry Veach of Los Angeles, and all entered with the prefix "Angeles". Griffin's Boss was the sire, and the dam was Angeles Queen who was also registered in the same volume. As she was whelped in May 1937, and her litter came in July 1938, she was a very young dam.

Wayne Alter continued to list. The first puppies from Altnacraig appeared, called Annora and Alair of Altnacraig (Duke of Hellingly x Maud of Hellingly), whelped in May 1938. Charles Ackerman listed a pair of pups, and also imported Rosamund of Deleval (A269,184) who was sired by Paladin of Deleval out of Gloriana of Deleval.

Two more Hellingly dogs were imported. Col. Titus acquired Dagmar of Hellingly (A256,505) who was a son of Duke of Hellingly out of Berenice of Hellingly. Rather confusingly, the Clarks imported Duke the same year. He was out of Josephine of Hellingly by Ajax of Hellingly, and his number was A225,559.

Also to Manthorne went Agrippa of Saxondale (A265,603), a male sired by Sir Timothy x Uda of Saxondale. Another import was Vancouver Corporal (A274,888), listed by Francis J. Garson of Trenton, NJ. The sire was Grenadier Brutus out of Prudence of Crestwood. Lastly, Stanley Rinehart, Jr. entered Wisdom of Goring (A251,141), by Despot out of Sybilla of Deleval, making six imports for the year.

The last year of the decade, 1939, was darkened by the war in Europe, but there were still two Hellingly dogs sent to Altnacraig. They were littermates, Kate and King of Hellingly (King Baldur of Hellingly x Elaine of Hellingly) whelped in 1936.

More of the Clarks' "A" litter were listed, plus the "B" litter of seven, which included the famous Boyce of Altnacraig (A342,848) whose photo has frequently been used to illustrate the standard of the Mastiff.

Dr. Veach entered a litter of four, sired by his Brian of Roxbroom, out of Goldhawk Elsie, who seems to have crossed the continent from Manthorne in Massachusetts to Los Angeles, California. Titus himself had but one of his breeding, Dianne of Manthorne (A299,977), who had been whelped in 1934, and was owned by R. G. Wahn. Alter had a few dogs listed, and Garson had one sired by his Vancouver Corporal out of Dorothy of Saxondale. There were a few entries of one dog by scattered breeders, few of which were ever heard of again. Registrations totaled 27.

U.S. MASTIFF REGISTRATIONS 1920-1939

1920 - 4	1930 - 11
1921 - 2	1931 - 4
1922 - 5	1932 - 6
1923 - 2	1933 - 12
1924 - 5	1934 - 5
1925 - 2	1935 - 27
1926 - 1	1936 - 13
1927 - none	1937 - 26
1928 - 4	1938 - 30
1929 - 2	1939 - 27

DOGS IMPORTED FROM ENGLAND, 1930-1939

1930 Vagabond King of Ileden (754,204) fawn
Breeder: Mrs. L. Woods
Owner: Wardwell Jones
Whelped: 30.4.1929 (Cleveland Premier x Honor of Hellingly)
Goldhawk Buster (735,006) fawn
Breeder: Mrs. R. M. Langton
Owner: F. J. A. Beier
Whelped: 9.10.1926 (Cleveland Chancellor x Woodbrook Princess)
Thor of the Isles (735,952) fawn
Breeder: Mrs. J. Evans
Owner: F. J. A. Beier
Whelped: 25.12.1926 (Prince x Jersey Queen)
Benardo of Pinetrees (739,223) red fawn
Breeder: G. C. P. Gudgeon
Owner: Johanna Chapman
Whelped: 2.9.27 (Prince x Nanette of Pinetrees)
Warrior (759,967) fawn
Breeder: Mrs. C. Kennett
Owner: F. J. A. Beier
Whelped: 9.8.27 (Blaise of Westcroft x Cleopatra of Westcroft)
Dagonturk (744,859) brindle
Breeder: Mrs. I. Bell
Owner: George S. Amory
Whelped: 20.7.29
Lady Marjorie of Beamsley (739,167) fawn
Breeder: G. Booth
Owner: Frances J. Hedfors
Whelped: 31.5.1929 (Anglesea Menai x Mary of Beamsley)
Mattesdon Tondelayo Goodbreed (739,224) red fawn
Breeder: H. J. White
Owner: Johanna Chapman
Whelped: 2.2.1927 (Duke x Flavia of Westcroft)

The History and Management of the Mastiff

1931   Stella Menai (763,284)
             Breeder: Thomas and Oliver
             Owner: Kenridge Kennels
             Whelped: 4.7.1928 (Anglesea Menai x Maida Menai)
         Lady Dinah of Eastburn (776,333) fawn
             Breeder: Mrs. Wesley Oliver
             Owner: G. E. Williams
             Whelped: 28.8.1930 (Plutarch x Queenie)
         Prince Patrick of Penn (783,275) fawn
             Breeder: Mrs. R. L. Kent
             Owner: Wardwell Jones
             Whelped: 1930 (King Peter of Penn x Lady Patricia of Penn)

1932   Benton Jasper (823,420) fawn
             Breeder: H. C. Liddell
             Owner: Emilie Hill
             Whelped: 22.8.1928 (Joseph of Hellingly x Benton Elisabeth)
         Revilow (837,341) Bitch, fawn
             Breeder: W. Oliver
             Owner: C. P. Williams
             Whelped: 13.12.1931 (Plutarch x Queenie)

1933   Goldhawk Elsie (854,780) fawn
             Breeder: Mrs. R. M. Langton
             Owner: Percy Hobart Titus
             Whelped: 18.4.1932 (Sioux Chief x Tess of Woodbrook)
         Milfold Lass (854,779) fawn
             Breeder: J. Peters
             Owner: Percy Hobart Titus
             Whelped: 17.4.1932 (Ajax of Hellingly x Sweet Memory)
         Roxbury Boy (854,778) fawn
             Breeder: J. Peters
             Owner: Percy Hobart Titus
             Whelped: 17.4.1932 (Ajax of Hellingly x Sweet Memory)
         Gem of Goring (877,427) fawn
             Breeder: Miss F. M. Crump
             Owner: H. Greenlee
             Whelped: 23.12.1932 (Thor x Wyndley Boadicia)
         Dantes of Dervot (895,154) fawn
             Breeder: H. Young
             Owner: Dudley Leland
             Whelped: 12.9.1929 (Cleveland Premier x Bretwalda Maid of
             Wantley)

1935   Buzzard Pride (979,365) Bitch, fawn
        Breeder: Mrs. N. W. Briscoe, Ireland
        Owner: William C. Josse
        Whelped: 23.3.1931 (Comet Menai x Judy of Hellingly)
    Brutus of Saxondale (993,445) fawn
        Breeder: H. Taylor
        Owner: Wayne Alter
        Whelped: 26.11.1931 (Arolite x Hilda of Hellingly)

1936   Black Mask of Broomcourt (A67,724) Dog, fawn
        Breeder: H. Cook
        Owner: Edward Griffin
        Whelped: 31.8.1931 (Cleveland Comedian x Arethusa of Hellingly)
    Broomcourt Nell (A67,723) fawn
        Breeder: J. Catchpole
        Owner: Edward Griffin
        Whelped: 11.3.1931 (Brigadier x Veldicea)
    Princess Bess of Tiddicar (A73,812) fawn
        Breeder: N. Clarke
        Owner: Mrs. Byron Rogers
        Whelped: 24.10.1933 (Ajax of Hellingly x Break of Day)
    Rex of Tiddicar (A87,260) fawn
        Breeder: L. Crook
        Owner: O. E. Bache
        Whelped: 14.9.1935 (Black Prince of Tiddicar x Beta)
    Samson of Lympne (A91,127) brindle
        Breeder: Mrs. F. Samuelson
        Owner: Brooks Stevens, Jr.
        Whelped: 28.3.1935 (Piers of Deleval x Morwena of Trelyon)

1937   Monarch of Hellingly (A119,356) fawn
        Breeder: Miss S. Reid
        Owner: Mrs. Byron Rogers
        Whelped: 14.2.1935 (Marksman of Hellingly x Girl of Trelyon)
    Kathleen of Hellingly (A146,181) fawn
        Breeder: Mrs. E. G. Oliver
        Owner: James Foster Clark
        Whelped: 22.7.1936 (King Baldur of Hellingly x Elaine of Hellingly)

    Katrina of Hellingly (A146,180) fawn
        Breeder: Mrs. E. G. Oliver
        Owner: James Foster Clark
        Whelped: 22.7.1936 (King Baldur of Hellingly x Elaine of Hellingly)

    Roger of Ancramdale (A161,317) fawn
        Breeder: Mrs. Arthur Barker
        Owner: Stanley Rinehart
        Whelped: 24.6.1936 (Sir Timothy x Sarah of Frearn)

Crusader of Goring (A174,361) fawn
  Breeder: Norah Dickin
  Owner: Anna Hoyt
  Whelped: 3.1.1937 (Robert of Goring x Deidre of Deleval)
Damon of Hellingly (A184,037) fawn
  Breeder: Mrs. E. G. Oliver
  Owner: James F. Clark
  Whelped: 4.4.1935 (Duke of Hellingly x Berenice of Hellingly)
Maud of Hellingly (A189,527) brindle
  Breeder: Miss S. S. Reid
  Owner: James F. Clark
  Whelped: 14.2.1935 (Marksman of Hellingly x Girl of Trelyon)

1938   Duke of Hellingly (A225,559) fawn
  Breeder: Mrs. E. Oliver
  Owner: James F. Clark
  Whelped: 27.6.1933 (Ajax of Hellingly x Josephine of Hellingly)
Dagmar of Hellingly (A256,505) fawn
  Breeder: Mrs. E. Oliver
  Owner: P. H. Titus
  Whelped: 4.4.1935 (Duke of Hellingly x Berenice of Hellingly)
Wisdom of Goring (A251,141) fawn
  Breeder: N. Dickin
  Owner: Stanley Rinehart, Jr.
  Whelped: 11.10.1936 (Despot x Sybilla of Deleval)
Agrippa of Saxondale (A265,603) Dog, fawn
  Breeder: H. Taylor
  Owner: P. H. Titus
  Whelped: 20.10.1936 (Sir Timothy x Uda of Saxondale)
Rosamund of Deleval (A269,184) fawn
  Breeder: Mrs. W. M. Edger
  Owner: Chas. A. Ackerman
  Whelped: 23.12.1934 (Paladin of Deleval x Gloriana of Deleval)
Vancouver Corporal (A274,888) fawn
  Breeder: J. J. Heaton
  Owner: Francis J. Garson
  Whelped: 3.10.35 (Grenadier Brutus x Prudence of Crestwood)

1939   Kate of Hellingly (A326,613) fawn
  Breeder: Mrs. E. G. Oliver
  Owner: James F. Clark
  Whelped: 22.7.1936 (King Baldur of Hellingly x Elaine of Hellingly)
King of Hellingly (A236,612) fawn
  Breeder: Mrs. E. G. Oliver
  Owner: James F. Clark
  Whelped: 22.7.1936 (King Baldur of Hellingly x Elaine of Hellingly)

4.1 Arolite, 1928. U.K.

4.2 Guy Greenwood's Hillcrest Mastiffs at the Gisborn Show, August 1928. Benvolio, Fantine, Bess of Bronygarth, Kundry, Ch. Duke. U.K.

4.3 Joy of Wantley, 1925 (Ch. King Baldur x Hecuba of Hellingly). Breeder H. Young, owners Mr. And Mrs. E.G. Oliver. U.K.

4.4 Miss Ianthe Bell with Withybush puppies, 1930's. U.K.

4.5 Agrippa of Saxondale, 1939 Owner/Breeder Mr. H. Taylor. U.K.

4.6 Miss Barbara Blackstone with Broomcourt Faithful and Defiant, 1938. U.K.

4.7 Guy Greenwood judging the Richmond Show, late 1930s Miss I. Bell at left, Mr. S.R. Anderson extreme right. U.K.

4.8 B. H. Titus with imports Goldhawk Elsie and Milford Lass, 1930's. USA

4.9 Aldwin of Altnacraig, ca. 1938 (Duke of Hellingly x Maud of Hellingly). Breeder/owner J. F. Clark. USA

4.10 Bruce and Jaime of Montrose, 1939 (Duke of Hellingly x Diana of Manthorne). Breeder/owner R. Wahn. USA

Chapter 5

1940-1960

The United Kingdom   *Elizabeth J. Baxter*

The fluctuations in fortune of our breed will have been described; the revival at the beginning of the nineteenth century, the popularity of the 1870's followed by decline in the early 1900's. Then an upswing which lasted until the First World War which was in turn followed by several years of great difficulty. In the twenty years preceding the Second World War, the breed went from strength to strength but then came the most dangerous and disastrous period of its entire history, when in the mid-1940's and because of the war there was only one bitch in the entire country of breeding age and it is to her and her alone that we owe the single line of continuity. This bitch was Sally of Coldblow, by Robin of Brunwins out of Hortia, the result of a mother/son mating. Her breeding goes back through Miss Bell's Uther Penarvon to Mrs. Scheerboom's Ch. Bill of Havengore and it is impossible to over-emphasise the important part she played, along with her breeder, in the survival of the breed as a whole.

Prior to the war, nearly all the Mastiffs had either been exported to America or were put down. The few that remained were, with the exception of Sally, not bred from and at the end of the war they were too old to be of help. For example, Rex of Havengore who was registered in 1946 was actually born in 1939.

Much as we owe a tremendous amount to Sally, we owe it equally to her mother, Hortia. This bitch, of Deleval breeding, was owned by Mrs. Park, the only person to actually breed a litter (according to Kennel Club records) during the war. Hortia was born 8th August 1937 and, mated to Ch. Christopher of Havengore, produced Robin of Brunwins on 5th December 1939. On 8th October 1943 having been mated back to her son Robin, Hortia whelped Sally being over six years of age at the time. Not only that but she actually had another litter, again sired by Robin, on the 15th May 1944, when she was seven. No trace can be found of this litter and there is no record of any of them having registered progeny.

In passing it might be mentioned how both dogs and bitches in the past seem to have been used for breeding at ages far exceeding anything that is currently acceptable. During the late 1800's, dogs are down as having sired litters at 10 and 11 years of age with bitches producing puppies at eight and 9.

In 1946 a registration of great significance is recorded in the Kennel Club breed supplement, i.e., Templecombe Taurus, registered in September of that year, further details unknown.

The story has often been recounted how a young brindle Mastiff was found wandering during the early war years; how he was rescued and accepted by the Kennel Club as a Mastiff; how mated to Sally of Coldblow this dog sired several puppies. Of these, the surviving puppy born on the 26th January 1947 was bought by Mr. K. Hulbert and registered as Nydia of Frithend. Like her grandmother Hortia and her mother Sally, it is quite impossible to over-emphasise her importance—without her, it is my conviction, that even with the imports which were later brought in from Canada and America, the breed would have died out in the United Kingdom.

The identity of Templecombe Taurus has long been a mystery and indeed a bone of contention as to whether he was a pure-bred Mastiff, a Bull Mastiff or a crossbred. In the summer (1984) issue of the Old English Mastiff Club newsletter there is an article about this dog written by Graham Hicks. The name here is given as Templecombe Toros but having checked with the Kennel Club they have confirmed that on their records the name is down as "Taurus" and so that is the spelling that I will use here. This article by Graham Hicks is interesting and well researched but unfortunately I have been absolutely forbidden to make any use of it for the purposes of clarification, in this book.

The bare bones of this dog's history, his master killed in the bombing on the South Coast, have been known for many years. What this article does do is give a much fuller picture as to how this dead master's friend handed him over to the lady with whom he was to spend the rest of his life. What it does not do unfortunately, is throw any definite light on to his parentage and, unless his papers and pedigree can ever be found, this will remain an area of speculation.

It has to be said that people who actually saw this dog were, and are, adamant that he was not a Bull Mastiff but I would now like to quote from a letter giving a different point of view. This was written to me by Mrs. Warren, owner and breeder of the Harbex Bull Mastiffs; written in 1983 when she was in fact herself 83 years of age, the original letter is of course available for inspection if required.

Harbex Tina had a litter in 1938 and a brindled bitch puppy (Lydia of Harbex) was sold to a Mrs. Button of Bexhill. Mrs. Button mated her to Ch. Springwell Major and Templecombe Taurus was the result. After intense consideration, I thought it was my duty to divulge this and so I had a private talk with Mrs. Dickin (the then secretary of the Old English Mastiff Club) and said that as the dog was from good Mastiff stock, and owing to the parlous state of the Mastiffs at that time, he could do nothing but good for the breed and if she wished it, that this conversation would go no further than the two of us. I left it to her. I heard nothing more from Mrs. Dickin and some time later saw the dog being exhibited—as a Mastiff—and had a quiet chuckle to myself.

Mrs. Warren very kindly enclosed a copy of Taurus's pedigree showing that, if what she said was correct, he was a red brindle Bull Mastiff descended on both sides from Ch. Roger of the Fens, the first male Bull Mastiff champion, and Roger was himself a greatgrandson of the Mastiff, Ch. King Baldur.

This version is denied by the protagonists of the pure-bred Mastiff theory, but I do not honestly think that after such a long space of time the mystery will ever be completely solved, unless papers are found for him.

According to Mr. Hicks' article, Mr. Warren attended the "Revival" meeting held in 1946, when Mastiff lovers gathered to discuss the saving of the breed, and signed a statement to the effect that he considered the dog, which was present, to be a Mastiff. According to Mrs. Warren, her husband returned from that meeting absolutely insistent that the dog was a Bull Mastiff and not a Mastiff.

Whatever the answer, he did as Mrs. Warren said in her letter to Mrs. Dickin do the breed nothing but good, so let us remember him for this fact and not because of the query as to his actual parentage. Without him there would have been no Nydia of Frithend and, repeating myself, without her there would be no Mastiffs, at least none that had continuity and complete British background. Survival would have had to come entirely from abroad; as it was, salvation at least in part, was produced at home.

Nydia was registered in 1947, the year that saw the faint start of revival. Other British registrations were her littermates, Ockite Wattagirl and Ockite Wattaboy, owned by Mr. White. However, these were not bred from. Honey of Parkhurst, bred by Mr. Parker, was imported by Mrs. P. Day from Canada, but although she produced one litter to the later imported Valiant Diadem, this line unfortunately died out, so cannot be said to be of lasting importance. The same is true of Victoria of Knockrivoch, imported from America by Mr. Bowles, as she too produced no progeny that was registered.

However, Mr. Bowles also registered Jana of Mansatta, born 17th January 1947, she was by the American dogs Sheba of Mansatta and Craig of Mansatta and her pedigree goes back through them to the English Saxondale Mastiffs of Mrs. Taylor on one side, and Canadian animals descended from Caractacus of Hellingly, Thor of the Isles and Weland on the other. Jana, through her daughter Ch. Vilna of Mansatta, is behind the Mansatta Mastiffs of the early 1950's. Havengore Comedian of Mansatta, Meps Jumbo of Mansatta, Petronella and Benedict of Mansatta, who are in most of today's pedigrees.

It is quite obvious from the above that despite six registrations being recorded for 1947, help was needed desperately, and it was essential to obtain fresh blood. To this end, Mrs. Dickin, the secretary, went to the United States and Canada, to try and obtain stock. One of the people to whom she spoke was Mr. Bob Burn, a young American breeder, as she wished to purchase a brindle puppy called Valiant Diadem, bred by Mr. Burn. But as he said in a letter to me, "she was talking ecumenical and I was talking economical" and so nothing came of this encounter. Diadem, born 30th June 1948 and by Hector of Knockrivoch out of Valiant Cythera, was a brindle who traced his pedigree back to the Hellingly imports of the 1930's and he was eventually bought and imported privately by, Mr. K. Hulbert. This was a most important and momentous purchase, because he and Nydia, between them, produced five litters, amounting to over 30 puppies, the last being born in September 1952. These 30 pups were a large proportion of the total births recorded—five litters between September 1949 and September 1952 deserve mention. One of the pups was Ch. Rodney of Havengore, 9th September 1949, the first post-war champion in the breed, and a brindle.

Mrs. Dickin's travels had not been entirely in vain as in 1948 a Mrs. Hyacinth Mellish of British Columbia supplied the Old English Mastiff Club with two puppies, both fawns, litter brother and sister. It was a life saving gift. Mrs. Mellish was born in England, but had gone to Canada in the early 1930's. She obtained her foundation stock from an American breeder, Mr. Merle Campbell, who in turn had bred from the English dogs exported to America in 1932 and 1934, i.e., Roxbury Boy, Buzzard Pride, Broomcourt Nell and Millfold Lass, who, as was shown in an earlier chapter, were an amalgam of all the British bloodlines. Mrs. Mellish mated one of her bitches, Can. Ch. Lady Heatherbelle Hyacinth, to Mr.

Parker's Canadian dog Rufus of Parkhurst and from this mating came Heatherbelle Sterling Silver and Heatherbelle Portia (later Heatherbelle Portia of Goring, as Goring was Mrs. Dickin's affix).

Faced with the very real possibility of the extinction of the breed, the English Kennel Club did what it had never done before nor since: it gave a breed club permission to register these two Mastiffs in the club's name, with the initials OEMC before their titles, hence OEMC Heatherbelle Sterling Silver, OEMC Heatherbelle Portia, etc. Portia went to Miss Bell (Withybush) who had been nominated as her "custodian" and Silver went to Mrs. Scheerboom. These are the only two registrations recorded for 1948.

In 1949 more Heatherbelle Mastiffs were imported privately, Heatherbelle Bearhill's Priscillia's Amelia, and Heatherbelle Bearhill's Rajah, both brought in by Mrs. Duke. I can trace no record of Amelia producing puppies, but Rajah was used at stud. Unfortunately, he was very closely related to the other two Canadian animals, as his sire was litter brother to Silver and Portia's sire and his dam was litter sister to Silver and Portia's dam. Even so, he was a valuable asset.

One other Canadian import was Heatherbelle Priscilla's Martha, a litter sister of Amelia, and imported by Dr. and Mrs. Mayne. She was by Eric of Knockrivoch (litter brother to the sire of Diadem, and although born in America, entirely British-bred from exported stock) out of Heatherbelle Hyacinth's Priscilla. Martha was the foundation bitch of the Mayne's kennel, producing one litter to Valiant and one litter to Rajah, but the kennel was disbanded when the Maynes emigrated to Australia in 1962. In 1978 they purchased another bitch from the writer, to start up in the breed again and were delighted to find that Martha was in the pedigree, about ten generations back.

By 1950 therefore, we have stock from five distinct sources: we have Nydia, the British born bitch; we have Valiant Diadem and Jana of Mansatta, both from the States, and we have two branches of the Heatherbelles, from Canada. The first generation of puppies produced from these animals were, for the most part, registered as being the property of the Old English Mastiff Club, thus we have OEMC Baroness, Prudence, Rodney, Baldur, Countess, Wolsey, Turk, Rowena, etc. The parents of the puppies registered appear to have been Valiant Diadem/Nydia and Valiant Diadem/Portia. As Diadem and Nydia were privately owned, it is obvious that Mr. Hulbert, their owner, most kindly made some of his stock available to the OEMC. The club owes him a great debt of gratitude.

When one studies closely the pedigrees of that time, one can be amused, appalled, or amazed at the amount of inbreeding that took place. Indeed, what else could be done? Valiant Diadem/Nydia offspring were mated to Valiant Diadem/Portia children and the resulting progeny were mated. Father mated daughter, mother—son, brother—sister, and so it went on. But it saved the breed. The OEMC bitches mated back to their fathers and brothers ensured survival and continuation.

We owe a lot to this very close inbreeding that took place then. We owe the very lovely "type" that emerged after the war and we also owe the unsoundness that was a legacy of this period.

It is fascinating to study the pedigrees of today's Mastiffs and see how they all (with the exception of one import in the sixties, one in the seventies and one in the 80's) funnel back to these original seven dogs, and how the lines then fan out to pre-war British animals, both those exported in the early 1930's and those exported just prior to the war.

In this immediate post-war period the brindle colour was comparatively common; Valiant Diadem was a brindle, Taurus had been a brindle, Ch. Rodney of Havengore was a brindle, as was Vyking Aethelwulf of Salying and OEMC Wolsey. Later on in the fifties, we get the beautiful brindles Ch. Withybush Aethelred and Ch. Drake of Havengore; but by 1960 the colour had once more become extremely rare.

To return to the earlier period: We have seen that up until 1950 the mainstay of the breed were our "pillars", and how over the years numbers gradually increased with 31 registrations in 1950, 32 in 1951 and 61 registrations being recorded for 1952 with the first *Stud Book* entries appearing for that year. At Crufts 1952, the first time Challenge Certificates (CC) were on offer since the war, Rodney won the dog CC and OEMC Countess the bitch. Both were by Valiant Diadem, with Rodney out of Nydia and Countess out of Portia.

Registrations crept up again; in 1953 we had 49, in 1954 there were 94 and in 1959 there were 58. This was a time of re-establishment and consolidation. Membership of the club increased and the outlook was good. The decade between 1940-1950 had been a terrible time; the next ten years saw hope and normality return. In actual fact the pedigrees of the early 1950's can be a little confusing, even misleading. Very few animals were registered with kennel prefixes, and we get names such as Valerie of Rayne, Cora of Wormhill, Jill of Flushdyke, Brevity of Bowerschurch, Semper Fidelis, Melita Salome, giving the impression of a plethora of unrelated breeding stock. This of course was not so; these bitches were all the result of breeding taking place between Valiant Diadem and

Nydia, or between the daughters of these two and Sterling Silver. Owned by different enthusiasts and not registered by specific kennels, it is somewhat hard to keep track of this first generation of post-war stock.

From 1950 to 1960 the two chief kennels were, as in pre-war days, Miss Bell's Withybush dogs and Mrs. Scheerboom's Havengore. Miss Bell being the custodian of Portia actually bred the majority of the Mastiffs registered as OEMC stock. The first litter born to Portia was on 13th August 1950, sired by our invaluable Diadem, and consisted of 12 puppies, amongst them being the first post-war bitch champion, OEMC Countess. She was subsequently purchased by Mrs. Edna Harrild, of the Moonsfield Great Danes. OEMC Boadicea, another of this litter, went to Mrs. Scheerboom. Portia's next litter was born on 21st June 1951, and was registered privately by Miss Bell; the sire was Ch. Rodney of Havengore (Diadem/Nydia) and consisted of nine puppies, three of which, Withybush Katherine, Rowena and Simon, were retained by their breeder. Miss Bell had also purchased OEMC Prudence (Diadem/Nydia) and on 28th June 1951, Prudence whelped five puppies to Heatherbelle Sterling Silver, one of them being Withybush Magnus who, as we will see, was sent to America subsequently to sire Wey Acres Lincoln. The Silver/Prudence mating was repeated a year later, with three more puppies, Withybush Lady Fayre, Lady Pearce and Lady Welcome, all of whom were kept by Miss Bell who by this time had sufficient stock to form a good nucleus of her post-war kennel.

Mrs. Scheerboom had charge of OEMC Sterling Silver, who was used so frequently on Diadem/Nydia daughters. She had also purchased the Diadem/Nydia son, Ch. Rodney of Havengore, an excellent stud force, together with his little sister OEMC Beatrix and the Diadem/Portia daughter, OEMC Boadicea. Apart from Rodney, the first post-war Havengore registration was for just one puppy, Ian of Havengore, born to Rodney and Boadicea on 25th February 1952, followed by two more litters in 1952 and 1953 by the litter brother and sister Rodney and Beatrix. These litters consisted of four and three puppies respectively. Like Miss Bell, Mrs. Scheerboom was enlarging and consolidating her kennel. Hugh of Havengore, the result of the litter brother/sister mating of Rodney and Beatrix was mated to OEMC Boadicea, his parent's half sister, and produced the beautiful Ch. Diann of Havengore; Hugh's full brother, Winston, sired Samson of Havengore. Mrs. Scheerboom also bought from Mr. Bowles Ch. Vilna of Mansatta (Heatherbelle Bearhill's Rajah) son, Havengore Comedian of Mansatta, who was mated to a Winston daughter, Cathie of Havengore, to produce the famous Minty of Havengore. Mated to Ch. Diann, their grandson was the superb Ch.

Hotspot of Havengore, who up until 1983, was the holder of the record number of Challenge Certificates won by a Mastiff dog. Numbers were increasing rapidly and it is hard to keep track of all the animals concerned without a sight of their pedigrees.

We must now mention the last import of this post-war period and another extremely interesting and important one. In the early part of 1953 Miss Bell imported Wey Acres Lincoln (born 13 November, 1952), a fawn dog bred by Mrs. Weyenberg in America. His father was Withybush Magnus, a dog sired by Heatherbelle Sterling Silver out of OEMC Prudence, who was a Diadem/Nydia daughter. Miss Bell sent Magnus to the States and in return took back one of his puppies, Lincoln, because Lincoln on his mother's side offered a little fresh blood. His mother was Peach Farm Priscilla and she had three or four generations of pure American breeding behind her before rejoining the English dogs. In fact, on her dam's side the American line goes back for seven generations before we find British names. A gap of about five years had elapsed between Lincoln coming here and the previous imports, so he was badly needed. Used extensively at stud he sired, among others, Ch. Withybush Aethelred, 27th January 1955, Ch. Withybush Crispin, 25th November 1956 and Jason of Copenore. It is probably through Jason that Lincoln has had the most influence on the breed as Jason, and *his* son, Ch. Threebees Friar of Copenore, appear in nearly every one of the pedigrees dominating the 1960's, complementing the breeding of the older kennels such as the Withybush and the Havengore, and producing magnificent stock. We will talk further about them a little later.

Other Mastiff breeders of the 1950 - 1960 period should be mentioned; one was Mrs. Day whose prefix of Hollesley is still so well known, and who had imported Honey of Parkhurst. From her bitch Ch. Dawn of Havengore Mrs. Day bred Larina, Leonora, Macushla, etc., the latter being behind all of the present-day Hollesley strain. Mr. and Mrs. Lindley founded the Copenore kennels; the Aberdeens, (owners of the Sparry Newfoundlands), bred Cleo of Sparry, Faithful Gilliard of Sparry and Crusader of Sparry, among others. Crusader was long coated but being otherwise a nice type was used at stud. Major and Mrs. Reardon founded their Buckhall kennels on a bitch purchased from the Aberdeens, Guinevere of Sparry. Mrs. Harrild, the owner of OEMC Countess, also owned her litter sister whom she bought and registered as Duchess of Moonsfield. Duchess was to become the mother of Ch. Baron of Moonsfield. Mr. Bowles, the importer of Craig and Sheba of Mansatta the parents of Jana, continued to breed, though not extensively, and we must not, of course, forget Mr. Hulbert, the owner of Diadem and Nydia, whose puppies were not registered with any specific kennel name. Mrs. Harvey, bred one litter which was registered as "of Salying" and one of these was the brindle dog Ch. Vyking Aethelwulf of Salying. He was by Heatherbelle, Bearhills Rajah out of Valerie of Rayne. The Saxondale Mastiffs, owned by Mr. and Mrs. Taylor who had been in the breed since the 1920's started up again and bred Boadicea of Saxondale and Cleopatra of Saxondale. Another small kennel was Meps, owned by Mr., Mrs. and Miss Perrenoud. Meps Basil was the sire of Ch. Hotspot of Havengore and was himself bred from the Perrenouds's foundation bitch, Withybush Beatrix; and Bill Hanson founded his Blackroc kennels on the Havengore line. The majority of these kennels actually reached their peak in the 1960's and will be discussed more fully in a later chapter.

There were 75 Mastiff registrations in 1957 and 92 in 1958. In this year the Crufts CC winners were Ch. Meps Angus (bred by the Perrenouds) and Ch. Vilna of Mansatta (Mr. Bowles). On the 11th February 1958 the wonderful fawn dog Ch. Hotspot of Havengore, already mentioned as being by Ch. Meps Basil, was born. He was one of the breed's all time "greats" and to my mind his pictures do him less than justice. 1959 was a Havengore year as far as Crufts was concerned with Ch. Drake (owned by Bill Hanson) winning the dog ticket at Crufts and Ch. Diann the bitch, although entries themselves were still fairly low. Seventeen dogs in all were entered and of these seven were Havengore, four were Withybush, with the Lindleys showing Jason of Copenore, Mrs. Reardon showing Guinevere of Sparry and Mesdames Lloyd Jones and Greenwell with Ch. Baron of Moonsfield. Mrs. Hector exhibited Olwen of Parcwood and Mr. Gray had Creola of Copenore. It is interesting to see that a bitch called Silver Queen of Zimapan, owned by a Comte Y de L"Arbre de Malander, of Cornwall, was offered for sale at a price of £ 200.

By 1960 the picture was very, very different from 1950. The future looked brighter. There were a few more Mastiffs, more newcomers, more breeders and more enthusiasts. The "old stalwarts" who had seen the club and the breed itself through its darkest days were still on hand to give advice and support and an atmosphere of optimism existed. Surely now the breed was safe; surely now the future was assured.

The United States of America   Patricia B. Hoffman
1940-1949

The year 1940 began a very difficult time for the breed. The complete loss of breeding stock in England is discussed above. In this country, though, it seemed at first that the breed might be on the upswing, as 31 were registered in 1940.

Robert Wahn, later Secretary of the Mastiff Club, registered a litter of six in 1940, *Stud Book* Volume LVII, by Duke of Hellingly out of his own Dianne of Manthorne. All the fawns, whelped in 1939, bore the suffix "of Montrose".

Peach Farm registered five; Wayne Alter, two. One of the latter's breeding, Alter's Big Jumbo (A444,636) went to Byron Parker's kennel in Canada and provided the base for later dogs that came to the United States (Buster of Saxondale x Angeles Victoria). Altnacraig's "D" litter of February 1940, consisted of Durwin, Dare and Drone (Aldwin of Altnacraig x Katrina of Hellingly). Eric of Altnacraig, the only listing from the "E" litter, was a brindle by King of Hellingly out of Maud of Hellingly.

Rather surprisingly, four dogs were listed from England, three of which went to Titus at Manthorne: Prunella (A428,823) was a 1935 bitch by Uther Penarvon x Hermia. She does not appear to have had progeny here. The second of Titus's three was Witch of Goring (A437,174), littermate to the previous import, Wisdom of Goring (Despot x Sybilla of Deleval), bred by Mrs. Dickin. She was only at Manthorne briefly, as she then went to Helen Weyenberg, Wey Acres, in Wisconsin, and produced. Remus of Hammercliffe (A428,822) was bred by F. Bowles (Pluto of Herga x Rosamund of Deleval).

The fourth import was Rolanda (A428,894), by Brockwell of Goring out of Boadicea of Deleval, who went to Dr. Harry Veach of Los Angeles (Angeles prefix) and produced several litters.

Merle Campbell of Oregon registered his first Mastiffs in 1940. One was C. A. Ackerman's Lady (A441,587), the other was Shanno of Lyme Hall (A443,545) from the same litter out of Campbell's Merle's Brunhilda of Lyme Hall, who was bred by Ackerman, owned by Campbell, and listed in the same volume.

The Mastiff Club of America held its first Specialty Show in 1940, and the OEMC Challenge Cup was awarded to Aldwin of Altnacraig. He was a fawn, sired by Duke of Hellingly out of Maud of Hellingly. The Cup had previously been awarded only at the Westminster Show, but henceforth was presented at the Club's annual show, and the names of each winner have been engraved on the trophy.

In 1941, the Cup was won by Boyce of Altnacraig, another son of Duke of Hellingly, but out of Kathleen of Hellingly. This was the last speciality to be held until 1949 after the war. Also in 1941, the Mastiff Club of America (MCOA) became a member club of the AKC, and the standard was officially adopted. No changes were to be made in the standard until 1982, when a section on "Gait" was added. The sequence of events was as follows:

June 3 1941—the Club adopted its Standard.

July 8 1941—Standard approved by AKC.

August 1941—MCOA applied for membership in AKC.

October 1941—membership approved by AKC. Clearly, matters moved more rapidly in those days!

Volume LVIII, 1941, had a total of 42 for the year. A large litter of nine, bred by H. M. Veach of Los Angeles, all with the "Angeles" prefix, were sired by his Angeles King out of the imported Rolanda. Merle Campbell sent a photo of King, who appeared to be a very large dog.

Dogs from earlier litters were entered by various breeders. Altnacraig accounted for several: the "F" litter (Boyce of Altnacraig x Maud of Hellingly) produced eight, both fawn and brindle. Aldwin of Altnacraig and Kathleen of Hellingly were the parents of the "G" litter of six registrations.

For the first time, Helen Weyenberg's name was shown as a breeder, with Wey Acres Noel (A514,831), a 1940 male by Manthorne Majesty out of Witch of Goring; and a female, Wey Acres Brenda. Mrs. Weyenberg's prefix would be seen in virtually every pedigree in the later years of the decade, in England as well as America, with her Wey Acres Lincoln.

One import crossed the Atlantic, Peter of Hammercliffe (A529,192), and he was sent to Altnacraig. His sire was Remus of Hammercliffe, already in America, and his dam was Alftruda of Deleval.

In 1941, Schuyler Baldwin bought his first Mastiff from Byron Parker of Canada. Donegal of Orchard Glen (Canadian registry 167,532) was out of Manthorne Joy by Alter's Big Jumbo: thus he was of completely United States stock. Donegal was a cherished member of the Baldwin family for ten years, and Mr. Baldwin was a stalwart supporter of MCOA until his death in 1992.

With the aftermath of Pearl Harbour in December 1941, Mastiff registrations fell dramatically, as indeed did those of all breeds. In 1942, only seven Mastiffs were listed in Volume LIX of the *Stud Book*. Wayne Alter had five entries, three of which were from 1939 and 1941 whelpings. One dog was imported from Canada, a littermate to the Baldwin's Donegal.

One English import, bred by Mrs. Scheerboom, was entered, Gyn of Hammercliffe (A539,084, Christopher of Havengore x Prunella). Gyn may have been imported well before 1942, as she was a 1939 bitch who went to Altnacraig and did have litters in this country.

A name that was to become familiar and would appear in many pedigrees was that of H. H. Peters, of Ohio. He acquired Duchess of St. Paul (A615,079, Buster of Saxondale x Angeles Victoria), from Wayne Alter. She was whelped in 1939.

Again, the records for 1943 show only a few Mastiffs, with the total of eight. All were bred by Alter, with one exception; another littermate of Donegal came in from Canada. Peters acquired Nero of Milton (A663,878, Buster of Saxondale x Angeles Princess), and Alter's breeding was basically the foundation of Peters' "Old Mill" line.

Eighteen Mastiffs were registered in Volume LXI of the *Stud Book* for 1944. One was an import from the same litter as Donegal: Sir Belden Burn (A726,089) went to R. B. Burn, then of Connecticut. Mr. Burn showed his dog extensively. Sir had the great distinction of being the very first Mastiff to obtain the Companion Dog (CD) certification from the AKC, in 1944.

Another dog of the same parentage (Alter's Big Jumbo x Manthorne Joy) was imported from Parker's kennel in Canada. H. H. Peters bred the pair he obtained from Wayne Alter and registered five: one, Sheba of Mansatta (A755,953) went to Waiter and Olive Frick whose suffix was to become well known in later years.

Eric of Knockrivoch (A751,003) was registered as bred and owned by John Leitch of Pennsylvania. He was by Eric of Altnacraig out of Gyn of Hammercliffe, so evidently the Clarks had sent the dam to a new owner. According to one report, the brindle dog stood 38 inches at the shoulder, and weighed 238 lb. If true, a real giant.

Dr. Marion Douglass of Cleveland bred Peter of Hammercliffe to Fenella of Altnacraig, with four of the litter registered, one as Patricia of Altnacraig. Alter had four entries from two litters, both from 1942 breedings.

In 1944, the first breed column for Mastiffs appeared in the AKC *Gazette* in January, giving little information except for a request for new members, dues, etc. It was written by the Secretary, Robert G. Wahn. In later columns it was stated that there were 41 members at the end of 1943, and that ten members attended the annual meeting of that year, a snowstorm being the cause of the low number. The column appeared rather irregularly, and gave few facts on activities for the year.

Mastiff material or references were rare, so the November 1944 article in the *Gazette* by Jones Wood was quite unusual. It was titled "Pinkerton's Symbol, 'The Eye'". According to a legend, Chicago's first detective agency, founded by Amos Pinkerton, had as its logo an eye, and the reason was as follows. Pinkerton was a cooper in Illinois, and owned a Mastiff named Argus (Argus, of course, means "eye"). One night the dog kept his owner awake, and finally stirred him to action, and the pair tracked horse thieves who had passed through the yard. For twenty miles the noble beast pursued the miscreants: "His massive head swung in deep left-right arcs; he closed one eye in wrinkled concentration while the other widened to glow in the dark." At last, the pair caught up with the thief, and "rolling on the earth, his throat caught fast in Argus' jaws was the culprit—dead before Pinkerton could call Argus off".

Although there were but six registered in 1945, there was more interest in the breed. A set of lists has figures from a 1945 questionnaire headed "Mastiff Club of America". Those interested in selling (1945 Questionnaire) gave ten names, nearly all familiar from the *Stud Book*. Another list "Those who show" also had ten names, but most seem to have been prospective, or very occasional, exhibitors. However, the final list "Those who would like to import" had seventeen members. This seems odd, considering the virtual absence of Mastiffs in England at the time.

Of the six entries in the *Stud Book*, three were of Leitch's breeding (Eric of Altnacraig x Gyn of Hammercliffe), the same litter as the dog previously registered. Peach Farm had one bitch, whelped in 1941, and H. H. Peters, a 1943 bitch. The final entry was from Douglass—also from a 1943 breeding.

There were a few Mastiff columns in the *Gazette*, at which time James Foster Clark was Treasurer. The $5 annual dues were paid to the Red Cross rather than to the Club, as its war effort, but the total amount donated was not stated.

Registrations in Volume LXIII of the *Stud Book* for 1946 began what was to be a steady upswing, with 22 Mastiffs. The first "of Mansatta" litter of eight was registered by Mr. and Mrs. Walter Frick. It was whelped in June of 1945, and the dam of the puppies was Blythe of Hampden and the sire Gail of Altnacraig.

Chaseway (William Chase) came into the picture with the "A" litter of 1945 by Angeles President out of Gwendolyn of Altnacraig. One of these, Austin of Chaseway, went back to Mrs. Clark and eventually to Mrs. Brill at Peach Farm.

Merle Campbell made one very significant pair of registrations. Heatherbelle Lady Diana (W3076) and Heatherbelle Lady Hyacinth (W3077) went to Mr. and Mrs. H. W. Mellish (to use the spelling given inU.S.and Canada) of Canada and were to be the foundation of their kennel and whose descendants helped to revive the Mastiff in England as discussed in the U.K. section above. Their sire was Shanno of Lyme Hall and their dam was Merle's Tanna. Mr. Campbell also registered a number of others of the same breeding. There was one import from Parker of Canada, Olga of Parkhurst (W15332) whose sire and dam, Emblem and Joy of Parkhurst, went back to American bloodlines.

In 1947 there were 30 registrations. Most of the breeders were familiar: Peach Farm, Merle Campbell, Frick, and for the first time, Valiant prefix appeared, a bitch bred by Ralph Higgins (Alter's Big Jumbo x Prospect Peg) who was owned by Robert B. Burn. Several Knockrivoch dogs were entered by John Leitch, sired by Boyce of Altnacraig out of Una of Knockrivoch. Another Parkhurst dog was imported from Canada. Burn also registered his "C" litter, (Alter's Big Jumbo x Olivia of Mansatta). One of these went to General Patch, whose family is still interested in the breed.

A leaflet called "Mastiff Owners of the United States and Their Registered Dogs, as shown by returns from the questionnaire of the Mastiff Club of America, Inc., and the Stud Book records of the American Kennel Club, January 1, 1949" listed sixty names, with the dogs owned by each person. Though it is clearly incomplete, it does give some indication of who owned what dog at the time. Since this information was gathered in 1948, it is interesting to note that there were only 15 Mastiffs in the Stud Book for that year. An entire litter of seven was registered by Robert B. Burn, one of which was the very important brindle dog Valiant Diadem, who played a large part in restoring the breed to Great Britain. The litter's sire was Hector of Knockrivoch and the dam was Valiant Cythera.

The Stud Book for 1949 (Volume LXVI) had 35 listings. Hector of Knockrivoch was used extensively at stud, and in 1948 had sired litters by Peach Farm Rosita, Peach Farm Polly, Patricia of Altnacraig, Valiant Debutante and Lady Diana. One puppy from the latter went to Wey Acres, Mr. Duke of Wey Acres (W113,378). Austin of Chaseway, then belonging to the Brills, sired a 1949 litter by Peach Farm Rosita who was evidently a good producer. It is interesting to note that color descriptions were not as yet standard: for example, Peach Farm Tiger Lily was listed as "orange fawn".

There were several imports from Canada entered. Burn imported Demon of Parkhurst (Emblem x Joy of Parkhurst) and used the dog at stud. Mrs. Mellish's two females, previously mentioned, provided several imports: Heatherbelle Diana's Cinderella, Hyacinth's Prudence and Hyacinth's Jane. Merle Campbell acquired Heatherbelle Bridget's Abigail, a granddaughter of his Heatherbelle Lady Hyacinth, sired by Hector of Knockrivoch out of Heatherbelle Hyacinth's Priscilla.

A Lady Diana and Hector puppy went to Mrs. Richard Patch, as did Peach Farm Cressida, continuing the Patch family's interest in the breed. (Donaghmore's Wahb W135,246, Hector x Lady Diana: Peach Farm Cressida, W136,342, Hector x Peach Farm Rosita.)

The Mastiff Club of America held its 20th Anniversary Show on 12th November 1949, which drew 18 entries, of which two were absent. Mrs. Walter Frick was the organizer. The winner was George Strawbridge (Wilco x Heather of Knockrivoch), a young dog, whelped in May of 1948. The show was written up in one of the very infrequent breed columns in the Gazette, and the article stated that there were "almost 100 Mastiffs in this country".

U.S. MASTIFF REGISTRATIONS 1940–1949

1940 - 31	1945 - 6
1941 - 42	1946 - 22
1942 - 7	1947 - 30
1943 - 8	1948 - 15
1944 - 18	1949 - 35

DOGS IMPORTED FROM ENGLAND 1940–1949

1940 Prunella (A428,823) fawn
Breeder: Miss I. Bell
Owner: P. H. Titus
Whelped: 1935 (Uther Penarvon x Hermia)
Remus of Hammercliffe (A428,822) fawn
Breeder: F. Bowles
Owner: P. H. Titus
Whelped: 1937 (Pluto of Herga x Rosamund of Deleval)
Rolanda (A428,894) fawn
Breeder: Mrs. H. H. Barwood
Owner: Harry Veach
Whelped: 1937 (Brockwell of Goring x Boadicea of Deleval)

Witch of Goring (A437,174) fawn
Breeder: Mrs. N. G. E. Dickin
Owner: P. H. Titus
Whelped: 1936 (Despot x Sybilla of Deleval)

1941   Peter of Hammercliffe (A529,192) fawn
Breeder: Mrs. F. Woolley
Owner: James Foster Clark
Whelped: 1940 (Remus of Hammercliffe x Alftruda of
Deleval)

1942   Gyn of Hammercliffe (A539,084) fawn
Breeder: Mrs. L. Scheerboom
Owner: James Foster Clark
Whelped: 1939 (Christopher of Havengore x Prunella)

The United States of America
1950-1959

Interest in the breed increased perceptibly during this decade. Registrations crept up from 24 in 1950 to a peak of 61 in 1959. Beginning in 1952, the *Stud Book* no longer listed every Mastiff, but included only those that had produced (sires and dams). Monthly and annual total registrations of each breed were published in the *Gazette*.

In the final years of listing all Mastiff registrations, it is interesting to note that of the 24 entries, four litters were sired by Hector of Knockrivoch, and two other sires were used—making a very narrow range of bloodlines. Two males were imported from the Mellish's Heatherbelle Kennels of Canada, but added little to the genetic pool.

Agatha of Chaseway (Angeles President x Gwendolyn of Altnacraig) won the Club Show. The following year Peach Farm Katrina, a daughter of Austin of Chaseway out of Peach Farm Belinda was the winner, followed in 1952 by a littermate, Peach Farm Hobo. The year 1951 saw 25 registrations and the first championship since 1937 was awarded to George Strawbridge (Wilco x Heather of Knockrivoch).

A much-needed boost to the breed was given in 1952, when Marie A. Moore became interested in Mastiffs. Her first dog was Peach Farm Michael (Austin of Chaseway x Peach Farm Belinda), acquired in that year. It is safe to say that without her kennel, Mooreleigh, and that of the Brills' Peach Farm, the breed in the United States would have virtually died out.

Registrations numbered 39, and the Mastiff Club had 60 members. Its president was Paul Hampshire. A very small breeding base; 17 of the 25 listings were sired by Austin of Chaseway and three by Hector of Knockrivoch.

There was a slight drop in numbers for 1953, to 33. As the *Stud Book* now listed only those Mastiffs who had progeny, detailed information is no longer available. For example, in this year only four Mastiffs were listed as breeding stock: Withybush Magnus, Heatherbelle Valentine's Prancer, Theodore Bozo, Peach Farm Michael.

We do have information on the 1952 litter from Peach Farm Priscilla by Withybush Magnus, owned by Helen Weyenberg (Wey Acres Kennels). It included Wey Acres Tars, Wey Acres Winnie, and the very important Wey Acres Lincoln, who was so prominent in restoring the breed in England.

The following year, 1954, saw but 37 registrations, no champions, and no Club show, but in 1955 45 Mastiffs were registered. Marie Moore's imported brindle bitch, Meps Berenice (Vyking Aethelwulf of Salying x Withybush Beatrix) won the Club show and went on to become a champion two years later—the first of many to be owned or bred by Mooreleigh Kennels.

The upward trend continued in 1956, with 56 listings. The Club speciality was won by Mooreleigh Kennels imported Adonis of Sparry. The first litter bred by Mrs. Frank Greco was entered, and her prefix "Greco's" was to become very well known in the breed. Another outstanding name was that of Adelaide Bolté , who later took the kennel name Reveille. Mrs. Bolté acquired her first Mastiff, Donaghmore's Charisse, in 1956.

It was also the year that marked the entrance of the well-known Willowledge Kennels (Stuart and Eve Olsen). The imports, Beowulf of Havengore and Twinkle of Havengore, were the foundation of their line.

There were only 30 registrations in 1957. Mooreleigh Moby Dick won the Speciality, and repeated his achievement in 1959. As noted earlier, Meps Berenice became a champion, the only one since 1951.

In 1958, Adonis of Sparry won the Club show, a feat he accomplished again in 1960, making him the first three-time winner of the Speciality.

In 1958 registrations doubled to 60. A welcome achievement was the award of Companion Dog to David and Carol Cole's Caesar of Seattle. This was the first degree to be awarded to a Mastiff since Robert Burn's Sir Belden Burn, in 1944.

In 1959 there was an outcross in the breed. This was the registration as a Mastiff of the imported Fidelle de Fenelon, who was actually a Bordeaux Dog, whelped in France, and bred by Van Cappel. She was acquired and registered by Merle Campbell, of Oregon. Her pedigree is shown in Appendix I.

At the time there was some controversy over the listing, but eventually Fidelle was allowed to be entered in the *Stud Book* and all her progeny were listed as Mastiffs. Her litter by Wey Acres Tars has had a profound effect on the breed. If one checks back on pedigrees of some of the most outstanding Mastiffs in both England and America, the outcross can be seen, and it must be admitted that it did nothing but good to the breed.

And so the decade ended. The establishment of several important kennels, Mooreleigh, Willowledge, Greco, plus the Peach Farm of the Brills, added immeasurably to the strength of the breed in America. Imports of excellent stock plus careful use of American-bred Mastiffs set the stage for an improvement and spread of interest in the coming decade.

U.S. MASTIFF REGISTRATIONS 1950-1959

1950 - 24	1955 - 45
1951 - 25	1956 - 56
1952 - 39	1957 - 30
1953 - 33	1958 - 60
1954 - 37	1959 - 61

The History and Management of the Mastiff

5.1 Buckhall Rillamill Cassandra and puppies, 1950. Owner Major & Mrs. Reardon Photo: C. Brasted. U.K.

5.2 Tudor King of Lexander, 15-10-55. (Heatherbelle Sterling Silver x Brevity of Bowerschurch). U.K.

5.3 Tudor King of Lexander and O.E.M.C. Elgiva, 13-8-56 (Valient Diadem x Heatherbelle Portia of Goriey.) Both parents imported. U.K.

The History and Management of the Mastiff

5.4 Tudor of Salander, 7-3-52. (Heatherbelle Sterling Silver x O.E.M.C. Elgira.) Breeder Anderson. U.K.

5.5 Ch. Vilna of Mansatta, 28-4-52. (Heatherbelle Bearhills Rajah x Jana of Mansatta.) Breeder Bowles. U.K.

5.6 Withybush Crispin and daughter, 25-11-56 (By Weyacres Lincoln, Am. Import in 1953). Owned & Bred by Miss Bell. U.K.

5.7 Fanifold Heatherbelle Priscilla's Martha, 24-5-49. (Eric of Knockrivoch x Heatherbelle Hyacinth's Priscilla). U.K.

5.8 Sir Belden Burn C.D. 1944. (Alter's Big Jumbo x Manthorne Joy). Owner R. Burn. Photo: Ylla. USA

5.9 Vancouver Island Dog Fanciers Show (Canada) 1949. From left: Ch. Parker's Jumbo of Parkhurst; Ch. Heatherbelle Lady Diana, handled by Mrs. Mellish; Ch. Heatherbelle Yorick; Ch Heatherbelle Lady Hyacinth. Canada.

5.10 Canadian Ch. Heatherbelle Diana and puppies. Breeder/owner H. Mellish. Canada

5.11 Wey Acres Wanda, ca. 1954 (Withybush Magnus x Peach Farm Priscilla). Breeder/owner H. Weyenberg. USA

5.12 Specialty Show 1955. Ch. Meps Berenice (Viking Aethelwulf of Saylyng x Withybush Beatrix). Breeder M. Perrenaud, owner M. Moore. USA

5.13 Wey Acres Tars and Wey Acres Wonder, ca. 1956 (Withybush Magnus x Peach Farm Priscilla). Breeder H. Weyenberg, owner M. Campbell. USA

5.14 Specialty Show 1956. Ch. Adonis of Sparry and Ch. Meps Berenice. Owner M. Moore. Photo Shafer. USA

5.15. Mooreleigh Munchausen 1958. Breeder/owner M. Moore. USA

5.16 Caesar of Seattle C.D. 1958. (Ch. Beowulf of Havengore x Twinkle of Havengore). Breeder E. Olsen, owners D. and C. Cole. USA

5.17. Angeles Galahad at 7 months, with breeder/owner H. Veach, 1959. USA

5.18. Ch. Mooreleigh Moby Dick, 1959. (Meps Bing x Wey Acres Wanda). Breeder M. Moore, owner F. Ewald. Photo: Brown. USA

Chapter 6

1960-1980

The United Kingdom   *Elizabeth J. Baxter*

In actual fact, 1960 began sadly for the Mastiff fancy with the death of one of its most stalwart supporters, Miss Ianthe Bell of the Withybush kennels. Active in the breed since 1925, she left her Mastiffs to her friend of many years, Miss Phylidda Blackstone, with strict instructions that all over the age of 18 months were to be put down. Miss P. Blackstone and her sister, Miss Barbara Blackstone, herself the secretary of the Old English Mastiff Club for many years during the 1960's and 1970's, had the heartbreaking task of seeing that these instructions were carried out. Survivors were Withybush Superbus, a grand light brindle dog, Withybush Etta and one other bitch, which three the Misses Blackstone and Mrs. Mary Hector took into "partnership" and kept, Superbus living with Mrs. Hector. One other bitch, Clarissa, who was nursing a litter was spared and found a pet home and the pups subsequently sold. It must have been a ghastly day; to put down healthy, happy dogs is terrible but Miss Bell's instructions were explicit and she had the ultimate welfare of her dogs at heart. The gap left by the loss of Miss Bell herself to the club was great and the loss of the breeding stock housed in her kennels an enormous blow to the breed, even though numbers had increased during the 1950's and extinction had been averted. The Withybush prefix and the Withybush Mastiffs will be remembered over the years with gratitude for their contribution to the breed itself.

Another loss to the club during this time was the death of Mrs. Dickin who had been secretary of the club in the difficult days at the end of the war and who had gone herself to Canada and the United States to search for fresh stock. She retired from the secretaryship in 1964, the occasion being a very happy and relaxed garden party where she was presented with a lovely glass goblet in commemoration of all that she had achieved. She died two years later and was much missed.

On a more cheerful note, the state of the breed itself was most encouraging with registrations starting in 1960 with 99 and rising in 1970 to 154. Numbers at shows increased and the numbers of Challenge Certificates allocated to the breed were also increased, as Mastiffs started to make their presence felt in the ring.

Brindles by now were almost non-existent and when the writer showed her Taddington Diamond Lil of Farnaby as a puppy at WELKS in 1964, people came running to "see the brindle". Lil was the only one on show and the only one to be shown for many months. A brindle, when seen, was something on which to comment. Happily, the numbers gradually increased until by the end of the 1960's they were no longer a rare species.

The early years of this period were overshadowed by Hotspot, who had won seven CC's in 1960, including Crufts and in 1961 he amassed another five with two more in 1962. The breed as a whole was still dominated by the Havengores, with this kennel "doing the double" at Crufts in 1962 with Ch. Hotspot winning the dog CC and Dore of Havengore winning the bitch. After this Mrs. Scheerboom slowly withdrew from the ring, and after the death of her husband rarely showed her dogs, although she did in fact show a bitch, Pindine of Sylvadown (out of a bitch called Clare of Havengore, and bred by Mrs. Barton) at the OEMC club show in 1971. But this was a rarity.

It would be easy merely to list show winners, especially Crufts winners for these years, but a breed consists of more than this and the interest for me is to observe the new kennels which were now very much to the fore. One of these was Mr. and Mrs. Lindley's Copenore line, which is known worldwide. Founded on a bitch called Cleo of Sparry (a daughter of Heatherbelle Sterling Silver, the Canadian dog) they bred Mastiffs whose names were, and still are, household words. Cleo, mated to the American import Wey Acres Lincoln produced one of the best known stud dogs of all time, Jason of Copenore, a fawn dog born in 1957. Unhappily he never attained his title but he sired, among others, Ch. Weatherhill Thor (4.10.1962), Ch. Bathsheba of Kisumu (13.1.1963) Ch. Taddington Diamond Lil of Farnaby (October 1963) and the truly beautiful Ch. Macushla of Hollesley (26.7.1964). Perhaps the greatest of his sons however was Ch. Threebees Friar of Copenore, born on 30th September 1964. The Copenore kennels were based in Sussex and the Lindleys did not breed in a large way, preferring quality to quantity. Their Mastiffs always acquired top honours in the show ring, usually for new owners, as Mrs. Lindley always seemed more interested in the breeding of really good stock than in showing them.

　　　　The History and Management of the Mastiff

Ch. Threebees Friar of Copenore was out of a bitch called Cleopatra of Saxondale. He had as big an influence on the breed as his sire and grandsire and appears over and over again in our pedigrees. He was a huge fawn dog, perhaps slightly plain in head although with a broad skull, but his bone, his size and his superb temperament made him outstanding. Major and Mrs. Reardon of the Buckhall kennels purchased him from his owner, Mrs. Barbara Baird, in 1967 as the Reardons could see his enormous potential. He certainly lived up to their expectations becoming one of the outstanding sires of the century. The Buckhall Mastiffs in Kent specialised in those lovely big bitches which today seem to be things of the past and all their dogs had the most gorgeous temperaments. In their heyday they were a kennel to rival any that had gone before.

To my mind the most beautiful and well-known Mastiff bitch of this period was Mrs. and Miss Day's fawn Ch. Macushla of Hollesley, by Jason out of Ch. Dawn of Havengore and bred by her owners. From her are descended such dogs as Ch. Hollesley Macushla's Sheba, Ch. Hollesley Macushla's Dagda, Ch. Dare Devil of Hollesley, Ch. Copenore Rab, Ch. Copenore Czarina, Ch. Devil's Advocate of Hollesley, Ch. Devil Dancer of Hollesley, down to the record holding Mastiff Ch. Hollesley Medicine Man and his sister Ch. Hollesley Rowella. I well remember Macushla winning the CC at Crufts in 1966 while still only a youngster and age did not wither her, as she went on to win Best of Breed at Crufts both in 1969 and 1970. To my mind she was one of the greatest bitches ever, slightly heavy coated perhaps for some, but what a record she has left behind her. Today, sadly, we seem to have lost the size and substance in bitches which she epitomised.

Another famous kennel (actually started in the 1950's) was the Kisumu establishment. Founded by Mrs. Irene Creigh, a lady in every sense of the word, it was based on a bitch called Bunty of Bardayle, bred by Mrs. Maisie Anderson. Mated to Hotspot, Bunty produced Ch. Fatima of Kisumu (1960) best bitch at Crufts in 1965; and Fatima in turn, mated to Jason of Copenore, gave Mrs. Creigh the fabulous Ch. Bathsheba of Kisumu who became a champion at 17 months winning the CC at Crufts in 1964, a year before her mother did so. The Kisumu kennels continued to produce good stock throughout the 1960's and the 1970's, including Ch. Jasper of Kisumu, Utopia of Kisumu, Lavinia of Kisumu and of course Beaucaris Marcus of Kisumu. I feel it is a great pity that this lady's knowledge of the breed could not have been better utilised as a judge.

Mr. Bill Hanson for many years a committee member of the OEMC and who had founded his kennels on the Havengore Mastiffs (Ch. Gipsy of Havengore and Ch. Drake of Havengore) maintained a small but strong kennel among which were Ch. Petrel of Blackroc (bitch CC Crufts 1963) Ch. Tuppence of Blackroc (bitch CC Crufts 1967) and Ch. Falcon of Blackroc. The last named, a sound, medium-sized brindle dog was exported to the United States and indeed Mr. Hanson himself went to America for a short time.

Two animals that deserve comment and which bridge the period between the end of the 1950's and the start of the 1960's were Dr. Allison's Ch. Weatherhill Milf Manetta who was by Ch. Hotspot of Havengore out of Serena of Sparry, and her son by Jason, Ch. Weatherhill Thor. Thor, a fawn dog of repute, was bought by Mesdames Lloyd Jones and Greenwell and did a good deal of winning. Mrs. Lindley acquired his brother, Weatherhill Bellringer.

Mention must also be made of Janet Roberts and her Cornhay kennels. One of the foundation bitches here was Mrs. Lindley's Copenore Bonny Helen, a Jason daughter. Janet did not breed extensively but what she did produce was good, her Ch. Cornhay Kennet, owned by Miss Fidler, going best dog at Crufts in 1970, being beaten for Best of Breed by Macushla. Janet continued to do well with her Cornhay dogs during the late 1960's and early 1970's but she then withdrew from the Mastiff world and her kennel has ceased to function.

Those who breed in a small way, keep quiet, and mind their own business, tend to get overlooked. Mr. Cogan has now, in 2003, almost entirely retired from the breed but his Craigavon prefix has been in existence for almost 40 years now. In that time he has produced quality stock. His foundation bitch was Taddington Emma, (Jason of Copenore x Tiger Lily of Kisumu) born in October 1963, and he and his dogs were always a force to be reckoned with. He was quiet, unassuming and unpushy. I feel his example of good sportsmanship and kindness was, and is, an example to many people. Would that there were more like him! His Taddington Emma was litter sister to my Ch. Taddington Diamond Lil of Farnaby, and Emma is to be remembered especially for winning a Challenge Certificate at the incredible age of nine years. She was worth her weight in gold as a brood bitch, although she never managed to win the elusive third Challenge Certificate and become a champion herself.

Lastly we must remember Miss Mercer and her Rhossnessneys, who were situated in Cornwall. Miss Mercer, because of distance and ill health, was not much seen in the show ring but she bred some good stock, founded mainly on Mrs. Taylor's Saxondale line. Mrs. Taylor was then living in Cornwall staying there until her death in 1990.

So we come into the 1970's and with the increase in Mastiff owners I would think it almost certain that unintentionally, I shall omit some dog or some person from this section and for this I apologise in advance. It is impossible in the interests of comparative brevity to list every single person who bred or showed a Mastiff at this time.

What must be remembered is that some of the people, dogs and kennels mentioned here will have been commented upon in the previous chapter. It is difficult to draw a hard and fast line between all those active over the last ten years and those active until today. There is, thankfully, a degree of continuity so many animals and people may be talked about again, others for the first time.

1970 was a period of expansion, more so perhaps than ever before. Registrations for 1971 were 154 and rose to 226 in 1973 the first time the breed had topped the 200 mark. They continued to rise, reaching 279 in 1978 and an astonishing 316 in 1980. 1975-1976 however were very poor years for puppies and only 87 registrations were recorded for 1976.

In 1970 Mr. and Mrs. Say bought President of Shute, a fawn dog puppy by Ch. Threebees Friar of Copenore out of Baroness Fiona of Buckhall. Thus started the Bulliff kennel so well known throughout the 1970's and 1980's. President, put to a bitch called Marnie of Hubbadane, bred by the writer but given away unregistered, sired Ch. Presidents Lad of Bulliff who was Best of Breed at Crufts in 1977 and Countess Caroline who won the bitch CC there in 1979. The Says, although breeding infrequently, are still interested, and involved, in the breed.

Another new personality was Mrs. Jones who founded her Gildasan kennels on a bitch called Whytefarm Katrina, bred by the Lindleys; she was by Weatherhill Bellringer out of Copenore Prima Donna. She was mated to Frideswide Kis Balint to produce Humoresque of Gildasan. She was then mated back to her son Humoresque and from the resulting litter came Gildasan Lovely Looker and the start of the Gildasan line. Another of their foundation bitches was Ragtime Dame Twisty, by Lucky Attempt of Farnaby out of Tiger Lily of Ragtime. The kennel grew and prospered although living in Norfolk, as they do, the Jones were unable to be as active as they perhaps would wish; the Mastiffs bred at the Gildasan kennels, however, were prominent in the awards during this period.

We must not forget Mrs. Sylvia Shorter, with her Canonbury dogs; the two best known must be Ch. Canonbury Eminence of Gildasan, best of breed at Crufts in 1972 (bred by Mrs. Jones, by Ch. Cornhay Kennet out of Whytefarm Katrina) and Ch. Canonbury Autobiography with whom she won Best of Breed at the same show in 1975. Unfortunately Mrs. Shorter subsequently emigrated to South Africa, taking her Mastiffs with her.

Two well-known bitches who won extensively were those belonging to Miss M. Perrenoud, whose father in the 1950's owned Meps Basil, sire of Hotspot. Her Ch. Meps Portia born in 1968, breeder Mr. Bradley, was by Ch. Balint of Havengore (himself a Hotspot son,) out of Ensign of Copenore. She won the bitch ticket at Crufts in 1972 and Portia's daughter Ch. Meps Nydia (by Ch. Overnoons Mr. Micawber of Buckhall) also won well.

Mention perhaps could be made of Nydia's sire. Ch. Overnoons Mr. Micawber of Buckhall, one of the last of the Buckhall dogs—along with his brother Ch. Lord Jim of Buckhall, belonging to Mrs. and Mr. Morgan—to be campaigned. Like his sire, Friar, he was a massive animal; a dark brindle, he was owned by Mrs. How and won best of breed at Crufts in both 1973 and 1974. He could be said to be the end of an era, for the Buckhalls had now almost retired from the ring and their loss was felt keenly. They had given the breed so much in size, substance, soundness and good temperament.

Meanwhile in Wales, untroubled by the happenings of the world as a whole, Mrs. Anne Davies bred her Nantymynydd Mastiffs as she had done since the 1960's; her foundation was a stud dog called Emrys O"Nantymynydd, by Ch. Balint of Havengore out of Kisumu Copenore Catherine. Because she never showed, she tended to be overlooked but her strain continues to this day, a distinct and unique line which is behind a great many kennels on the Continent, Belgium and Holland in particular.

Mrs. Mary Denton is another breeder whose stock is perhaps better known on the Continent than in this country (U.K.). Again, a person who seemed to prefer breeding Mastiffs than to showing them, she owned a small but strong kennel founded on Baroness Anthea of Buckhall. This bitch was by Ch. Weatherhill Thor, and from her came both Bournewood Sophie and Bournewood Index Vicki.

More converts to the breed in 1970 were Mr. and Mrs. Hicks and their son Graham. Their foundation bitch was the apricot Lisken Rowena of Kisumu born 25th April 1970. They also bought Inniscorrig Sir Arthur Crown, bred by Mrs. Stamper, by Sebastian of Hollesley out of

Oxhaege Uffhild. Both Rowena and Arthur were apricots and mated, they produced Ch. Jilgrajon Lady Victoria and Jilgrajon Sir Caleb Wyndham. The Hicks also obtained from Mr. and Mrs. Phillips the medium sized yet sound and substantial fawn dog, Ch. Cemaes King Edward of Jilgrajon—commonly known as Spud. The combination of Spud and Lady Victoria produced the big handsome dog, Ch. Jilgrajon Sir Gladstone who to my mind was a loss to the breed inasmuch as he was not used, as he should have been, at stud. Lady Victoria was then mated to a dog that my husband had bred, the beautiful headed Lesdon the Lord Alexander and from this mating came Ch. Jilgrajon Rebecca West, born 31st August 1978.

The brindle bitch Ch. Artifax Arabella of Farnaby, whom I had the honour to own, won well at this time and gave me a great deal of pleasure with her loyalty and love. I shall always remember her, my darling Bella.

To my mind, however, one of the most intriguing aspects of the 1970's was the emergence of Mrs. E. Degerdon as one of the breed's leading owners. Up until this time she had been living in the Home Counties and unable to keep dogs in large numbers, but, following her move to Wales, she was able to start her Grangemoor kennel and the way she did it was fascinating. From Mrs. Day, who throughout all this time continued to show, win with, and breed her Hollesley Mastiffs (being by now surely the breeder with the longest experience) Mrs. Degerdon acquired Ch. Hollesley Macushla's Dagda, by Baron Spencer of Buckhall out of the wonderful Ch. Hollesley Macushla. This dog was eventually mated to Mrs. Lindley's Ch. Copenore Mary Ellen, to produce just two puppies, Ch. Copenore Rab and Ch. Copenore Czarina, both of whom Mrs. Degerdon purchased from Mrs. Lindley. Rab was a magnificent Mastiff, albeit fiery with other males, and he combined the best of the Copenore and the Hollesley strains. He came out in 1972, annexing four CC's in 1973 and still winning them in 1976. He will perhaps be best remembered as the sire of Ch. Hollesley Medicine Man.

Vivien Corbett at that time had the Jakote prefix and had bred and shown her Mastiffs with success in the period 1971-1975 but domestic difficulties meant that she had to give up her dogs. She had imported from America the brindle, The Devil From Wayside (by Lord Marcus of Kenacres out of Wayside Delilah, d.o.b. 1973, and bred by Mr. Thornsbrough): Mrs. Degerdon now purchased The Devil from Vivien Corbett and he was mated to Dagda's sister, Ch. Hollesley Macushla's Sheba owned by Mesdames Lloyd Jones & Greenwell. From this mating came Ch. Dare Devil of Hollesley, Ch. Devil's Advocate of Hollesley, and Ch.

Devil Dancer from Hollesley, Mrs. Greenwell registering the puppies, with Mrs. Day's permission, with the Hollesley prefix, so as to carry on the bitch line. The Dare Devil was acquired from his breeders by Mrs. Degerdon, and he was the same type as his cousin Rab, a Mastiff of size, substance, correct head type and true nobility.

The co-operation between Mrs. Day, Mrs. Lindley (the owner of Rab's dam) Mesdames Greenwell and Lloyd Jones and Mrs. Degerdon, produced a spate of superb Mastiffs who dominated the ring in the mid and late 1970's. Personally, I find it a little difficult to keep track of the intricacies of their breeding and ownership, and therefore include their pedigrees in Appendix I.

Mrs. Degerdon continued to own Mastiffs at her home in Wales but appeared to be concentrating more on the breeding aspect rather than the show ring though in 1979 she did win the CC at Crufts with her Ch. Grangemoor Bevis.

The Devil from Wayside did not only produce winners to bitches of the Hollesley line, he was also the sire of Ch. Jakote Lady Glencora (out of Ashley House Beth of Jakote) the Cowe's big brindle, Ch. Forefoot Prince of Darkness (out of Nina of Remargae from Forefoot) and the Rice's Ch. Darkling Bridie (out of Darkling Arabella). He was a controversial dog; five generations back he had an outcross to a Dogue de Bordeaux and this damned him in the eyes of some. Certainly, he had his faults and he had his detractors and it was possible in many cases to pick out his descendants in the ring because, despite the superb type of Mastiff which he sired to the Hollesley bred bitches as already mentioned, I think it is true to say that many of his descendants have heads and expressions which are not typical. This is sad, as with so many head types already in circulation, breeders should be concentrating on the difficult task of breeding the correct head, not a St. Bernard head, a Bullmastiff head, a Newfoundland head or a Dogue de Bordeaux head. Having said all that, however, we have to be honest and ask ourselves is there a Mastiff in the world today who does not have an outcross somewhere in the background, to one of the breeds mentioned above? The answer has to be "No". The fact remains as far as the Devil is concerned that his progeny do include some of the finest and it is by these that he should perhaps be judged.

Lastly we should mention Mr. and Mrs. Cowe whose foundation bitch was Nina of Remargae and whose prefix was Forefoot. They owned Ch. Forefoot Prince of Darkness, who won the dog C. C. at Crufts in

1978 but a tragic and severe illness meant that Mrs. Cowe could no longer keep and show her Mastiffs so again we have a strain of dogs and an enthusiastic breeder, lost to the breed because of ill health.

In the closing years of this decade occurred the death of Mrs. Lucy Scheerboom for so long a supporter of the breed, President of the OEMC club from 1967-1977 and one of those who had helped the breed and the club through the dark and difficult days of the 1940's. Her death could truthfully be said to end an era.

The period covered in this chapter, 1960-1980 saw the death, therefore, of both Miss Bell and Mrs. Scheerboom, who had started in the breed at almost the same time and who had served it so well.

It also saw the demise of the very large multi-dog kennels and the emergence of smaller, "amateur" kennels and this trend still continues. A few breeders kept 20 or 30 Mastiffs but in the main breeders kept numbers down to levels where the dogs were mostly house-pets for all or part of the time, and perhaps bred one or two litters a year. With a breed such as ours, craving human companionship, this was, and is, a good thing.

The United States of America   *Patricia B. Hoffman*
1960-1969

The 1960's marked the period of what might be called the Renaissance of the Mastiff in America. From the very low figure of 43 registrations in 1960, the number rose to 230 in 1969. The position of the breed at last seemed secure.

In 1961, there were 75 registered. The Olsens' Beowulf of Havengore (Hugh of Havengore and Havengore Petronella of Mansatta) became a champion, and won the Club show over an entry of 11.

Mastiff news was very scarce, with few breed columns appearing in the *Gazette*. The only news, in fact, appeared in June, under the heading "Bull Mastiffs"! The column listed the officers of the MCOA: President, Patty Brill; Vice-President, Stuart Olsen; Secretary, Lloyd Watner; Treasurer, Sidney Scott; and Schuyler Baldwin, a new Board Member.

The years 1962 and 1963 each had 63 entries, and one champion for each year. Sheba of Zimapan (Adam of Havengore x Silver Queen of Zimapan) was the earlier. There was no Club show that year.

The year 1963 saw the first American-bred bitch to become a champion in 26 years. This was Titan Tangela (Wey Acres Tars x Merle's Princess) owned by Zita Deviny and bred by Merle Campbell.

Mr. Campbell's Baron of Wey Acres Tars (Wey Acres Tars x Fidelle de Fenelon), owned by J. Parker, was the very first Mastiff to gain the advanced degree of Companion Dog Excellent (CDX). Three others won CD certificates, the Club show was won by the imported Felton of Kisumu.

In 1964 registrations picked up a bit, rising to 79, and two champions finished. One was Mrs. Deviny's Titan Victor, sired by Peach Farm Amos out of Ch. Titan Tangela. The other was Gaynor of Bardayle (Samson of Havengore x Patricia of Bardayle), imported by Mrs. Greco. This bitch and Edgemount Withybush Wilfred were important additions to her kennel.

The 1964 Club Show was won by Eng. Ch. Rhinehart of Blackroc, who won his American title the following year, making him the first dual title holder. He was a very important addition to the breed in this country, and his offspring were to be prominent in the following years. His importer was Marie Moore, and his sire and dam were Drake of Havengore and Gipsy of Havengore; his breeder Bill Hanson. Mrs. Moore later brought in his full brother, Falcon of Blackroc, also a notable sire.

In 1965 registrations passed the 100 mark for the first time during the century, with a total of 110. Five champions finished in addition to Rhinehart. Two were bred by Mooreleigh, one by Willowledge (the first registered under that kennel name), and, one imported bitch.

Adelaide Bolté owned Mooreleigh Joyce (Mooreleigh David x Mooreleigh Barbara) who produced three litters sired by Rhinehart, and many of these went on to become champions and top producers. The Club show drew 17 entries, and Rhinehart won again.

Beginning in 1965, a regular Mastiff column appeared in the *Gazette*, for many years written by Mrs. Moore. Also in 1965, Volume 1, Number 1 of the Mastiff Club Newsletter was issued. It has been published ever since, with occasional lapses. Its originator and first editor was Schuyler Baldwin, followed by me, then various writers were in charge.

There were 124 Mastiffs registered in 1966, and five championships awarded. One was Reveille Defender, a Rhinehart-Joyce offspring, bred by Mrs. Bolté. Mrs. Greco owned two, one an import, Ginna of Havengore; the other American-bred Prince Valiant d"Orleans. Mrs. Moore's import, Werburga, and the American-bred Justine of Rainbow Mountain (H. Newbold, breeder) complete the roster.

The Club show was won by Windsor's McTavish (Duncan of Windsor x Willowledge Evelyn), bred, owned, and shown by Charlotte Strong, whose Windsor Kennels have played an important role in the improvement of the Mastiff in America.

McTavish finished his title in 1967, with seven others, only one an import. This was a sister of Falcon and Rhinehart of Blackroc, Raven of Blackroc, imported by Willowledge. The Club show had 24 entries, and was won by Reveille Juggernaut, who repeated his triumph the following year (1968) with an entry of 28, also completing his championship.

In addition to the total of ten championships in 1968, a Companion Dog certificate was awarded to the Coles' Ieda's Thor (later a champion). Six of the title holders were bred by Willowledge, surely a record! A total of 182 Mastiffs was registered.

The last year of the decade had 230 listings and 16 champions, only five being imported. Many of these Mastiffs went on to add to the roster of important breeding stock. One was Ch. Nelson of Hollesley (Weatherhill Thor x Leonora of Hollesley), bred by Mrs. P. Day and imported by Mrs. Greco. A Rhinehart son, Ch. Ballyherugh's Cormac O'Conn, bred by Gerry Danaher, won the Club show, weighing in at 178 pounds, in a competition of 36 entries.

Truly, the breed was in better shape than it had been in decades; what would the 1970's bring?

U.S. MASTIFF REGISTRATIONS 1960-1969

1960 - 43	1965 - 110
1961 - 75	1966 - 124
1962 - 63	1967 - 145
1963 - 63	1968 - 182
1964 - 79	1969 - 230

1970-1979

The decade of the seventies was a time of rapid growth and increasing popularity of the Mastiff, as it was for all the large breeds. These two factors brought problems: indiscriminate and ignorant breeding; new owners and breeders unfamiliar with the background, bloodlines, and difficulties of our breed; "puppy mills"; increasing commercialism.

1970 began the period with 285 registrations. Sixteen championships were given, only two to imported dogs, a contrast to some previous years when the majority of title winners was English imports.

The Club Specialty was won by Ch. Ballyherugh's Cormac O'Conn (a Rhinehart x Willowledge Tammy son), over an entry of 37. This was his second win, and he also had the rare distinction of winning Working Group at the Canadian Sportsman Show.

In 1971 the Mastiff Club experimented with a second Speciality Show, and it was not well attended, drawing but 10 entries. The winner was Ch. Rumblin Eko's His Majesty Thor (Bowat's Roar N Rumble of Corgeen x Frideswide Susan). The regular show was won by Ch. Reveille Defender (Ch. Rhinehart of Blackroc x Ch. Mooreleigh Joyce) with an entry of 40. There were 15 champions listed for the year, with 325 Mastiffs registered.

Entries in 1972 jumped to 394, with 30 champions. It was obvious that showing Mastiffs was gaining in popularity and interest in the breed was accelerating. However, the Club show drew only 30, and "Thor" was the winner. The next year, 1973, he repeated his win, over 44 entries.

Registrations continued to rise, with 516 in 1973 and 641 in 1974. The Club show for 1973, 1974 and 1975 was won by Ch. Reveille Big Thunder (Ch. Renrock's Brian O"Dare x Reveille Tribute). Championships for the years were 30, 24 and 48, respectively.

A number of Mastiffs were obedience trained and won their certificates, CD. Two CDX (Companion Dog Excellent) were given, and one UD degree. This Utility Dog was Spice Hills Memory of Jeremy (Berngarth Humphrey x Berngarth Victoria). "Jenny", to use her call name, was owned and trained by LeRoy Pilarski, of Minnesota. Probably the most unusual award was that of Schutzhund A, to Ch. Willowledge Bartholomew, owned and trained by H. Woolf.

1975 had only a slight rise in numbers with 651 listings, and 48 champions, but in 1976 the registrations jumped to 810. There were 55 champions, and the Club show was won by Ch. Reveille Big Thunder for the third time, over the largest entry to date—79.

The same number of champions achieved the title in 1977, all of which were American-bred. 936 Mastiffs were registered, and the Speciality was won by Ch. Greenbrier's Shambeau. He was sired by Ch. Meps Tristan out of Rojondo's Ramona, owned by S. Lyons and bred by Mrs. E. D. Funk.

In 1978 the first book on Mastiffs since M. B. Wynn's book of 1886 was published. This was Marie A. Moore's *The Mastiff*, a mine of information, and lavishly illustrated in both black-and-white and color. That year 48 American-bred champions were listed, and a total of 948 registrations entered. The Specialty was won by Ch. Russo's Rommel of Colossus (Willow Point's Colossus x Ch. Big Bertha of Colossus) over an entry of 50.

In the last year of the decade registrations went over one thousand—1,097 to be exact. All champions, 53 of them, were bred in this country, and obedience gained in popularity, with seven Mastiffs winning CD certificates. Over 80 dogs were entered in the Speciality, which was won by Ch. Deer Run Zen CD (Deer Run Noah Massalane x Deer Run Jennifer).

An influential kennel of the 1970's was Deer Run, owned by Tobin Jackson. Breeding on a very large scale, this prefix is found in almost every pedigree today. Its contribution to the breed cannot be underestimated.

U. S. MASTIFF REGISTRATIONS 1970-1979

1970 - 285	1975 - 651
1971 - 325	1976 - 810
1972 - 394	1977 - 936
1973 - 516	1978 - 948
1974 - 641	1979 - 1,097

6.1 Stanley Dangerfield judging the OEMC Show, 1960's. From left: W. Hanson, R. Creigh, B. Baxter, L. Scheerboom. U.K.

6.2 Ch. Macushla of Hollesley, 1960's (Jason of Capenore x Dawn of Havengore). Born 26.7.64. Breeder Mrs. P. Day. U.K.

6.3 Ch. Jilgrajon Sir Gladstone, late 1970's (Ch. Caemes King Edward of Jilgrajon x Ch. Jilgrajon Lady Victoria). Born 1977. Breeders W. and G. Hicks. U.K.

6.4 Ch. Artifax Arabella of Farnaby (Lucky Attempt of Farnaby x Mistress Jennifer of Buckhall). Born 1972. Breeder E. Baxter. Photo: D. Pearce. U.K.

6.5 Ch. Hollesley Medicine Man (Ch. Copenore Rab x Ch. Devil Dancer of Hollesley). Born 1978. Owners Lloyd-Jones and Greenwell. Photo: D. Pearce. U.K.

6.6 Alice of Shute, 1969 (Ch. Threebees Friar of Copenore x Baroness Fiona of Buckhall). Bred by Harris. U.K.

6.7 Ch. Yarme Susan, 23-7-1975 (Hubbastone Tristan x Ragtime Ma Piggins). Breeder Forshaw. U.K.

6.8 Ch. Forefoot King Kong, 27-7-78 (Forefoot Prince of Darkness x Forefoot Rosa Dartle). Breeder Cowe. U.K.

6.9 Bulliff Captain Hanilco, January 1975 (Ch. The Devil from Waytide x Ch. Astelle Oven Ready). U.K.

6.10 Eng. and Am. Ch. Rhinehart of Blackroc ca. 1960 (Drake of Havengore x Gipsy of Havengore). Breeder W. Hansen, owner M. Moore. Photo: Pearl. USA

6.11 Eight-month-old puppies (Ch. Goliath of Kisumu x Willowledge Margo). Breeders/owners E. and P. Gaar. USA

6.12 Eng. and Am. Ch. Falcon of Blackroc, 1960's. (Drake of Havengore x Gipsy of Havengore). Breeder W. Hansen, owner M. Moore. Photo Pearl. USA

6.13 Peach Farm Amos, mid-1960's (Donaghmore Arthur x Peach Farm Dulcie). Breeder P. Brill, owner Z. Deviny. USA

6.14 Ch. Mooreleigh Joyce and friends. Breeder M. Moore, owner D. Bolté. USA

6.15 Ch. Helena of Rainbow Mountain, ca. 1965 (Henry of Havengore x Greco's Heather). Owner H. Newbold. USA

6.16 Reveille Sentinel, 1965 (Ch. Rhinehart of Blackroc x Mooreleigh Joyce). Breeder A. Bolte, owner L. Finley. Photo: Gilbert. USA

6.17 Club Specialty. Ch. Willowledge Merri Christmas (Willowledge Ali Khan x Ch. Willowledge Bathsheba). Breeder/owner E Olsen. Judge, Mrs. L. Scheerboom of Havengore Mastiffs 1968. Photo: Shafer. USA

6.18 Argument of Carinthia, 1974 (Ch. Tiberias of Kisumu x Ch. Ballyherugh Doire Carinthia). Breeder/owner P.B. Hoffman. USA

6.19 Ch. Renrock Sean O'Dare, 1975 (Ch. Renrock Brian O'Dare x Ch. Reveille Tribute). Breeder/owner W.R. Newman. USA

6.20 Ch. Agnes of Carintha, 1975. (Ch. Tiberias of Kisumu x Ch. Ballyherugh Doire of Carinthia). Breeder P.B. Hoffman, owner J. Hartman. Photo: Thacker. USA

Chapter 7

1980-1990

The United Kingdom   *Elizabeth J. Baxter*

For me, this decade was principally notable for three things—the dominance of Ch. Hollesley Medicine Man, the tragedy cum scandal of Mrs. Degerdon and her Grangemoors, and the importation by Messrs Thomas and Tugwell of the Bredwardine kennel, of Am. Ch. Arciniega's Lion.

Before touching on any of these events, let us first look at the kennels of the 1970's which were still active. Among these were the Says with the Bulliffs, Mrs. Robson Jones and the Gildasans, Mr. Cogan with his long established Craigavons, Mr. and Mrs. Hicks and the Jilgrajons (although they wound down their activities during this decade) my husband and I with the Lesdons and Farnabys, and of course Mrs. Pam Day with her Hollesley Mastiffs.

As well as newly established kennels which we will talk about shortly, there were also losses both in people and breeding establishments. Mrs. Scheerboom, had of course died and her place as president of Old English Mastiff Club was taken by Mrs. Pam Day. Tragically, Major Reardon of the Buckhall dogs died suddenly in the early 1980's. That meant the end of this famous kennel. Another sad loss was the death of Rene Creigh of the Kisumu Mastiffs; the death of Mrs. Lindsay of the Copenore dogs and the death of Bill Hanson, a stalwart supporter of the breed and an OEMC committee member. The Celerity kennel also ceased operations, following the death of Mr. A. Norfolk.

I have already mentioned Messrs Thomas and Tugwell and the Bredwardine Kennels. This is surely one of the best known kennels of both the 1980's and 1990's. They were actually founded in 1976, when they bought a brindle bitch puppy, Farnaby Voodoo Princess. Although she never attained her title I think it can safely be said that she was the foundation bitch for these gentlemen. Mated to the big apricot dog Ch. Forefoot Prince Igor of Bredwardine, she produced the top winning female Ch. Bredwardine Beau I'Deal, an apricot like her father. Since their inception, these kennels have been extremely successful in the show ring and house some excellent stock.

Raymond Boatwright started his Glynpedrs with Ch. Forefoot Little Emily of Bredwardine (by Ch. Overnoons Mr. Micawber of Buckhall out of Nina of Remargae of Forefoot) who was bred by the Cowes. She was the top winning bitch at the start of the decade but unfortunately has left very few descendants, although her grand daughter Ch. Glynpedr Tat-tinger enjoyed considerable success in the show ring. Raymond owned among others Ch. Misty Moondrops of Glynpedr, Ch. Captain Morgan of Glynpedr and Ch. Glynpedr Dom Perignon. He was also a successful breeder. Like the Bredwardines, the Glynpedrs probably became even better known in the following decade, and they will certainly be commented on in the next chapter.

Several other well-known names came into the breed at this time, some specialising in breeding, others taking more interest in simply exhibiting. One of the larger kennels was David Blaxter with his Na-mous and Masnou dogs. The two prefixes tend to muddle me but one belongs to David (Namous) and the other to his wife Sylvia (Masnou). He bought as his foundation bitch a brindle called Lesdon Lady Better-ess, and when he and his wife moved to France in the very early 1980's, they took her with them and made her into an international champion. Mated to a French dog, Fr. Ch. Ramuncho des Verts Tilleuls, she pro-duced Ch. Überacht of Namous (born 14.9.83) who went Best of Breed at Crufts both in 1988 and 1989. As Betteress was by Ch. Parcwood W. Bear Esq. of Lesdon x Ch. Yarme Jane of Farnaby, this kennel is founded on a mixture of British and French blood, as when the Blaxters returned from France in the mid 1980's they brought back with them Mastiffs carrying fresh bloodlines, and since their return they have also imported other animals from France. The Namous/Masnou kennel continue to be a major force with which to be reckoned.

Another important breeding establishment was Prixcan, owned by Julia Manfredi. Her original bitch was Trevabyn Spring Fever, (13.1.82), the mother of her first champion, Ch. Prixcan Serenity Almeria. This was followed by Ch. Prixcan Contach, and Ch. Prixcan Espada. This kennel became even more influential in the 1990's and produced, and produces, Mastiffs with excellent heads.

David and Mary Joynes founded their Damaria kennels in 1980 with a dog, Ch. Celerity Powerful Sort, bred by Mrs. Denise Norfolk. They then obtained Zanfi Princess Tanya of Damaria, bred by Nick Waters, and Nandina Shady Lady of Damaria. From Shady Lady they bred perhaps their best known dog, Ch. Damaria Count Magnum. This kennel enjoyed a great deal of success and bred good dogs.

Jill and Richard Sargeant started the Trevabyns in 1980, with a dog called Belbeck Plantation Boss. They then bought Farnaby Feudal Countess and produced a string of good quality Mastiffs. Their Ch. Trevabyn Black Ice was a much used stud dog and their Trevabyn Spring Fever mated to Black Ice produced the Prixcan foundation bitch, Serenity Almeria.

A kennel which seemed to specialise in exhibiting rather than breeding was Louis McDonald and his Longendales. He enjoyed considerable success with Ch. Longendale King Louis (born in 1977 and became a champion in 1981) and Ch. Lord Bernard of Longendale. He continued to exhibit and win right through the 1980's.

Mrs. Duval seemingly obtained her first bitch, Balclutha Minerva, in 1980, and made her up into a champion; but the Mastiff of hers that I remember best was her beautiful Ch. Chevelu Blodeuwedd of Bredwardine, who won the CC at Crufts in 1990 beating my Ch. Farnaby Fraze and Fable in the process! This fawn bitch was gorgeous, and had been bought and campaigned by Richard Thomas. Mrs. Duval breeds only infrequently but when she does have a litter, they are of good quality.

A kennel that started in the early 1980's was Quixhill, owned by Hilary Sargeant and Norman Clarke. Their foundation bitch was Trevabyn Winter Solstice (22.12.81) and the stud dog Trevabyn Sirius. These two dogs produced Quixhill True Britt, born in 1985, but the Quixhills became better known in the 1990's and in any case, only bred an occasional litter.

Here I must apologise to anybody whose dogs or kennel I inadvertently omitted. It is hard to name everybody.

From the foregoing it will be seen that several of today's well known kennels started in the 1980's carrying on where others had left off. Perhaps we could have a look at what was happening in Ireland at that time. Sarah Windham owned a big brindle dog, Int. Ch. Langton of Falmorehall (brother to my husband's Ch. Parcwood W. Bear Esq. of Lesdon) and this dog won the Open Class at Crufts in 1980. She also owned Irish Ch. Farnaby Fighting Faith of Falmorehall, who went Best of Breed at Crufts in 1983, the only bitch ever to beat Medicine Man. Sarah Windham was almost alone in her efforts to keep the breed going in the Republic.

Before going into details of Medicine Man and his achievements, perhaps it could be mentioned that at the very start of the 1980's, brindles were on almost equal pegging with fawns, and were doing a lot of winning. As stated above, Langton won at Crufts in 1980, and in the same year his brother Parcwood W. Bear, went best in show at the Old English Club Championship show, under the American breed specialist Marie Moore. Fighting Faith, as already noted won Best Of Breed at Crufts in 1983. Throughout this decade, there seemed to be more and more brindles taking top honours.

Let us now turn our attention to the dominant dog of the decade, Ch. Hollesley Medicine Man, bred by Mrs. Pam Day, by Ch. Copenore Rab x Ch. Devil Dancer of Hollesley, and born on the 25th January 1978. He was owned by Mrs. Lloyd-Jones and Phil Greenwell, the latter always handling him in the ring. He was the record holder for the breed, and was almost unbeatable. To be hyper critical, he was perhaps about one inch too short in back, but even so he was magnificent. He had what is so often lacking in a Mastiff, showmanship and ring presence, and when he strode into the ring he could not be denied. A true ambassador for the breed. He was Best of Breed at Crufts in 1981, 1982 (where his sister Hollesley Rowella got the bitch ticket) and 1984. In 1983 he won the Challenge Certificate but was beaten for Best of Breed—the only time. He was also best of breed at the Old English Mastiff Club's championship show in 1982. He retired after his 1984 win, covered with honours. He, and his owner Phil Greenwell, made the show ring their own! And speaking personally, I am sorry he was not shown at Crufts 1985, where my husband gave the CC to a young up and coming dog, Ch. Bulliff Warrior, from the Junior class. I would dearly have liked to have seen these two meet, but it was not to be. Medicine Man will always be remembered with great affection, as an example to the breed.

Now, to the Grangemoor tragedy. During the 1970's and into the '80's they had been one of the leading kennels, and Mrs. Degerdon had owned Mastiffs since the very early 1960's, when she acquired Milf Murias. She owned Ch. Copenore Rab, Ch. Copenore Czarina, Grangemoor Bevis, and others. However, and apparently out of the blue, in March 1985, she suddenly flew out of the country, in a hired plane, with over 40 Mastiffs. The trouble was that although the intention had been to go into partnership with somebody living in the States, Mrs. Degerdon arrived without a work permit and with the planned kennels not even built. The results were catastrophic—for the dogs. They were farmed out, having nowhere to go, there was no money to feed them. The American Mastiff Club did its best to help, but to no avail. Most were put down, and a video made of them at the time is heartbreaking. Eventually Mrs. Degerdon was forced to return and of the 40 something dogs that had left the country with her, five or six made the return journey. These were then put into quarantine kennels and it is believed that with no money to pay for them, they simply spent the rest of their lives there. Nothing more, as far as I am aware, was ever heard of their owner. The Grangemoor kennels had come to a miserable conclusion.

To proceed to a happier subject, we will return to Messrs Thomas and Tugwell and the Bredwardine kennels. Having been judging in the United States, Richard Thomas saw a big apricot dog, Arciniegas Lion, and determined to purchase him. He was eventually imported in 1987, and his pedigree is in Appendix I. He was by Am. Ch. Groppetti's Wallon out of Groppetti's Arciniega Saga, and was born 19th October 1984. He soon became an English champion, and in fact took the country by storm. Like the Devil from Wayside, bringing some fresh blood into the country, he was used extensively at stud and it would be hard, today, to find dogs that do not go back to him. Having said that, there are a handful that are still "Lion Free!" His progeny dominated the ring in the early 1990's and will be discussed later, but his most famous sons, Ch. Brigadier of Bredwardine and Ch. Bredwardine Brongest were also most successful stud dogs and his champion daughters include Ch. Bredwardine Bedwyn and Ch. Chevelu Blodeuwedd of Bredwardine. His influence will be felt for many many years. Like The Devil, he carried on his sire's side the blood of Fidelle de Fenelon, as Wallon's great grandsire was Ina Pauls Ben of Lovecreek; the rest of his breeding is pure Deer Run, and goes back to Ch. Deer Run Wycliff and Deer Run Sophie. Most unhappily, he died young, and left a great gap in his owners' hearts because as well as being an enormous prize winner, he was also their house dog and house pet.

Registrations for the breed remained fairly stable during the 1980's, being 303 for 1980 and 446 for 1989. I know this is an increase of nearly 150 but for a ten year period that does not seem to be excessive.

Finally, and speaking personally, I feel that after the 1970's which produced superb head types as personified by Rab, the Dare Devil, Devil Dancer, etc., heads were not quite as good as they had been. Movement certainly improved, and when we look at the 1990's we will have to see whether we got the head type back again, and whether overall type and soundness have also improved, or perhaps deteriorated.

The United States of America   *Patricia B. Hoffman*

Upward went the registrations for 1980, totaling 1,198. Sixty-four championships were awarded, and five Mastiffs became holders of CD degrees. There were nearly 60 entries in the annual show, which was won by Ch. Gulph Mills Mugger (Ch. Alexander of Dahlseid x Ch. Massalane's Dinah-Might).

The Statistics for 1981 indicated that no fewer than 383 litters were entered, with 1,367 individual registrations. Four CDX awards were won. The club show was won by Ch. Tamarack Sheba (Ch. Acadian Konigstiger x Ch. Tamarack Peaches Love Creek), the first time in many years that the winner had been a bitch.

Continuing the steady increase, 1982 showed 1,419 in the AKC registry, with 97 champions, the same number of titles won the previous year. The very large entry of the national specialty as won by Ch. Gulph Mills Resounder (Ch. Ramsgate Job x Ch. Greenbranch Dame Sybil). The first puppy sweepstakes was held at this show. A major loss to the breed occurred with the death of Patty Brill, owner of Peach Farm Kennel (see Chapter 16 "Cameo Portraits").

In 1983 there were 1,580 registrations. The Mastiff Club of America held its very first Independent Speciality Show, with a very satisfactory entry of 65. Its winner was a female, Ch. Old School's Ursa Major (Deer Run Florister Bruce x Old School's Trouble). Puppy Sweepstakes winner was won by Windsor's Pippin (Tamarack Donner x Ch. Windsor's Plum.) Mrs. Baxter judged regular classes and I judged the Sweepstakes.

Registrations for 1984 rose only slightly to 1,584. The Specialty was won by Ch. Quellwater Deer Run Antique.

CHAMPIONS, A View of the Mastiff in America, by Joan Hahn with Judith Powers (now out of print) was published by the Mastiff Club of America in 1984. A large book, copiously illustrated, its 270 pages presented a superb account of the breed to the date of issue, and has been a valuable reference work for anyone interested in the breed.

In mid-decade many new breeders entered the picture, and many of the kennels of the previous ten years had disappeared. Registrations continued to increase—1,777 for 1985. Although the club show was not held independently, and no sweepstakes took place, there was a substantial entry of 89. The winner was Ch. Oak Ridge's Heath Mor Galahad (Riverside Farms Berserker x Oak Ridge's Margaise).

1,841 registrations were listed in 1986, and the National Specialty drew a record entry of 163. The winner was Arciniega's Lion (Ch. Groppetti's Wallon x Arciniega's Saba), who was soon exported to England.

The following year, 1987, over 2,000 Mastiffs were registered with the AKC. Interest in training was also on the increase: 15 dogs gained CD titles, two went on to become CDX holders, and the first Mastiff to become a UD in over 12 years was Ch. Classics Rubilee O Fourells.

The Specialty was won by Ch. Gelwils Brandy Alexander (Ch. Gelwil's Alexander x Buffy's Brandy) over an entry of 214.

Marie A. Moore died in 1987. One of the most prominent figures in the breed, her Mooreleigh Kennel produced many champions, and provided stock for numerous breeders. (See "Cameo Portraits").

Interest in the genetic problems affecting Mastiffs also increased. More were being checked for hip dysplasia and eye problems. These ailments were (and are) checked by outside agencies and results published in the Club's quarterly *Journal*.

As the breed grew in popularity, more and more reports of Mastiffs in trouble began to surface. Dogs in animal shelters, pet shops, strays and problems with unsuitable owners became all too frequent. Therefore, the Mastiff Club of America organized its official rescue operation in 1988. This has continued to expand and is now on a nationwide basis. It is tragic that this magnificent breed should need so much help.

Registrations were up, with a total of 2,129. Winner of the Specialty was Ch. Old School's Primo Remo Major (Ch. Deer Run Ezekiel x Ch. Old School's Ursa Major), with an entry of 148.

Interest in genetic testing continued, and more and more Mastiffs were being certified free of such ailments as hip dysplasia, progressive retinal atrophy, and Von Willebrand's disease. On a happy note, many more were passing temperament tests.

176 dogs made up a record entry at the 1989 show, which was won by C. Iron Hills War Wagon (Ch. Lionsire Iron Hills Warleggen x Ch. Iron Hills Elbereth). The first Obedience trials were held at the show, with a good entry of 25, of which a significant number qualified. Annual registrations totalled 2,247.

The year also marked the closing of the famous Willowledge Kennel, owned by Eve Olsen-Fisher (see "Cameo Portraits"). Another event of 1989 was the recognition by the AKC of the Redwood Empire Mastiff Club, based on the west coast—the first and thus far the only regional club to have official sanction.

In addition to the increasing number of Mastiffs winning CD titles, the Utility Dog award was achieved by Ch. J.G.'s Mr. T. (Deer Run Tuff Stuff x J.G.'s Crossbow Lady Tigress).

The years 1980 through 1989 were a period of rapid growth for the breed. To summarize: registrations with the AKC went from 1,198 to 2,247, almost doubling the numbers. Activities other than showing increased, many Obedience titles were won, including advanced degrees. Show entries jumped, and competition became more demanding and intense. Genetic testing became more frequent, and the outlook for the next decade was hopeful.

Registrations for 1984 rose, as did the number of champions made up. The Club's Second Independent Specialty Show again brought a good number of dogs. Its winner was Ch. Quellwater Deer Run Antique.

As the popularity of the Mastiff increased, more and more breeders entered the picture. Many of the names that were prominent in the preceding decade no longer bred, although in several cases still owned dogs and showed them.

Looking at the list of kennel names for the '70's, it was startling to find that only a handful of names occurred in the '80's list, and many of those remaining were responsible for only a litter a year. At the time Willowledge, Greco, Windsor, Reveille and Titan were still active. Of these, the first two dated back to the '50's, and the others from the '60's.

U.S. MASTIFF REGISTRATIONS 1980-1989

1980 - 1,198	1985 - 1,777
1981 - 1,367	1986 - 1,841
1982 - 1,419	1987 - 2,088
1983 - 1,580	1988 - 2,129
1984 - 1,584	1989 - 2,247

7.1 Irish Ch. Bannwater Sorly Boy and son, 1980. Owner/breeder W. Blackwell. U.K.

7.2 Ch. Parcwood W. Bear, Esq of Lesdon, 1983. Breeder M. Hector, owner D. Baxter. Photo: D. Pearce. U.K.

The History and Management of the Mastiff

7.3 Ch. Bredwardine Beau Ideal, 18-10-80 (Ch. Forefoot Prince Igor of Bredwardine x Farnaby Voodoo Princess). U.K.

7.4 Ch. Bredwardine Brongest, 29-9-87 (Am. Ch. Arciniegas Lion of Bredwardine x Bredwardine Berthvedw). Breeder Thomas Trywell. U.K.

7.5 Ch. Bulliff Warrior, 13-10-83 (Bulliff Ranger of Bonners x Bulliff Saith). Best of Breed at Crufts, 1985. U.K.

7.6 Farnaby Touch of Class at Trevabyn, 28-11-85 (Ch. Trevabyn Blank Ice x Farnaby Special Features). U.K.

7.7 Ch. Quellwater Deer Run Antique (Ch. Deer Run Zachary x Quellwater Akee). Whelped 1982, shown here at age 11. Breeder H. Fass. Owner D. Sather. USA

7.8 Ch. Old School's Ursa Major, 1983 (Deer Run Florister Bruce x Old School's Trouble). Breeder/owner D. Bahlman. USA

7.9 Ch. Gulph Mills Mulcher, 1980. (Ch. Gulph Mills Mugger x Green-branch Macushla). Breeders/owners D. and M. Gensburger. USA

7.10 Ch. Caledonia Eric the Red (Fiddlewood Acco of Carinthia x Caledonia Mary of Love Creek). Breeder/owner S. Farber. USA

7.11 Ch. Altom's Paula's Pride (Ch. Beauregard Sasquatch Axtell x Altom's Smiling Paula). Breeders/owners T. and A. Bowman. USA

Chapter 8

1990 To Date

The United Kingdom   *Elizabeth J. Baxter*

When I started this chapter it was to conclude in 1999, but delays mean that it is now 2003 as I complete this section, and as the last 3 years seem to be quite at variance with the preceeding 10, I have decided to divide it into two parts; 1990-1999, and then up to date. This is a relief because quite honestly in 1999 I was feeling extremely gloomy about the overall state of the breed. The last three years seem to give far more hope.

So the 1990's seem a rather strange decade. As a Victorian novelist put it "like the curate's egg—good in parts." Well known kennels, which we will discuss later, continued to flourish and new ones were established, but it seems that these early years of the period were notable for the number of people who came into the breed and left it again quite quickly. Perhaps they did not make the profit they had hoped. It is obvious that to have a well known kennel and prefix takes many, many years; it is not something that can be achieved overnight. Yet this seems to be what some people were trying to do.

Show catalogues of this time are full of names that appear to be fleeting and insubstantial. Listed are dogs of no specific breeding, of unknown parentage, bred by unknown people. It was almost as if a large proportion of new Mastiff owners were trying to bypass tried and tested, but time consuming methods, to get to the top immediately.

Unfortunately this seemed to go hand in hand with ignorance of the breed, of bloodlines, of line breeding, or how to set about establishing a specific line. I am sorry if I sound supercilious, but the fact remains that quality in the 1990's, with of course honourable exceptions, seems to have suffered. When people come into a breed like Mastiffs to make money, they are disappointed and the breed suffers. A few people produced many excellent dogs; a great many people produced mediocre stock.

On a happier note let us now look at the kennels which were mentioned previously, and the biggest and best known and most prolific was, and is, the Bredwardines owned by Messrs Thomas and Tugwell. We saw the influence exerted by their American import, Ch. Arciniegas Lion who produced a galaxy of champions. As top stud dog, he was followed by his son, Ch. Bredwardine Brongest, and between them they sired Ch. Bredwardine Bedwyr, Ch. Bredwardine Bwlchllan, Ch. Bredwardine Boysfafawr of Watlands. Ch. Chevelu Blodeuwedd of Bredwardine, Ch. Bredwardine Brenhines of Brookview, Ch. Darkling Finbar of Bredwardine, Ch. Darkling Finn Mac Cumhal of Bredwardine, and Ch. Bredwardine Bryntowydd.

Another kennel well known and reputable who gave the Bredwardines a run for their money was Raymond Boatwright's Glynpedrs. His Ch. Glynpedr Dom Perignon (born 27th June 1982, by the famous Ch. Hollesley Medicine Man out of the top winning bitch Glynpedr Bollinger) was just as influential a stud dog as any that Bredwardine produced, and he exerted a considerable influence on the breed. Other Glynpedr dogs were Ch. Glynpedr Ruinart, Ch. Glynpedr Tattinger, Ch. Brave Chaka at Glynpedr, who went best of breed at Crufts in both 1992 and 1993, and Ch. Glynpedr Napoleon who, owned by Mr. and Mrs. Bromley, was Best in Show at the Old English Mastiff Club championship show in 1993. In 1991 Raymond imported the American dog, Fantasy's in the Night, and made him up into a champion, but unfortunately this dog was used only infrequently at stud. When talking about kennels such as Bredwardine and Glynpedr, it must be remembered that their activities spanned both the 1980's and the 1990's and it is sometimes hard to catalogue all their successes or separate them into specific times.

The next kennel which really "took off" in the 1990's was Julia Manfredi's Prixcan. Mention has already been made of Ch. Prixcan Contach and Ch. Prixcan Espada, and these were followed by Ch. Prixcan Druses (owned by Mr. and Mrs. Pass) Ch. Prixcan Poseuse, Ch. Prixcan Morgan La Fee, Ch. Prixcan Esprit, Ch. Prixcan Eclat and Ch. Prixcan Blasine. In 1991 Prixcan "did the double" at Crufts winning both challenge certificates, with Contach and Poseuse.

Louis McDonald continued to exhibit and win well and in 1990 I see that he had Ch. Glynpedr Sandeman of Longendale entered at Crufts. Other kennels such as Namous, Chevelu, Trevabyn, Damaria, and of course Farnaby, were still much in evidence. Again I apologize to all those whose names I have inadvertently omitted.

In addition to the older kennels mentioned, several new ones came into being. Perhaps the best known was that of Thelma Green with her Jengren dogs. One of these, Ch. Jengren Pluto, was a big brindle winner towards the end of the 1990's. Her first and most famous dog however was Ch. Dignified John at Jengren, who was by Ch. Glynpedr Dom Perignon x Meps Dark Ranee. Unfortunately, although only active in the breed for a comparitvely short time, and despite her many successes, ill health has meant that Thelma is yet another breeder who at present is seen less frequently.

It is probably true to say that during the 1990's, and at the start of the 21st century, that the largest kennel and one of the most important was that belonging to Mr. and Mrs. Knight. Elaine Knight's prefix is Kumormai and her husband's is Klanzman. I say "is" because they are still very much to the fore and have a reputable and successful establishment. Although based in the north of Scotland they manage to attend nearly every championship show held in the United Kingdom and do a considerable amount of winning. They have taken the time and the trouble to get properly founded and this time and trouble has paid off.

The Faerdorn prefix is becoming even better known and yet another newcomer, although he had Mastiffs well before 1990, is David Collinson with the Massalovs. He returned from the United States in the late 1980's and his first bitch seems to have been Ch. Glynpedr Irish Velvet of Massalov. At the end of this decade he is becoming more and more successful in the show ring.

We must not forget to mention Liz and Gordon Davies with their Ceninpedr dogs. Although they do not appear to do a great deal of breeding, what they do breed is good.

A dog that did a great deal of winning in the earlier part of the 1990's was the apricot Ch. Darkling Paddington Bear (3.4.91). He was by Ch. Trevabyn Mr. Snowman of Andwell x Darkling Magic Mistress and bred by Webberly and Rice. When he and Janet Webberly went to Australia he was much missed.

Solocroft, with Mr. and Mrs. Mitchell made their appearance in 1992 while Kim Dodds owned the outstanding fawn bitch, Ch. Marcolian Rhannas Flower of Luvalump. Pam Chidwick of the long established Cedwalla kennels had great success with her almost unbeatable fawn bitch, Ch. Cedwalla Sweet Charity, by Cedwalla Warwick x Cedwalla Harriet.

Two other top winning fawn bitches were Ch. Dawn Roseanne (by Bugeilyn of Bredwardine x Rosetta St. Michael) and Ch. Brookview Bo-Filette (Monte de Lion Brookview x Bredwardine Brenhlines of Brookview).

Although I know it will be as if I am sounding my own trumpet, I would like to mention my trio of brindles who did so well at that time. In 1990 Big Bertha (Ch. Farnaby Fraze and Fable) was Mastiff bitch of the year, and in 1995 her son Ch. Farnaby Fringe Benefit was Mastiff of the year, and best dog at the Old English Mastiff Club championship show. Fred, as he was called, finished his show career by going best veteran in show at the Mastiff Association show in 1999. His mother died of bloat when he and his siblings were only two weeks of age—a devastating loss.

I entered Fringe Benefit's sire, Farnaby Touch of Class at Trevabyn, for the OEMC championship show in 1991, where to my joy he went Best in Show. However, he was shown infrequently as I concentrated on campaigning his son. Touch of Class was also a most successful and much used stud dog. The brindle colour was certainly holding its own against the fawns.

There were many other notable brindle winners, with often more brindles than fawns in the ring. Some of the best known were Ch. Bredwardine Brongest, together with many of his offspring including including Ch. Darkling Finbar of Bredwardine; Ch. Jengren Pluto, Ch. Brave Chaka at Glynpedr, Ch. Prixcan Morgan La Fee, Ch. Quixhill True Brit, Ch. Rothero Belonga Judd and many others. I will mention the top brindle winners of the next few years later in this chapter.

To balance the gains, we have to look at the losses. Although Glynpedr had been one of the most dominant kennels, Raymond Boatwright has now given up the breed and embarked on a new career, that of nurse. Another great loss, because I feel they had not reached their potential, was Damaria. The tragic and early death of Mary Joynes meant that this line too, was lost to the breed, after so much success in both exhibiting and breeding. Mr. Cogan who founded his Craigavon kennel back in 1963 does not enjoy good health and breeds infrequently. Mr. and Mrs. Say of the famous Bulliffs have also withdrawn to a great extent from showing and breeding, although at the Mastiff Association championship show in the year 2002 they produced a brother and sister Bulliff Dom and Bulliff Dacie, who took both the dog and bitch Challenge Certificates, thus doing the double. They are now both champions and it is to be hoped that this means that the Bulliffs will be seen more frequently in the show ring. Mrs. Say is the vice president of the Old English Mastiff Club and judged their show in 1998.

Norman Clarke who with Hilary Sargeant had the Quixhall Mastiffs, died very young and very suddenly, and with the death of my husband in 1996, the Lesdon prefix ceased to exist. This prefix had in fact belonged to my mother and started in 1912. It must have been one of the oldest in existence.

Also in this period occurred the death of Miss Barbara Blackstone (see Chapter 16 "Cameo Portraits"). This lady, and she was indeed a lady, died at the age of 98 just after Christmas 1998. This meant that another link with the very early history of the breed was severed. Mrs. Lindley, of the well known Copenore Mastiffs died in 1992, and of course Mrs. Day, of the renowned Hollesley Mastiffs s died on New Years Day 1996. So it will be apparent that the 1990's was a decade of great loss, both in people and in kennels, as well as some gains. A sad decade in many ways.

As mentioned at the start of this chapter, I said that the period was "good in parts". Perhaps I should enlarge a little more. I mentioned that people seemed to come and go, and the impression given was that they were in it for profit, and not for the benefit of the breed. This, I fear, was probably true. More and more Mastiff puppies seem to find their way into the hands of dealers, even pet shops, although this is strictly against the Code of Ethics enshrined in the rules of the two Mastiff clubs. It means that there are plenty of unscrupulous people, not members, of either of the clubs, who are behaving in this manner.

I would like to finish this chapter with a reflection on what I consider to be the state of the breed in the 1990's its strengths and weaknesses. I would be the first to admit that there were some good typy dogs, which one can call a strength, but there is no getting away from the fact that movement was, in a great many cases apalling, and a cause of great concern.

The breed Standard covers the appearance of the dog. It is, or should be, easy to follow so that one can see at a glance whether a Mastiff has a good head, good bone, good size. The Mastiff is a very head-conscious breed and at that time the majority of the dogs were of an adequate type. We had some nice looking Mastiffs with the required breed features. Of course there were and always will be, differences and people interpret the Standard in different ways.

Movement, however, is governed by correct construction, correct proportions and correct balance. One of the things in the past that has been blamed for poor movement is hip dysplasia. This of course is caused by the poor fit of the hip joint into the socket. While the majority of views is that it is hereditary, others hold that environment and diet play a large part in the condition. I believe that during the 1990's H.D. was not as big a problem as it had been in the past, say 20 years ago. Many breeders now have their animal's hip scored and I wish that more would do so. Elbow dysplasia is also known, but again we do not seem to hear so much about it, and it can of course be corrected by surgery. According to The Animal Health Trust our breed does not seem to suffer from eye problems — I insert this here although it has nothing to do with movement!

Mastiffs seem to go through phases of being sound and having good movement and then for some reason or the other the opposite holds true. In the 1990's we saw so many dogs who appeard to have difficulty moving their hindquarters; walking seemed stitlted, even painful. I truly believe that this could well have been due to a condition known as "Wobblers," or Wobbler Syndrome.

This is something that plagues many large breeds, such as Great Danes, Borzois, Dobermans, etc. We are told that it does not affect Mastiffs, but this is incorrect. It has somehow got into the breed. If we can bring ourselves to acknowledge this and work to eliminate it, we will succeed. We need to act, because it is a comparatively, and I say comparatively, new problem and shutting our eyes to it will not make it go away.

The correct name for Wobblers is Hereditary Cervical Spondalopathy. It is a neurological condition caused by damage to the spinal cord. To try to be brief, this damage is caused when vertebrae in the neck grow out of shape. The nerve is pinched and the whole of the back and hindquarters can be affected. The trouble is that nerve damage does not show up on x-rays so there is no easy way of confirming a diagnosis. Also the condition can vary greatly from slight disability and reluctance to move to total paralysis. Very often a dog with wobbly hindquarters will have its back and rear end x-rayed but the damage is actually high up in the neck. So anybody with a dog who does not move freely — stop and think. "Would it possibly be nerve damage that is the cause?" The word to worry about here of course is *Hereditary* Cervical Spondalopathy.

If I appear to be labouring the point then I apologise, but I feel it is important to look facts in the face. It is no sin to have a dog with a fault, hereditary or otherwise, the only sin is to shut our eyes, and/or breed from the animal concerned. Faults can crop up unexpectedly at any time and it should be realized that many hereditary faults can skip one or more generations. We certainly do not want a witch hunt, just honesty and the realisation of the possibility that this condition now exists within our breed.

To complete my thoughts on the 1990's I will touch on Registrations before going on to the last 3 years. These rose from 396 in 1990, to 535 in 1995, and 528 in 1999. Registrations for the first half of 2002 came to just 252. It must be borne in mind however, that these figures do not include puppies that are not registered but sold by dealers.

We have had some good Mastiffs in the last decade, but unfortunately we also had several that did the breed no favours at all.

And so we come to the start of the 21st century, and I can say in all honesty that I feel far more optimtistic. Quality certainly seems to be on the "up" once more and movement much improved. Perhaps the penny has dropped at last. However it is no good having a Mastiff that looks superb when posed, but which is incapable of getting round the ring.

There have been a plethora of promising animals in the last three years. New champions, all good movers, include Ch. Cassanova of Bredwardine, Chs. Bulliff Dom and Bulliff Dacie, Ch. Darkling Hector, Ch. Fearnaught the Barbarian, Ch. Kumormai All Gold, and Ch. Dajenis Peace Maker of DoBunni. Bredwardine are producing a crop of promising youngsters, and all in all quality and movement both seem to be improving. I hope the breed is undergoing a real revival.

I was particularly heartened by the critique written by the judge of the Mastiff Association Championship Show, David Blaxter, in February 2003. He praised both the quality and the movement of the majority of the animals entered under him, in particular his two main winners, which I am proud to say were litter brother and sister, Farnaby Floating Voter and Farnaby Fallen Woman at Wickhaven. The movement of both of these was, he said, excellent.

So perhaps after a very lean period the corner has been turned, and we can look forward to better times ahead.

The United States of America   *Patricia B. Hoffman*

1990 showed registrations increasing to 2,712. Ch. Iron Hills War Wagon, who had won the previous year, won the National Specialty. A total of 157 Mastiffs was entered. It might be noted that while 157 Mastiffs were actually entered, the catalogue total of over 400 included multiple entries of one dog: that is, it might be entered in several classes or events. 31 competed in Obedience at the show.

The most important occurrence of 1991 was the revision of the Official Standard of the Breed (see Chapter 11). This became effective December 21, 1991.

The year's statistics showed more interest in activities other than conformation. 15 CD titles were won, and three Mastiffs achieved the advanced CDX. A brindle bitch, Ch. Miyaka Misha CDX won a Tracking title—only the third in the breed to do so. Showing, of course, continued more intensively, and 156 champions were made up. A grand total of 2,886 Mastiffs was registered with the AKC.

The 1991 Specialty drew an entry of 166 (catalogue total 422) and the winner was Ch. Stonehouse Country Squire (Ch. Groppetti Sir Arthur x Ch. McBee's Golden Nugget).

In 1992 registrations passed the three thousand mark (3,237). That year marked a new feature at the club show. For the first time, colors were divided, but in Open Classes only: fawn, apricot and brindle being judged separately. This was in part due to the widespread belief that brindles were not given equal attention with other colors. The winner was a fawn female, Ch. Smok"n Lad's Stormy Dominic (Ch. Groppetti Sir Arthur x Smok"n Lad's Stormy Bernadette) over an entry of 236.

In 1993 the entry at the National Specialty was 272, and the winner was Ch. Matts Joshua of Dogwood Knoll (Ch. Burns Hall Zachary x Burns Hall Nicole). The first Futurity event was held at the show.

The most important event of that year was the publication of Joan Hahn's *GRANDEUR AND GOOD NATURE, The Character of the Mastiff* (now out of print and very rare). Its over 700 large pages included articles on various topics, history and a rich collection of photographs and reproductions. It provided an unequaled look at the breed to date.

Also to appear in 1993 was the first *STUD DOG REGISTER*, compiled and issued by Debora Jones. Owners could submit complete information on sires: a three generation pedigree, data on health, including testing for hip dysplasia and other genetic factors, physical description and comments on temperament and other traits.

1994 brought another large entry for the annual Club show, which was won by Ch. Iron Hills Earned Interest (Ch. Iron Hills War Wagon x Ch. Brite Star Lionsire Addition), a female.

Norma Jean Greco died. Her kennel dated back to the 1960's, and her kennel name "Greco" appears in many pedigrees. Among her imports were Ch. Nelson of Hollesley, Edgemount Withybush Wilfred and Gaynor of Bardayle. Registrations continued to climb, with a total for 1994 of 3,824.

The Specialty for 1995 drew a record entry of 467 and a bitch, Ch. Iguards T & T Magic Moment (Ch. Lionsire Cantankerous Earl x Ch. Iguards Tinker Belle) took the top spot.

Registrations were over four thousand (4,245) and the Rescue Committee sadly reported that over 200 Mastiffs were handled. A Rescue Parade was held at the Specialty of dogs that were placed and happy with new owners. This was to become an annual event.

In 1993 a committee was formed to set up a Working Dog (WD) award to be given by the Club. A point system was formulated based on a number of criteria. For a complete description of the award, see Chapter 15 "Mastiff Activities". At the annual meeting of the Club 20 WD titles were presented.

1996 entries in the AKC records totalled 4,807. The National Specialty added a Draft Dog and Carting Test with five dogs qualifying. Ch. Ridgewood's Otis (Ch. Iron Hills Orpheus x Kaylin Brandee) was the conformation winner.

A brindle won the 1997 Specialty: Ch. Iron Hills Into The Night (Ch. Iron Hills Paint Your Wagon x Kara Stonehage) over an entry of 296.

Registrations soared to 5,270. Sad to report, in one six month period the Rescue Committee had 149 Mastiffs to deal with.

Canadian breeder Hyacinth Mellish died. Her Heatherbelle prefix was well known here and in England. (See "Cameo Portraits" for details).

A very slight drop in registrations occurred for the first time—down to 5148. The Specialty continued to draw an enormous entry of 457. Its winner was Ch. Iron Hills Into The Night, last year's winner. Obedience had an entry of 39 in the tenth competition held with the show.

During 1998 194 Mastiffs became Champions of Record; 14 won CD titles; two achieved CDX. One Tracking title went to Beowulf Nordic Traveller.

The Mastiff Club ended that year with a total membership of 818.

With 5,306 registrations in 1999, almost double the number listed in 1990, it was clear that the popularity of our once-rare breed was still on the increase. The National Specialty had a very large entry, with the top award going to Ch. Regal Hills Sudden Impact (Paladins Ob Wan Kinobie x Ch. Nightstalkers Enchantress).

Registrations for 2000 totalled 5,576, but 2001 showed a very slight drop—5,434. The rescue statistics, sadly, continued to rise. The horrifying figure for 2001 was 442, plus many dogs from the previous year as yet unplaced.

But to return to the National Specialty—now an event lasting several days. It includes, in addition to regular conformation and obedience, carting, temperament testing, health checks and seminars, among other activities. Plus, of course the annual meeting and awards.

In 2000 the Specialty had 292 entries, and the winner was Ch. Regal Hills Sudden Impact, the previous year's winner.

The 2001 Specialty had the very large total of 400 Mastiffs, and its winner was Ch. Golem Moses George E (Ch. Groppetti Genghis Moses E x Ch. Groppetti Gar Hannah E).

However, 2002 drew a smaller number, with 287 dogs competing. Best in show went to Ch. Ironclad's Ironhill Ivana (Ch. Acorn Hill Uther Pendragon x Ironhill's Ironclad Alibi).

The last decade of the century was a period not only of the overwhelming increase in numbers, but also of many, many problems. The latter range from ignorant and indiscriminate breeding (and breeders) to major health problems.

Looking back over the years since my entry into Mastiffs in 1961, I am amazed at what has happened to the breed. At that time, with a total of 75 registrations, it was possible to be familiar with almost all the dogs, and certainly to know all the breeders. Today, with literally hundreds of entries at the Club Specialty, and very large numbers at regular shows, one sees many dogs of unfamiliar lineage and many "in and out" owners and breeders.

It would be impossible to list breeders of the final decade: the roster would cover pages. Many kennels have come and gone, and very few that were extant in the early years of the 90's still function.

8.1 Ch. Farnaby Fraze and Fable, 1990 (Ch. Demarier Count Magnum x Farnaby Special Features). Breeder/owner E. Baxter. Photo: D. Pearce. U.K.

8.2 Ch. Fearnaught the Barbarian, 2001 (Helmlake Rock 'n Roll for Fearnaught x Wyecaple Tosca of Fearnaught). Breeder G. Payne. Photo: D. Young. U.K.

8.3 Ch. Kumormai All Gold, 1999. Breeder/owner E.Knight.
Photo: A. Walker. U.K.

8.4 Rhilaubekan Benjamin, 1-10-99 (Ch. Bwlchygwyn of Bredwardine x
Silver Blossom over Rhilaubekan). Owner John Chris Rischmiller. U.K.

8.5 Ch. Brookview Beau Filette, 21-10-96 (Monti De Leone Brookview x Bredwardine Brenhines of Brookview). BIS at Mastiff Association Millenium Show 2000. Breeder/owner Seager & Lewis. U.K.

8.6 Ch. Cassanova of Bredwardine, 10-9-00 (Bredwardine Mastdoch Like a Tiger x Penrichlar Peep). Breeder Budd. U.K.

8.7 Ch. Glynpedr Napoleon at 12 months, 12-10-86 (Ch. Damaria Count Magnum x Glynpedr Fanta). BIS at O.E.M.C. Show, 1993. Owner/breeder John & Bromley. U.K.

8.8 Ch. Smok'n Lad's Stormy Dominic, 1992. (Ch. Groppetti Sir Arthur x Smok'n Lad's Stormy Bernadette). Breeders/owners M. and J. Jackson. USA

8.9 Ch. Misty Meadows Dusty Miller (Ch. Groppetti Sir Arthur x Ch. Lefholz Pretty Peaches N Cream). Breeder M. Blethen, owners M. Blethen and D. Bolté. USA

8.10 Arrabelle of Acorn Hill (Ch. Deer Run Ivan x Deer Run Lucride). Breeder/owner M.L. Owens. USA

8.11 Am. and Can. Ch. Medallion Miss Innocence C.D. (Ch. Lionsire Ironhills Warleggen x Monty's Dixie Derbe C.D.). Breeders/owners W. Brown and J. Margraf. USA

8.12 Am. and Can. Ch. Greiner Hall Jedadiah (Ch. Greiner Hall Chadwick x Greiner Hall Isnor). Breeders S. and L. Napotnik. Owners G. and C. Cuthbert. USA

8.13 High Country Ginger of Brown's Haven. Breeders J. and P. Lange. Owners M. and D. Brown. USA

Chapter 9
Mastiffs World Wide

In the original book published in the early 1980's the emphasis was on Mastiffs in the United Kingdom and the United States. In this revision we want to give details about Mastiffs in other countries, their history, numbers, etc. To this end I have the task of covering Europe and Patricia Hoffman will be tackling Australia, New Zealand and Canada. Countries that are not mentioned are those for which we have received no information, or that have very few Mastiffs resident. Thank you to all the people who have kindly sent us the details required. *E.J.B*

For American readers who may not be au fait with show arrangements and government in Europe, let me explain that although each country has its own national Kennel Club, the overall governing body is the Federation Cynologique International—known as the F.C.I. This regulates all matters canine, including the making up of champions and the running of shows. The F.C.I. is based in France but covers the whole continent. To become a champion in the country of its residence a dog must win three CAC's—Certificat d'Aptitude au Championnat. To become an international champion he must win three CACIBs—Certificat d'Aptitude au Championnat de Beaute, and he must do this in three different countries. One of the wins must be at the club show; what Americans call the Speciality.

AUSTRIA

There are probably only about 20 Mastiffs in Austria, and their needs are catered for by the Molosser Club, which embraces all the Molosser breeds, Bullmastiffs, Filas, Mastini, Dogue de Bordeaux, etc. There are many more Fila Brasileiros than any other breed and the Mastiffs are only a very small group. The dogs have been imported from the United Kingdom, the Netherlands, Germany, Czechoslovakia (as it was then) and the United States. There is only one breeder, Sabine Gruber and Klaus Nothnagl, and their kennel name is "Of Wincliff". I believe there have been only three litters in the last ten years.

The first litter of Mastiffs in Austria was born in 1881, and the second appears 111 years later. This first registration was a dog called Casar, owned by a Mrs. Hollfeld of Vienna, and was born on the 8th December 1881. This could well be the first actual Mastiff to be born in Europe, but this is not definite.

The two Mastiffs from the United States are from Donna Bahlman's Old School kennels and are Ch. Old School Robin Major and Old School Merlin Major.

Mastiffs continue to be a minority breed.

BELGIUM

The first Belgian known to have owned Mastiffs was a Rev. H. van Doorne, who lived in London in the 1880's. He was a judge of the breed and also bred in 1886 two champions, Frigga and Jack Rhyr. Nothing more seems to be known about such dogs until 1969 when a Mrs. Verbeke of Dagrau imported a pair, Dagrau O'Nantymynydd and Oxhaege Biorn, in 1970. These two animals were the cornerstone of the breed both in Belgium and in Holland, where Dutch breeders such as Desaal, Sanguis Nobilis and Ircomara (these are the names of the kennels not the owners!) used their bloodlines and built on this pair. One of their offspring, Xsuleika of Dagrau became the great grandmother of the Belgian bred champion Joancy's Graf Gotthard, who was "top dog of the year" in 1985, beating all other breeds in the Netherlands. His sister Ch. Joancy's Galatea was World Champion bitch in 1986. Belgian kennels of this period have imported principally from the U.K. but also from the Netherlands. The Gwenstone/Backside kennels owned by Carl and Rina van Bael were an important element within the breed for this period, and their bloodlines included Hubbadane and Falmorehall.

There is a flourishing Mastiff Club, the Belgian Old English Mastiff Club, and although numbers may not be high, nevertheless interest is keen and shows well attended. At this club's championship show in 2001 I gave the famous veteran dog Lazybone Lincoln the dog CAC and his daughter Danish Ch. Augusta the bitch CAC, grading them both as "Excellent". However, I actually made a Belgian dog who came up from the youth class, Best in Show. As a Junior he was not eligible to challenge for the CAC. This was Zirion Erebor. I was much impressed with the overall quality shown under me.

Perhaps one of the leading kennels in the country a the moment is that belonging to Mr. Cuypers, "Erebor." Erebor's Zirion was Best Of Breed at the Belgium championship show, as mentioned above, and Int. Ch. Lady Celine The Might Molosser was world winner and BOB in 2002.

DENMARK

The first Mastiff in Denmark after the Second World War was Bournewood Emma (by Sebastian of Hollesley out of Baroness Anthea of Buckhall) imported in 1972. There are still many of her descendants in the country. Since that date development has been slow but steady, and there are now approximately 100-120 Mastiffs in Denmark. Most of them have been bred in the country, but there have also been imports from England, Holland and the USA During the 1980's there were quite a few fertility problems but recently the breeding results have been much more promising, with three to four litters a year.

From the 1970's onwards there was no specific Mastiff club, and the Joint Club for Breeds without a Special Club catered for them under the auspices of the Danish Kennel Club. However in 1993 a joint club was formed for Bullmastiffs, Neapolitan Mastiffs, Dogue de Bordeaux and Fila de Brasileiro. This club was called The Danish Molosso Club. One problem was that being so small in numbers it was difficult to obtain the services of a "specialist" judge because all rounders were not necessarily satisfactory when it came to judging the Mastiff breed.

In 1995 The Danish Mastiff Club was established, and although not large, it now has approximately 70 members. It holds one show a year and the officers do their best to obtain a "specialist" judge from overseas. These shows are popular and attract exhibitors not only from Denmark but from other European countries. The shows are always held at a castle, nothing else being good enough for the Mastiffs! Great importance is attached to the social gathering with lunch after the show.

When I think of Denmark, the name of one Mastiff in particular comes to mind, and that is Danish, Swedish and Int. Ch. Augusta. I made her best bitch at the Belgian club show in 2001, and her offspring show every sign of continuing to win, both in their own country and overseas.

Her breeder is Birte Christoffersen, of the Hugedogge kennel, which is considered to be one of the best kennels in Europe. Among the dogs which this kennel has imported are Int. Ch. Groppetti Mr. And Int. Ch. Willeyway Conrad, together with two females, all from the USA, and her latest American import, Int. Ch. Massy Milly of Audley went Best

Of Breed at the Netherland championship show in 2001 while her Ch. Hugedogge Anna Bella was Best Of Show at the 2002 Swedish show. This kennel can be justified in being proud of these achievements.

FINLAND

Although some individual Mastiffs were registered in 1967 and 1978, it is probably true to say that Mastiffs became an established breed in Finland in 1982. This is the time when Mrs. Marja Karjalainen started her kennel with an import from the U.K., Bulliff Roamer. She was by Ch. Honeycroft Danny Boy x Bulliff Giselt and was Mrs. Karjalainen's foundation bitch. The next year her owner brought in, from Sweden, Powerfull's Crassus, born 16th September 1981. This dog had an illustrious show career but is more important because he and Roamer between them produced two litters, and their progeny included Fin. Ch. Roamer's Costly Eleonor (Mrs. Karjalainen took her first bitch's name as her kennel prefix) who is herself behind other early stock. Roamer's second litter to Fin. Ch. Bredwardine Blaenlluest produced the famous and beautiful female Fin. Ch. Roamer's Sylvie who won best of breed at the Finnish Speciality Show four times, in 1989, 90, 92 and 93.

So it could well be said that Mrs. Karjalainen brought Mastiffs to Finland, produced many litters, and other Finnish breeders obtained their foundation stock from her lines. She has now ceased breeding Mastiffs.

Other important kennels are Xeriex's, Cassandran and Tamarixin. These have all been active since the beginning and are still with us; they have also imported most of the breeding stock, and all breed high quality puppies.

Riitta Martin-Koivisto imported Bredwardine Blaenlluest and owned the Wonghoff kennel, but she did not stay in the breed for any great length of time.

Other well known dogs are Fin. and Est. Ch. Mascamua Sir Lancelot (by Damaria the Chiefton x Lesdon Lady Grace) born 21.11.91. A big brindle, with good hips, he does not appear to have been used at stud.

Mrs. Mytty's Xeriex's kennel has imported more dogs than most, her latest acquisition is a Jengren puppy from Thelma Green. Before that she was always faithful to the Bulliff kennels, perhaps her most famous dog being Fin. Ch. Bulliff Undine Ulti, born 31.5.90. This is when the brindle colour started to appear. Both she and her kennels are still very active within the breed.

Mrs. Jokinen with the Tamarixin has imported a brindle male, Namous Snax, and a fawn bitch Masnou Fancy Fair. Mrs. Ramo of the Cassandran kennels imported an American bitch, Tamarack American Dream, bred by Carole Smith. She was by Am. Ch. Tamarack Top Gun Gunner x Tamarack Annastasia. Although she never became a champion, she did produce a few litters.

All these kennels co-operate with each other, and perhaps if they did not, there would not be any Mastiffs in Finland when one considers the cost of importing English breeding stock.

According to the Finnish Kennel Club, the total number of Mastiffs registered between 1963 and 1998 is 282 and there are about 200 Mastiffs living in the country at present.

All breeding stock must have their hips and elbows X-rayed at 18 months of age. The results must be adequate as far as the hips are concerned, as otherwise the offspring will not be registered. Hips are compulsory, the elbows only a "must" which does not limit registrations. The statistics are published by the Finnish Kennel Club and the breed club publishes the results in their magazine. This breed club is The Bullmastiff and Mastiff Club and is supervised by the Finnish Kennel Club. It is allowed to arrange an official annual specialty show and has about 500 members. The club also does its best to disseminate information, arrange matches, training, etc., and publishes a magazine four times a year.

Perhaps a few more words could be said about the American bitch imported by the Tamarixin kennel. One of her daughters, Fin. Ch. Cassandran Colorado Spring, when mated to Namous Snax, produced the famous litter sisters Finnish International Champion (in 1997, at the age of three years) Tamarixin Betsy, and Tamarixin Big Bertha, also an International Champion. Not only are these two top winners, they have also produced two litters each—surely they must be worth their weight in gold.

Another famous Tamarixin dog is Finnish, Latvian and Estonian champion Tamarixin Concord owned by Satu Leitenen. This dog also holds the titles of Finnish Winner 1999, Finnish Speciality winner 1999 and Estonian and Latvian Winner 2000.

As well as being behind Big Bertha and Betsy, the imported Tamarack American Dream also produced Cassandran Freshwater, who is a Finish, Swedish and Estonian champion, and Cassandran Fawley, who is a Finnish champion. It must cost even more to import a dog from America than it does from the U.K., but in this case it was certainly worth it.

Registration numbers fluctuate, from 6 in 1995, to 52 in 1996, back to 8 in 1999 and 28 for 2001. The most influential sire appears to be Fin. Ch. Bulliff Bay, imported from the Bulliff kennels in England, but there have also been numerous other imports over the past three or four years; one from England in 1998 and another from England in 2000, and a Swedish puppy in 2001. The last import to date is a dog puppy from the Kumormai kennels in Scotland.

Since the year 2000, there have been four confirmed international champions, Tamarixin Captain Concorde, Cassandran Freshwater, Wakonda's Anastase, and Ocobo Igor. Of these, three were Finnish bred while Igor came from the U.K. It is hoped that Fin. Ch. Farnaby Facile Princeps will attain his iInternational championship in the near future.

FRANCE
France of course has its own Mastiff breed, the Dogue de Bordeaux. Since the early 1900's only the occasional Mastiff appeared in France and there was little interest in the British breed. Importations really began in the 1970's, when Monsieur Boiret imported Samson of Shute. As the 1970's progressed, a small number of enthusiasts began to breed a few litters, from dogs brought in, in the main, from the U.K.and Holland. A Bullmastiff breed club had been founded in 1957 and in 1970 Mastiffs were admitted and the name "Mastiff" was added to the breed title.

After Mr. Boiret imported Samson and started the kennel of Castel du Bouyset, other owners started breeding operations. The kennel of La Vidoquerie obtained stock, as far as can be ascertained, from England. Following them came Mrs. Tompousky with her Chenaies de Kompys-tou kennel, which was based on dogs from Holland. Madame Benedetti started her de Belgodere kennel with a bitch from Mr. Boiret and a dog from la Vidoquerie, followed by a dog from Mrs. Wartel, of Dutch and English breeding. This dog was Ramuncho des Verts Tilleuls. Just after this Mr. Ruiz started his de Quelque Part kennel, with some Dutch stock from the von Sanguis Nobilis kennel.

During the 1970's a number of imports made a considerable difference to the available breeding stock. David Blaxter took Lesdon Lady Betteresse of Namous, a brindle bitch bred by Denis Baxter, to France from England. She was shown at a number of shows with great success. She was then bred to Ch. Ramuncho des Verts Tilleuls, a fawn dog owned by Mme. Benedetti, a son of Ch. Arpad v.d. Titanen, imported from Holland. The resultant puppies included English Champion Uber-acht of Namous, and French and Int. Ch. U'King Kong of Namous. These three dogs, Ramuncho, Arpad and U'King Kong made a tremendous difference to and had an enormous influence on, the breed. They and their offspring formed the major part of the growth of the breed, of which Mme. Benedetti was probably the major breeder in France. It must also be remembered that most of the Dutch dogs were only one or two generations away from English dogs imported into Holland in the recent past.

Another great influence was Mr. and Mme. Berthou's importation of Warbuff of Bulliff and a Bredwardine bitch. The Berthous had been heavily involved with Bullmastiffs since the 1950's and began very successfully showing and breeding Mastiffs, under the prefix of de Mollossie kennel. They have dominated the breed up to the present day in producing sound winning dogs of both breeds.

A major disaster occurred when a dog imported from England was found to suffer from Wobblers. This was after he had become a champion and after he had sired several litters. Using the powers invested in it, the club declared the champion and all his offspring to be unable to breed, and stock already registered was de-confirmed. This almost split the club apart.

Currently the Mastiff is going strong, with over 100 registrations a year, from 12 or so active breeders. Each produces on average of one litter a year. Kennels currently active include De Molossie, de la Tivolliere, The Little Big Man, des Brumes d'Avalon, de Mingoval, de Quelque Part, du Mas d'Eole, de la Lande de Tamara, among others. Before becoming a champion, or being declared a Selected Sire, a Mastiff must have an acceptable hip X-ray and all Mastiffs must pass a test of character.

The Club is very strict in checking health disorders considered to be genetic in origin and has the power to control what happens in the breed.

It is also extremely difficult to make up a French champion. To do this a Mastiff must have excellent hips, pass a stringent character test, obtain a CACs at the National d'Elevage, plus one CAC at a Mastiff Speciality (there are only five of these during any year in international dog shows) plus one CACs in an international dog show in France. Then there is the "conformation" with a Mastiff judge at 15 months of age. This eliminates youngsters of poor quality or those with long hair. These dogs cannot obtain their official pedigrees from the Society Centrale Canine for breeding.

One of the dogs doing a considerable amount of winning in the country at the moment is the Danish import, Ch. Hugedogge B. Sir Purcel belonging to Mr. Bernard Le Courtois. Sir Purcel is the sire of Sagamore Stableboy Brullemail and his sister Sugar and Spice Brullemail, who are also owned by Mr. Le Courtois. Perhaps I should say here that although Sire Purcel's name is frequently shortened to Hugedogge B. Sir Purcel, his full name is Ch. Hugedogge Barbarolli Sir Purcel!

GERMANY

It has been difficult to get information about the breed in Germany, and I am indebted to Mr. J. Feldmann for enabling me to include the following information:

The first litter to be entered in the stud book was in 1972, the breeder being a Mr. Flad using the prefix of v. Grafen Wlatow, with bloodlines from Belgium and England. In 1973 a Mr. Abt, prefix Broad Mein Baer, had a litter using one of Mr. Flad's bitches which had been mated to an English dog called Lisken Lancelot. Next in 1976 came Mr. Trimborn who bred fairly extensively, having about six liters in all, with the prefix of Meadowground. Again, a Broad Mein Baer bitch was the foundation.

In 1977 Isolde Schmidt started the Of Seven Oaks kennel, which is one of the few establishments still in operation in the early 2000's.

From 1979 to 1992 Mr. Lohmann ran his very successful Stonehage kennel based on Dutch bloodlines. He was the first person to import Mastiffs from the U.K. and from the United States direct. Mr. Flad had his stock originally from Belgium, and these lines went back to English dogs but they were not directly imported from the U.K.

From 1980 to 1982 Mr. Mueller had his kennel with the prefix Baerengrund, and he bred quite extensively. Mr. Alexander was also active in the breed from 1981 to 1983 under the title of Blacksmith. He too used Dutch bloodlines, and also used Mr. Lohmann's English Import, Theseus of Forefoot. Two other breeders of about this time were Fam Lotz with the Babylon kennels and Mr. Deinat with the Res Rusticae. Fam Ulyatts Griffon of Rufford started her kennel with the same line as Isolde Schmidt's, that is from a Mrs. Wolf Wittenberg's "Cheviot Hills" Mastiffs. Fam Ulyatt imported Bredwardine Bronant, a daughter of Ch. Bredwardine Brongest and Isolde Schmidt imported Damaria Princess-Marleda from England, and Erebor Magic Maggie May from Belgium.

At the end of the 1990's the importation of two dogs by Ch. Brigadier of Bredwardine and a complete litter of three males and two females by Ch. Darkling Finn MacCumhal of Bredwardine introduced fresh blood into the country. It was hoped that this would give the breed a boost. However, as of 2002 the situation in the country is becoming increasingly difficult because of the draconian laws against certain breeds of dogs (Breed Specific Legislation) of which the Mastiff is one. The result is diminishing interest in large dogs as a whole.

This means that there are now only two old, well known and long established kennels left which produce puppies with any regularity. One of these is Of Seven Oaks, mentioned above, and now owned in partnership by Isolde Schmidt and Dieter Lessner. This kennel was based on a granddaughter of Ch. Hollesley Medicine Man and a Dutch male, Lazybones Lord Lincoln, in 1977. It has been influenced by Bulliff, Farnaby and American blood, and their most famous Mastiff daughter, Diva d.d. Freezing Wrinkles was a big winner and a well-known champion on the Continent. Her offspring by Dutch Ch. Lazybones Lincoln carry the hopes of the Seven Oaks Kennel into the future. Mention should also be made of the top winning Mastiff in Germany in the late 1990's, Ch. Her Dea of Seven Oaks. Unhappily, in 2002 this kennel lost its most famous male, Ch. McBeth of Seven Oaks. He is much missed.

The other long established kennel is from the Burning Mountain (Sybella Nodues). Two of her well known winners are Ch. Francis from the Burning Mountain and Billa from the Burning Mountain.

In the past there have been other small kennels that have started with high hopes but most have stopped, either because of personal reasons or because of the Breed Specific Legislation. So the situation in Germany at the moment is one of almost despair.

ITALY

Mastiffs in Italy can really be called a rare breed; the oldest registration found is one dog in 1965. In 1970 and 1980 there was an average of 20-30 registrations a year, with a minimum of just one in 1970. The highest number of these two decades was 1980 when 48 Mastiffs were registered with the Italian Kennel Club. However, during the 1990's registrations rose to 50 to 80, with the highest number being 96 in 1998.

There is no Italian Mastiff club. The breed is catered for, as in Austria, by a multi breed club which covers nine different Molosser breeds, such as Bullmastiffs, Dogo Argentino, Mastini, etc. Because their numbers are higher, they tend to get more attention from the club. This club was established in 1988, and CACs have only been on offer for Mastiffs since the early 1990's.

At shows the breed is always judged by all rounders and there are no judges who are also Mastiff breeders or owners. The genetic pool is extremely small, and the situation means that quality is mixed.

There are some good imported specimens, mainly from the Bulliff and Bredwardine kennels, plus two Damaria dogs which were sent to Italy in the late 1980's. At the moment, some homebred dogs have in fact obtained the title of Champion (Italian and/or International) but these are the exceptions. The most famous dogs in the late 1990's were Bulliff Mighty Mamaluke, Bulliff Yddin Ystebrod, Bredwardine Bryneinon, Bredwardine Bwlchibau, all imports, plus two Italian bred Mastiffs Albireobetacignus and Allfmyfad. The sire of the latter was Ch. Bulliff Yddin Ystebrod.

It is hoped that both numbers and quality will improve over the next few years, however, Mastiffs are in competition with all the other Molosser breeds, such as Cane Corso, Neapolitan Mastiffs, etc. etc. whose numbers are much higher.

Mastiffs are kept in small numbers, in each breeder's home, and litters are rare. There are very few Mastiff breeders—only about four in all, these being Dr. L. Barberio, C. Gilardi, U. Gasche and Z. Zizzi.

THE NETHERLANDS

Mastiffs are popular in the Netherlands, and I often say that they have more than we do in the U.K. The majority are excellent specimens and there is a strong breed club, the Dutch Old English Mastiff Club whose members are enthusiastic and knowledgeable. Many of them make the trip to England to attend the club shows here.

The first mention of a Mastiff in the Netherlands appears in 1894. This was a male, Eldee's Duke, owned by a Mr. Dobbelman. Other important dogs, most from the U.K., were Max von Rotterdam, Black Prince, Ch. Orlando and Beau Boy. It must be remembered that in the 1900's there were no quarantine restrictions so dogs were free to travel to and from the continent.

The next importation came after the Second World War. There appears to be very little information on the breed during the first half the 20th century. In 1953 a dog called Fanifold Wulfstan, bred by Dr. Andy Mayne, was acquired. He was out of Heatherbelle Priscillas Martha, one of the Canadian bitches brought into England in the late 1940's early 1950's to help save the breed from extinction. Wulstan was a most important purchase and is behind many of today's Dutch Mastiffs. Then in 1971, Dagrau O'Nantymynydd from Belgium, became the first Dutch champion. She was bred by Mrs. Ann Davis, in Wales, and as already mentioned in the Belgian section, she and Oxhaege Biorn are ancestors of many of today's Dutch dogs. One of Dagrau's puppies, born in 1971, was sold to an early Mastiff breeder in Holland, a Mrs. Schiettekatte, whose kennel name was Ircomara. This puppy was Ustalinda of Dagrau and was a beautiful bitch.

Two other Dutch breeders at this time were Mr. van der Vorst, of the Sanguis Nobilis kennels and Mr. Kraay whose prefix was van Desaal. Neither of these kennels is still in existence. In 1974 Hans Rosingh, who is still breeding Mastiffs under the Lazybones prefix, and who is still an active club member, imported a brindle dog Artifax Addendum (by Lucky Attempt of Farnaby x Mistress Jennifer of Buckhall.) He was used at stud only seven times but even today his head type is still evident, as is his movement and strong character. Other imports were Danvor of Ragtime, by President of Shute, Crouch Hall Polly and Grangemoor Serena. Addendum and Danvor were outstanding stud dogs and their influence can still be felt.

A dog called Beno van Muhleteich was brought in from Switzerland and sired four litters. He was by Heath of Shute out of Hephzibah of Kisumu. In 1976, 11 dogs were imported, mostly from the U.K. The mid 1970's were a very good time for the breed in the Netherlands with more importations being made in the latter part of the decade. Hans Rosingh bred a litter by Int. Ch. Artifax Addendum out of Grangemoor Serena which appears to have been most outstanding. Serena was by Ch. Copenore Rab out of Ch. Jakote Lady Glencora and these two just "clicked" as the saying goes. Serena produced some beautiful puppies that are still remembered and discussed. These puppies added to the number of good breeding stock. Since 1979 there have been far fewer imports, mainly I think because Holland now has excellent Mastiffs and does not need to go outside for further "foreign" dogs!

The Dutch Mastiff Club started in 1977 with 56 members and the first Club match attracted 34 Mastiffs. In 1978, Mrs. Greenwell judged the show in Eindhoven where she made Ferro van de Ircomara best of breed, saying that ". . . he could win in every country, and certainly in Great Britain. He is a real Mastiff type and has everything that a Mastiff needs."

The first championship show was held in 1980 and again Mrs. Greenwell was the judge. She made Ferro best of breed. Since the 1980's the breed has gone from strength to strength. My late husband and I judged there in 1995 and thought the quality as a whole was exceptionally high. I feel sure that we here could benefit from some of the good quality stock now that quarantine has been abolished.

There are some well known kennels who have been breeding for more than 20 years, these being Mrs. Trijn Pool of the Cathalijanda kennel; Mr. And Mrs. Pieterson with the Jakotes; Mr. Marten Martens of the Lost Mill kennel; all of the above have breed several well known and good quality animals among them Ch. Dana down of Jakote, Ch. Honey

Hornet v.d. Ircmara, Ch. Lucky Lady v.d. Cathalijanda and the Ch. Grizzly of the Lost Mill. One of the Dutch dogs that I feel had had the most influence is Hans Rosingh's Ch. Lazybones Lincoln and his kennel goes back further than most, to the very early 1970's. Lazybones Lincoln is a credit to the breed and the sire of lovely Mastiffs, among them being the famous Danish Ch. Augusta.

Of the slightly "newer" breeders mention should be made of Mrs. Wil Tigchelaar, who has had considerable success with her Might Molosser kennel, one of these being Ch. Celine the Might Molossor and Ch. Clever Charles.

One other well known champion that springs to mind is Amigo Madock from the Black Mask, many times a Best in Show winner.

NORWAY

The English Mastiff is a rare breed in Norway. Today there are only about 100 Mastiffs in the country, most of them living in the eastern part of the country. The first imported Mastiff was born in 1904 and was owned by a William Mustad. The dog's name was Rita. The next one to be brought into Norway was 70 years later, and in 1981 a bitch was imported from Finland. Since then there have been several other imports, many from the Bulliff kennels in the U.K. and the first Norwegian puppies were born in 1990.

It is not expected that the breed will grow in numbers in the near future. Only about ten puppies per year are born, so there does not appear to be much chance of the population increasing. The number remains stable and in the hands of people who have the breed and do not wish to see it exploited.

There is a Norwegian Mastiff club and every year it holds its own Mastiff show. Usually about half the Mastiffs in the country attend and the club is working actively to make sure that only suitable animals are used for breeding. It also does its best to spread information about Mastiffs.

In 1999 a tragedy occurred when Ch. Doggertunet's Majestix, owned by Kare and Nina Konradsen, picked up rat poison while staying overnight at a holiday chalet on his way to the Swedish clubs show. It was not possible to save him, and the Konradsens returned home immediately. This dog was a successful stud dog and is a great loss to the breed.

Another very sad loss has occurred in the loss of the brindle bitch, Nor. Ch. Farnaby Festina Lente, owned by Thor of Hundstad; she died along with all he puppies after undergoing a caesarian, in August 2002.

There are still a few Norwegian breeders, who are listed on the Club's website, but many of the older breeders seem to have left, either temporarily or for good. Another unfortunate happening was the extensive use in the years 2000 and 2001 of animals who had not been checked for hip dysplasia, which resulted in quite a few problems, with some puppies having to be put down.

To help solve this problem the club formed a breeding council so that rules can be laid down. Lately several breedings have taken place which have followed these guidelines and it is hoped that improvements will take, and are taking, place. The Club considers producing healthy stock to be an important priority. Some breeders have spent a lot of time and trouble achieving this and they deserve all the support that the Club can give them.

The Club also feels that when dogs are imported from other countries, they should also be accompanied by complete information as regards to their health and any hereditary problems. Unfortunately this is not always the case; of the 110 Mastiffs mentioned at the beginning of this chapter only about 65% belong to club members.

RUSSIA

Mastiffs in Russia are extremely scattered, and amount to about 130-150 animals, perhaps less. Nobody can say the exact number because the situation with breeding stock has gone beyond control.

Some dogs are imported, some sold to neighbouring, former U.S.S.R., countries. They die, change owners, etc. New owners do not become members of any of the various Kennel Clubs as they are not interested in breeding. Show entries are low, from one or two dogs up to thirteen to sixteen dogs.

In Russia there are several big canine organizations but these all operate independently, and Mastiffs can be, and are, registered with any one of these. That is one of the reasons why it is so hard to get information about either numbers, or breeders.

Importations started in 1988 or 1989 from Germany and from Holland. The first was Alex Fleiers Moor Hauw and the second Elsa v.d.Ircomara. Later in 1992, four dogs were imported from England, all males and from the Bredwardine kennels, Bredwardine Bronenlog, (Chevelu Barrwg of Bredwardine x Bredwardine Bronyddmaw), Blejivride of Bredwardine, Bredwardine Bouspha and—not a Bredwardine this time, Cennenpedr Naughty Marietta (by Cennenpedr Kyar x Princess Cabeca at Cennenpedr.) These are the dogs that appear to have been most used for breeding and so can be said to be the foundation stock, at least for the Moscow area. Others have been imported from Sweden, and the United States. In 1994, a Namous bitch was brought in, Namous Sweet Grass, another Bredwardine Brithdir of Bredwardine and three more American dogs.

It will be seen from the above that the breed is scattered in the extreme, and does not appear to have a great many enthusiastic owners. The country is so large, and the various kennel clubs and organisations so diverse, the situation would not appear to be a very satisfactory one as far as the Mastiff is concerned. It would be of great benefit if the various Kennel Clubs could amalgamate or at least work together.

SPAIN

The Mastiff is a minority breed in Spain and has to contend with the Spanish Mastiff. Obviously most of the general public prefers their national breed rather than its foreign cousin.

There have been a few imports, mostly from the United Kingdom, and mostly to private homes as family dogs rather than for showing or breeding. In 1973 Jose Castillo and his wife brought in what appears to be the first import, Kisumu Happy, bred by Rene Creigh.

Then in 1979 Grangemoor, Cennenpedr, Bulliff and Bredwardine dogs appeared on the scene, although again, only a few were bred from with extremely few litters being registered to date. What were available went as pets and were all home bred with no planned breeding programme in mind.

Mastiff champions were as follows. 1982, Grangemoor Leo; 1983 Bredwardine Balad; 1985 Grangemoor Arnold; 1990 Mascamus Sir Charles and Jose Castillo's brindle bitch Rose of Spain at Mansiff; 1991 Deer Run Washington (an American import); 1992 Kosmos del Masset del Leo, Prixcan Marquise, Mansiff Justine (World Junior Champion); 1994 Prixcan Diva and a dog called simply Tyson.

There is no Mastiff club in Spain. As in Austria and Italy, the breed comes under the aegis of the Molossus Club (of Spain) that caters for Bullmastiffs, Dogue de Bordeaux, Filas, etc.

Apparently a main problem that Spanish Mastiff owners contend with is a lack of knowledge on the part of local judges. It is felt that judges from Italy and Spain, are influenced by their own national breed and as far as the Mastiff is concerned, untypical stock can win. There are only three breeders in Spain, and the number of puppies per year registered in the last five years, never exceeds 10 or 12. This is, it is felt, good for the breed since it will not become commercial.

SWEDEN

In the 1930's Mastiffs were kept, and possibly bred, by the Wacht-meister family, but these dogs have made no mark on today's pedigrees.

In 1962 a pair of Mastiffs were imported from Mrs. Lindley's Co-penore kennels by the von Geijer family. These did produce a litter but none of these were bred from, so the line died out. However, Mrs. Von Geijer has kept up her enthusiasm for the breed, showing, and breeding, and is still a Mastiff owner.

Interest in the breed was broadened somewhat in the 1970's and playing an active part were Ingmer Rosen, Eva Olsson, Ann-Marie and Gosta Norman and Hans Troedsson. Unfortunately all these have by now retired from the scene.

Towards the end of the 1970's and at the beginning of the 1980's, the Mastiff had a small popularity boost and soon the first kennel prefixes were registered with the Swedish Kennel Club. These were Inger and Tommy Ortberg's Mastino kennels; Harrieth Sandberg's Moloss; Kris-tina Lundberg's Old English kennel; Ruth and Gunnar Falk's Powerful; and Siv Jonasson's Thorarp's.

There were still not enough Mastiffs or Mastiff enthusiasts around with which to form a breed club so forces were joined with the Bullmas-tiff people, and the Bullmastiff and Mastiff Club was formed. Mastiffs were represented in the first committee by Eva Olsson as secretary, with Ruth Falk as treasurer, and Gunnar Falk on the committee. This co-operation lasted until 1997 when it was decided that both breeds had gained enough strength to become separate entities; so the Mastiff Club of Sweden was formed. This club at present has Harrieth Sandberg as secretary and Ruth Falk still carrying on as treasurer.

During the 1990's a number of new Mastiff fanciers have joined the ranks, among them Taina Ohman's Alvedor's kennel; Rod Mundenius's Atlasdog; Born and Gerd Karlsson's Classic; Annelie and Rosie Petters-son's Proudfoot; Ase Andersson's Skamandro and Onerva Nilsson's Ugly Dog.

A long term profile among Swedish breeders is Ingemar Ohman, associated so successfully with both the Moloss and Alvedor kennels. Unfortunately in 1999 he moved to the United States and was thus lost to the Swedish Mastiff scene.

The Mastiff is still a very small breed in numbers and during the 1980's the whole population was probably less than 100 dogs at any one time. In some years no puppies would be born at all and in the 1990's new registrations, both litters and imports have been between 10 and 35 a year. As of 2000 the total number of Mastiffs did not exceed 200.

It is not thought that Mastiffs will ever be "big" in breed numbers. People are spread thinly, making it impractical to take a bitch to somebody else's stud dog. Added to which, some dog owner/breeders live a long way from a well equipped veterinary surgery and we all know that sometimes Mastiffs can have difficulty whelping.

Swedish breeders have always relied heavily on the United Kingdom for new stock; a few animals have come from Holland, Ireland, Australia and even a couple from America. Sweden also exports some of its home bred puppies to Norway, Denmark and Finland.

The tradition in Sweden has never been one of keeping a large number of dogs and there are not very many really big kennels of any breed. Most breeders keep only one stud dog, and perhaps one or two or three bitches. As a result of the small number of dogs available, the lack of new blood has been continuous problem over the years.

In the mid 1980's Kristina Lundberg experimented, in co-operation with Raymond Boatright, with importing frozen semen from the Glynpedr stud dogs in the U.K. in an attempt to bring new blood into Sweden. At that time the techniques for the handling of frozen semen were not fully developed and the experiments failed.

In 1986 Ruth and Gunnar Falk were successful in bringing over fresh semen from Denmark and the artificial insemination (AI) resulted in a pregnancy. Unfortunately, only one puppy survived, but he, Ch. Powerful's Livius Emperor, was the pride and joy of the kennels for a number of years.

Artificial insemination of dogs has not, so far, caught on in Sweden as the procedure in dogs is so much more complicated than it is for horses or cattle. Perhaps as techniques improve, it will become more widely used, and this would be of great help to the Swedish Mastiff population.

SWITZERLAND

It seems that Switzerland, being a small and rather overcrowded country, has neither room nor liking for such a large dog as a Mastiff. However, there must have been the odd representative of the breed during the last two centuries, judging from their presence in art. The English animal painter, Landseer (1802-73) depicted a massively built dog with medium long hair and the caption "Alpine Mastiff" which bears an astonishing resemblance to today's long haired Mastiffs. Another painting by an unknown artist depicts a very nice typical dog with a good black mask, barking at some cows. The indigenous St. Bernards used to look very similar to Mastiffs apart from their white markings and of course Mr. Lukey's kennels in the middle to late 19th century was founded, to a large extent, on "Alpine Mastiffs" imported from Switzerland.

From that time until the 1960's there is no information about English Mastiffs in the country, although there might have been one or two imported from France prior to that date. Consulting Swiss dog show catalogues, it seems that there were a pair living near Bern in the mid-1960's, with another in Zurich and one in Bienne. As these last two were not exhibited, there is no record of them.

In the early 1970's dogs were imported in very small numbers from Holland (Sanguis Nobilis dogs) and from the U.K. From 1971 to 1993 according to show catalogues there were 41 males and 34 females shown in Switzerland. In 1994 at the World Exhibition in Bern, there were 24 males and 17 females entered, more than half as much as had been shown in the 22 previous years. However, none of them were bred in Switzerland. The reason being that there were only two Swiss dogs entered, the rest coming from Germany, France, Holland, etc.

Since 1985 there have been only five litters (21 puppies) whelped in the country, and Mrs. Mueller-Naegli's Swiss Ch. Falmorehall Brigadoon sired two of these litters. Mrs. Mueller-Naegli has imported dogs from both the U.K. and Ireland and can probably be said to have been the only Swiss breeder at that time.

From these figures it is easy to see that breeding Mastiffs does not figure largely in Switzerland, and in the mid 1990's there were only about 25 Mastiffs living in the country, with the males outnumbering the bitches. There is now no active breeding taking place.

Most Mastiff owners are members of the Swiss Molosser Club, which keeps a watchful eye on them and screens prospective customers. There may not be many Mastiffs living in Switzerland and even fewer will go to a dog show but all of them live as much beloved and cared for companions in their owners' homes.

AUSTRALIA AND NEW ZEALAND

The early history of the Mastiff in Australia is well documented in *The Dog in Australasia,* by Walter Beilby, published in 1897. According to the author, there were a few Mastiffs in Australia prior to 1882, but none of the earlier stock survived. He mentions shows in 1864 and 1871 at which some of the breed was shown. During the 1880's and 1890's many dogs were imported, from such well-known breeders as Taunton and Turner. Several progeny of the notorious Crown Prince are mentioned. New Zealand is referred to very briefly.

The 1960's brought renewed interest in the breed at which time various fanciers made several imports. Among these were dogs from prominent English kennels: Conrad of Havengore and Mutch of Bardayle in 1963; Cornhaye Ban Quo and Alexandra of Rhossnessney in 1964. This was just the beginning. A dozen or more were brought in during the latter part of the 1970's, and this has continued to date.

The Mastiff Club of Australia was established in 1985 by Dr. Andy Mayne. Dr. Mayne had owned the Fanifold kennels in the U.K. after the war and had in fact imported one of the Canadian Mastiffs, Heatherbelle Priscillas Martha in 1952. After emigrating to Australia he found, in the early 1960's, that Mastiffs were few and far between and decided to start the Fanifolds up again. To this end in the 1970's he imported Dear Diana of Farnaby and started the club for the benefit of all Mastiff enthusiasts. Ill health and his death in the late 1990's meant that the club has now ceased to exist. The Mastiff Club of Victoria founded in 1990 has, in part, succeeded the original and is recognized by the Victorian Canine Association. It held its first open show in 1993 and this was followed by its first Championship show in 1994, with a record entry of 42. Its winner was Ch. Kalcavalier Fire N Rain. Incidentally, the winner is called "Best Exhibit in Show."

As a rule, shows do not have large entries—20 is considered a big number even at the prestigious Royals, at Melbourne, Sydney, Canberra, etc. At club events higher numbers are the norm.

In the 1980's and 1990's the leading breeder was Mrs. A. Caffyn with her Hunzeal kennels. She exhibited and bred on a large scale and made a lasting impression on the Mastiffs in Australia and is still active on a lesser scale. Other leading kennels are Fay and Brian Gunson with Kalcavalier, Jannine Morrfew with Argenjes, and Mr. Ernie Warren with the Kalataras.

Anne Briglia has over the past few years been doing extremely well with her Breton dogs, proving almost unbeatable at the championship shows run by the Mastiff Club of Victoria. However, she may now face some competition as Janet Webberly from the U.K.has moved to Australia and from Eng. Ch. Darkling Paddington Bear and Marcolian Mormaer at Darkling she has bred two excellent youngsters, Aust. Ch. Darkling Simply Red and Darkling Cockney Rebel. These, combined with another English Import, Kingrock Prince Albert, should make the next few years in Victoria very interesting.

The leading kennel in New South Wales is Mastdoch, owned by Peter and Karen Docherty. This is based on old Australian lines coupled with Bredwardine imports. They house excellent animals and have qual-

The History and Management of the Mastiff

ity in depth. They bred and own Australian Grand Ch. Mastdoch Dier Coady. To become a Grand Champion a dog has to win 1,000 points instead of the 100 needed to become a champion. This kennel should prove very important to the breed "Down Under."

New Zealand began to bring in Mastiffs in the 1960's. One breeder, Mr. L. Kalis owned Delilah of Havengore and Sampson of Havengore—but what happened to that bloodline is not known. He also imported some dogs during the 1970's. Then there were no introductions until 1985, and a few more have been imported to date.

Mrs. Hobbs brought in two dogs from the British Kisumu kennels in 1976 and 1977, but the main source of supply was from the Bulliffs, with both Mrs. Hobbs and Mrs. Wilson-Salt importing dogs from there. The Ansells obtained stock from Bredwardine, and by the 1990's there was a small, but good, basic nucleus of animals. The best known kennel was Mrs. Wilson-Salt's, Lymehall, but at the beginning of the 21st century others are beginning to make their mark. An important step has been to import semen from America, which will enlarge the bloodlines, and dogs have also been imported from Australia, notably from the Hunzeal kennels. At the moment although there is a flourishing Mastiff Club, the authorities have not yet granted them permission to organize championship events, but they do hold ribbon parades, and social get togethers. The Mastiff owners and breeders of New Zealand are an enthusiastic bunch and although, as in Australia, the distances involved make for difficulties, Mastiffs in New Zealand are surely there to stay.

From this brief account of the Mastiff in New Zealand and Australia, it can be seen that the breed has recovered from its near disappearance prior to 1960. With many imports from different bloodlines, it appears that there is now a firm basis for the future. It is interesting to see that the history of the Mastiff in Australia and New Zealand is a parallel to that in the United States and Great Britain—popularity, followed by virtual extinction, with the breed being restored by dedicated owners and careful selection of stock.

CANADA

The history of the Mastiff in Canada has been closely connected with that of the breed in the United States. The Canadian Kennel Club (CKC) was established in 1888, four years after the American Kennel Club was founded in 1884. The two groups worked together. In fact, the AKC at one time actually handled Canadian registrations and managed their dog shows. The early problems of the CKC were eventually solved, and the arrangement was cancelled. It might be noted that for the years

1892 to 1896 no *Stud Book* was issued. Later difficulties occurred in the 1960's—all of which has made it difficult (if not impossible) to track down information on Mastiffs in Canada.

Fortunately, we do have some data from the years 1918 to the 1970's. In 1918 a fawn male was sent to W.O. Ingle, of Rochester, N.Y. This dog, Beowulf, later a champion, was bred by C.W. Dickinson, of Toronto, and was the first of many Mastiffs from Wingfield kennels sent to Canada. Beowulf's sire was Priam of Wingfield and the dam was Parkgate Duchess (see Appendix I). In 1919 all the entries in the AKC records were from Wingfield. The Wingfield kennels were based on British animals exported to Canada during the First World War, and a great deal of in-breeding took place because of the restricted bloodlines.

Another breeder of the time was F.J. Montgomery, also of Toronto, who sent Mary of Knollwood to the Ingles. She was sired by Woden the Saxon out of Princess Mary. Further information on this kennel and its dogs has not been found. At the same time, Dickinson registered a litter with the same parentage, making one wonder who actually owned the dogs. Records of the period were not always accurate!

An interesting point was the importation into Canada of the English Weland. He was a dog that was considered "pure" Mastiff—that is, he had no Bullmastiff in his pedigree. Although used at stud, his line unfortunately died out. Bullmastiff blood was introduced by another import, Thor of the Isles. His bloodline can be found in almost all Mastiffs because Thor was mated to Betty, the last Mastiff bitch bred by the Wingfields, and Betty is behind both the Peach Farm dogs of Patty Brill, and the animals that were sent back to England after the Second World War.

In 1920 a "Mastiff Club of America" (U.S. and Canada) was founded in Toronto with Dickinson as president and W.O. Ingle as Treasurer and Secretary. The organization lasted only a short time, but it does indicate the close ties between the two countries. Dickinson died in 1929, and his kennel dispersed. Eanfelda of Wingfield (Weland x Gwenfra of Wingfield) was his last export to the U.S.

In the 1940's the famous Heatherbelle Kennels of Vancouver came on the scene. Their contribution to the re-establishment of the Mastiff in England is discussed in (the United Kingdom section) of Chapter Five. Again, the close relationship of the countries is emphasized: Mr. and Mrs. Mellish acquired the first two Mastiffs from Merle Campbell of Oregon. Sired by Shanno of Lyme Hall out of Merle's Tanna, the pair were littermates: Heatherbelle Lady Diana and Heatherbelle Lady Hyacinth. These were later bred to Byron Parker's King Rufus of Parkhurst.

Again, note the connection, as Parker began with American stock, Alter's Big Jumbo and Manthorne Joy. Jumbo and Joy produced a litter that included Sir Belden Burn, the first Mastiff to win the Companion Dog title for his owner R.B. Burn.

Both Parkhust and Heatherbelle sent dogs to the U.S. for some years. In 1958 Heatherbelle Priscilla's Leo went back to Campbell. The sire of the dog was an American-bred Mastiff, Eric of Knochrivoch, and the dam was Heatherbelle Hyacinth's Priscilla. Another example of American-Canadian breeding was that of Heatherbelle Lady's Panther and an American dam, Lady of Clear View. It seems that the last of the Mellish's exports to the U.S. was early in 1971, and Parker had not sent any for several years.

Berngarth Kennels entered the picture in the 1970's. Owner Mrs. Eda Mitchell imported Frideswide Hereward, a Balint of Havengore son out of Taddington Emma. She acquired Peach Farm Ann from the Brills, and there were several litters from the pair. Later Hereward was bred to the imported Elation of Copenore.

The present Canadian Mastiff Club was organized in 1984. Barbara Goom, owner of Kilburnie Mastiffs, was the moving spirit. The first gathering of ten owners met at her home and set matters going. The Canadian Kennel Club recognized the group in 1984, and since then the Canadian Mastiff Club has been very active. Their first Specialty Show was held in 1994 and it is now an annual event. In addition, a newsletter is published, there are fun matches, social occasions and conformation training classes.

9.1 Ch. Hugedogge Barbirolli Sir Purcel, born 1998 (Ch. Groppetti I x Ch. Augusta). Owner Bernard le Courtois. France

9.2 Ch. Macbeth of Seven Oaks. Breeder/owner Isolde Schmidt. Germany

9.3 Zeus of Seven Oaks at 5 weeks. Germany

9.4 Diva v.d. Freezing Wrinkles, 1991 (Ch. Macbeth of Seven Oaks x Ch. Big Foot v.d. Freezing Wrinkles). Germany

9.5 Ch. Cosmos del Masset del Lleo, Breeder/owner J.M. Castillo. Spain

9.6 Valiant Jason at 18 months. Owner Ursula Müller-Naegel.
Switzerland

The History and Management of the Mastiff

9.7 Ch. Augusta. Breeder/owner Kennel Hugedogge. Denmark

9.8 Jengren Porthos, 10-5-1991. Owned by G. Martens. Denmark

9.9 Lazybones Lincoln (Easy Rider of Jakote x Lazbones Molley Malone). Breeder/owner Hans Rosingh. Denmark

9.10 Tamarixin Betsy (Namous Snax – Cassandran Colorado Spring). Breeder P. Jokinen, owner S. Tannermaki. Finland

9.11 Int, Est, Lv, & Fin Ch. Tamarixin Captain Concorde, 7-7-1996. Tamarizin Quintana Roo x. Xeriex's Playful Pat). Breeder P Jokinen, Owner Satu Laitinen. Finland

9.12 Fanifold Heatherbelle Priscilla's Martha, 1950. Bred by H. Mellish, imported by Dr. Andy Mayne. Foundation bitch of Fanifold Kennels. Australia

9.13 Ch. Mastdoch Dier Coady (Bredwardine Bythyngwn, x Maskhal Gypsy Queen). Born 21.12.93. Breeders/owners P. and K. Docherty. Australia

Chapter 10

The History of the Mastiff Clubs

The United Kingdom   *Elizabeth J. Baxter*

Unlike America, we do not have just one club. All breeds, if their numbers warrant it, can have more than one club looking after their interests. At the moment Mastiffs in this country have two.

The first is the Old English Mastiff Club (OEMC). This long established and well-known club was founded only ten years after the Kennel Club itself, that is to say, in 1883. A meeting was called at the Crystal Palace, with Dr. Forbes Winslow in the chair, with founder members being Mr. Mark Beaufoy, Mr. Nichols, Mr. R. Cook, Dr. Sydney Turner, and Mr. W. Taunton. (It will be noted, no ladies!) Mr. Turner and Mr. Taunton served on the committee for many years, and right through the First World War. Sidney Turner died in 1920 and W. Taunton in 1926.

The club took on the task of drawing up a breed Standard (which has remained almost unaltered until today) and club rules. They also arranged classes at shows. The First World War saw the breed suffer a great set back, but the club continued to work for the good of Mastiffs in general, and during the late 1920's and into the 1930's, numbers and quality improved. Many championship shows put on classes for them, and several most beautiful and valuable trophies were on offer for the winning animals. The names of the Scheerbooms, Miss Bell, and the Olivers appear in the club's list of members at this time.

The Second World War once again dealt the breed a devastating blow. During the 1930's many far sighted people sent some or all, of their dogs to America for safety, but when war broke out, nearly all the others were put down. At the end of the war there were only seven Mastiffs left in the country, of which only one was a bitch of breeding age. The club therefore called a meeting in 1946, to consider the state of the breed; 15 members attended and they promised to do everything in their power to save them from extinction.

Eventually Mastiffs were imported from Canada, and also from America, all being descendents of dogs that had been exported before the war. Because it was a state of emergency, and for the first and only time, the Kennel Club allowed these Canadian Mastiffs to be registered under the title of OEMC—never before or since has the Kennel Club allowed a breed club's title to become a registered prefix. Mastiffs appeared at Crufts for the first time in 1951, although they were entered "Not for Competition." During the coming years numbers increased, and the club ran its centenary show in 1983. It continues to run a championship show every August, and put on events such as seminars and talks as well as Fun Days.

Since the war we have had, I think, only three Presidents, the first being Mrs. Scheerboom, the second Mrs. Pam Day and the third, and present, Mrs. Phil Greenwell. Membership fluctuates but at present there seem to be 470 subscribers.

The second club is the Mastiff Association. This was started in 1984, because, it must be admitted, of dissatisfaction at the way the OEMC was being run. The prime mover was Douglas Oliff and after quite a battle, and in the teeth of opposition from the existing club, the Kennel Club gave its approval in 1987. The first open show was held in 1987 and the first championship show in 1994. There have been five presidents since its inception, the first being Mrs. Mary Hector, the second Mrs. Florrie Taylor, the third Mrs. Ben How, the fourth Mr. Douglas Oliff and the fifth, Hilary Sargeant. Competition seemed to spur the older club into new activity and at present both clubs work together. Mastiff Association Membership now stands at a little over 600.

The United States of America   *Patricia B. Hoffman*

The present Mastiff Club of America was formed in 1929. Two other clubs preceded it. The first organization, the "American Mastiff Club", was founded in 1879, thus antedating the American Kennel Club of 1884. Not much is known of this first group, but it was quite active during its existence.

Its first President was Robert Lenox Belknap, and the Secretary, Dr. Richard Derby. The first information I could find about the club was a notice of its Second Annual Meeting held in 1888; what had occurred during the years between that date and its founding is unknown. There were 50 members, of which six were associates. Dues were $5 yearly, or on payment of $25 one could have been a life member.

At some time the American Mastiff Club became a member of the American Kennel Club, but it neglected to pay its dues in 1893 and was dropped in 1897 and apparently ceased to exist shortly thereafter.

This early club owned several trophies, one of which was the Westminster Cup, presented to a club member at the show of that name for several years. The Old English Mastiff Club of England sent two trophies to be awarded to American members of that club. These were returned to England. For details on these Challenge Cups and the relationship of the two organizations, see Chapter 2. What happened to the American Mastiff Club records, minute books, and trophies is not known.

The second club was called "The Mastiff Club of America" and was organized in Toronto, Canada, in 1920. Its first President was C. W. Dickinson of that city, owner of Wingfield Mastiffs. The Secretary-Treasurer was W. O. Ingle, of Rochester, New York. Later Mr. Ingle became President and Miss K. McGuire the Secretary. It existed for only a few years and again all records of this club have been lost.

The present Mastiff Club of America (MCOA) was founded in 1929, but it was not until 1941 that it became a member club of the American Kennel Club. It is very sad to report that all the minute books, correspondence and records of the club prior to 1970 have been lost. This has made it very difficult to trace MCOA's progress in much detail. The only information on the early years is to be found in various periodicals, mostly in the *AKC Gazette* and such data are very rare.

From these infrequent references, we learn that in 1943 there were 41 members. The first Specialty of the club was held in 1940, another in 1941, then none until after the war in 1949. Details of the Specialties are given in the relevant chapters.

In 1945, the club donated its dues to the Red Cross for the war effort, but the total amount was not stated. That year the club kept "statistical data" on pedigrees, and would supply "cards" to those interested. Several litters were whelped, but again no details.

The next report found was from 1948, when the Annual Meeting was held at the Ritz-Carlton in New York. The only other information was that each breeder was to contribute $5 to the advertising fund.

In 1949, according to the *Gazette* column, written by C. R. Williams, the club held its Twentieth Anniversary Show. Nine dogs and nine bitches were entered, but two were absent. It was stated that there were "almost 100 Mastiffs in this country." "The English Mastiff Club (England) handed us a beautiful sterling Challenge Cup away back in 1932." This Cup was awarded every year to the Specialty winner until 1983, when it was lost and never recovered.

To return to 1949: a leaflet, *"Mastiff Owners of the United States and Their Registered Dogs"* listed 60 owners.

After the 1949 notes and brochure, there were no reports on the breed until 1965, when regular columns began to appear in the *Gazette*. Marie A. Moore was the first writer, and continued for many years. She also wrote for *Popular Dogs*, which ceased publication many years ago.

The year 1965 also marked the first issue of the club's newsletter, still published, as a very informative and well-illustrated quarterly.

The club has continued to grow and become more active with the years. In 1975, Patty Brill donated a trophy in memory of her husband, John Brill, to be awarded to the member who had done the most for the club, other than monetary, the previous year. Mrs. Brill was the first recipient; others have been Eve Olsen-Fisher and Marie Moore.

Membership continued to rise, with 200 in 1971, up to over 500 in 1984. At the end of the century, MCOA had well over 800 listed. The Specialty shows, formerly held at Devon, Pennsylvania, are now rotated to various parts of the country. There are several regional groups that support local shows, provide educational sessions, work in rescue and generally promote the breed.

The club now has a Genetic Data Collection. Dogs are tested and certified for several diseases and conditions. In addition to hip and elbow dysplaysia, Mastiffs may be tested for Von Willebrand's disease, thyroid conditions and other problems occurring in the breed. All tests are voluntary on the part of the owners and are conducted by outside organizations, the Orthopedic Foundation, for example.

A major problem, and one that is on the increase, is that of rescue. With the enormous rise in the number of dogs being bred, more and more Mastiffs need to be removed from bad situations. Careless breeders and ignorant owners contribute to the problem.

The Mastiff Club's Rescue Program, begun in 1988, now has a nationwide network of volunteers. Many of the dogs now rescued need veterinary treatment, or temporary boarding, which be extremely expensive. However, through the generosity of members of the club, funds are available. Not all rescues can be saved—some must be euthanized because of incurable illness or severe temperament problems. The numbers that are re-homed and restored to health make this program well worthwhile.

To give some idea of the magnitude of the rescue operation in 1999, 366 Mastiffs were rescued, and 50 could not be placed. The 2001 Statistics were even more distressing with the shocking total of 442.

At the Annual Meeting, awards are presented to outsdanding sires and dams, top winners in Working and Obedience as well as Conformation. Club members are also recognized for service to the oganization during the past year.

In addition to the quarterly *Journal*, which succeeded the earlier *News* an occasional *Bulletin* is issued to keep members informed of important events. Also sponsored by the club are the *Stud Dog Register* and the *Genetic Data Supplement*. The latter lists Mastiff free of certain hereditary problems. There are several committees that are aggressively attacking such problems.

As we proceed into the new millennium the Mastiff Club of American can can be proud of its progress since its foundation and is prepared to cope with the ever-increasing problems caused by popularity of the breed.

Chapter 11
The Breed Standard

The United Kingdom   *Elizabeth J. Baxter*

Any breed Standard is, or should be, the blueprint for a particular breed; a person reading this Standard should be able to visualise the animal described. Unfortunately this is not always possible. In any case, any breed Standard can be interpreted in slightly different ways by judges, as observers round a Mastiff ring at any dog show will be quick to realise. There are, as already mentioned in a previous chapter, so many different "types" in Mastiffs; the Dane, the Bloodhound, the Bullmastiff, the St. Bernard, the Newfoundland, etc. When one realises that all these breeds have had a hand in reshaping the present day Mastiff this is perhaps not surprising. What is surprising is that by now the correct, i.e. as set out in the breed Standard, type, has not been firmly established. I find it extremely worrying that new owners who have perhaps seen a predominance of one particular, incorrect, type in the ring—and winning!—should come to the conclusion that this is indeed the right one, just because the ring seems to be swamped by it. All too often it is not and another generation of breeders/judges is established with an eye for something that is incorrect.

Let us look at the Mastiff Standard; what does it tell us? It is printed below and I would suggest that the reader should study it in detail. I will then try to examine those parts that may need explanation, bearing in mind that what I say is my interpretation-based on many years experience but with which others may disagree.

Firstly, the Mastiff Standard is one of the very few that has no mention of height or weight; it merely says that the animal should be massive, powerful, symmetrical, a combination of grandeur and good nature, courage and docility.

We therefore envisage an animal that is above all big, but in proportion. The height should be made up more from the body than from the leg, unlike the Dane. The Standard specifically says that the girth should be one third more than the height at the shoulder. The chest must be wide and deep and well let down between the legs.

The Standard calls for ribs deep and well set back; therefore it follows that we are not looking for a "square" dog. Unlike the Bullmastiff, the Mastiff should be slightly longer than high. Today over and over again we see the squareness of a Bullmastiff in the Mastiff, and this is not to be desired.

As with all "working" breeds there should be a good bend of stifle and a well-developed second thigh. So often in the Mastiff the hind legs are straight up and down and in some cases this is so bad as to appear almost Chow-like. This particular fault appears down the generations and is one that should be bred out if possible. These straight hind legs with, in some cases, the dogs appearing to move on tiptoe on the hind feet, are to be strongly discouraged. Hindquarters lead us, naturally enough, to the question of gait, or movement, something else that is not mentioned in the breed Standard.

A Mastiff MU.S.T be able to move strongly, freely and soundly, but unhappily, this is not the case. In Chapter 8 I have mentioned a condition that I truly believe to be at the root of much of today's problems with movement—Wobblers or Hereditary Cervical Spondalopathy. It has always been difficult to combine enormous size with soundness and good movement. It can of course be done, and it must be done. What must also be borne in mind is that a Mastiff should be allowed to have a certain degree of ponderousness; an animal of this size and weight cannot be expected to move like an Afghan Hound or a Great Dane and should certainly not be penalized if it does not do so!

Mastiffs are, truly, a very head-conscious breed and as we have seen, there have been more disagreements and more arguments throughout the breed's history as to the correct head, than any other. A Mastiff head should be massive—the paragraph on this is explicit. The muzzle must be short, broad under the eyes (any suggestion of shallowness or snipeyness is to be deplored), blunt and "cut off" but not upturned. The under jaw is broad to the end, the nose also broad. The length of the muzzle to the head is as 1:3.

A really typical Mastiff head has a grandeur that once seen cannot be forgotten. The slightly goggle eyed look which we are now getting is completely foreign, as is excessive cheekiness. The Standard also calls for the forehead to be flat but "wrinkled when attention is excited". This must be noted because so many people seem to think that heavy wrinkling is a MU.S.T instead of a MU.S.T NOT. This overwrinkling makes a Mastiff look more like a Bloodhound than a Mastiff and is completely wrong. "Wrinkled when excited", not otherwise. The question of wrinkle is perhaps the main difference between the breed standards of the U.S. and the U.K. We call for wrinkle only "when alert" wheras the U.S. standard calls for more wrinkle than we really like. Otherwise the standards are very similar.

Another point that should be mentioned is mouths. How often, showing in a variety class, has the variety judge looked at an undershot Mastiff mouth, shuddered and turned away? Yet the Standard specifically states that the incisors may be level or the lower projecting beyond the upper but never so much as to become visible when the mouth is closed. This means in effect that a Mastiff may be undershot to a certain degree. Indeed, how can it be otherwise with the short deep muzzle that is required by the breed Standard? To have the correct head and muzzle combined with a scissor bite is almost anatomically impossible. It can be seen but infrequently. Indeed, a writer of the 1880's says of the breed that: "I have examined several . . . a little underhung, the lower jaw beyond the upper." Perhaps we should aim for a scissor bite but this must not be obtained at the expense of the short deep muzzle.

Coats are another point on which there is a good degree of variation. I consider coats to be almost cosmetic while other people think them very important. Coats vary from the sleek Dane coat through to the heavy thick coat inherited from the Newfoundland and St. Bernard. If a Mastiff puppy has "fringes" on its ears and tail, and riding breeches, you can safely say it will be long coated and of pet quality only. (The pity of this is that almost invariably the long-coated Mastiff is of superb head quality and structure.) A puppy with a few "guard hairs" on its head and back may well grow into a merely slightly heavy coated adult who is perfectly show worthy.

Lastly, the character of the animal must, as stated, be courageous yet docile. Yet it cannot be denied that in the breed there is often a high degree of nervousness. This is nearly always due to environment and upbringing; I have yet to find a breed that is as bad as a Mastiff for drawing into itself and shunning human company if it is not taken out and about and socialised when young.

It is essential that a Mastiff be a "family" dog mixing with humans if it is to reach its full potential as far as character is concerned. A Mastiff is not a pack dog, it is not a kennel dog. It is a human companion and must be regarded as such. For loyalty and courage there is nothing to compare with a good Mastiff; excellent with children, tolerant of other animals, and an excellent but unfiery guard. The size is a deterrent and like all giant things gentleness predominates unless the need for a display of strength should arise. And the strength of a Mastiff is enormous.

So there we have a Mastiff—a pen portrait should show a huge dog (weighing in the stud dog up to 16 stone or more) that yet moves well; a dog with a beautiful massive head set on a deep strong yet not square body; a dog of exceptional character and loyalty. A dog of which any owner can be proud.

It is essential that any body thinking of obtaining a Mastiff should read and re-read and understand the breed Standard because this is, as it were, the basic design of the animal. If all Mastiff enthusiasts adhere to this breed Standard then we will, in time, have just one Mastiff and not several types of Mastiff, as Shakespeare would say: "A consummation devoutly to be wished."

Official Kennel Club (of Britain) Standard for the Mastiff
Established in 1883 and changed very little since then.

General Appearance
Large, massive, powerful, symmetrical and well-knit frame. A combination of grandeur and good nature, courage and docility. The head, in general outline giving a square appearance when viewed from any point. Breadth greatly to be desired, and should be in ratio to length of the whole head and face as two to 3. Body, massive, broad, deep, long, powerfully built, on legs wide apart and squarely set. Muscles sharply defined. Size a great desideratum, if combined with quality. Height and substance important if both points are proportionately combined.

Head and Skull
Skull broad between the ears, forehead flat, but wrinkled when attention is excited. Brows (superciliary ridges) slightly raised. Muscles of the temples and cheeks (temporal and masseter) well developed. Arch across the skull of a rounded, flattened curve, with a depression up the centre of the forehead from the median line between the eyes, to halfway up the sagittal suture. Face or muzzle, short, broad under the eyes, and keeping nearly parallel in width to the end of the nose; truncated, i.e., blunt and cut off squarely, thus forming a right-angle with the upper line of the face, of great depth from the point of the nose to under jaw. Underjaw broad to the end. Nose broad, with widely spreading nostrils

when viewed from the front, flat (not pointed or turned up) in profile. Lips diverging at obtuse angles with the septum, and slightly pendulous so as to show a square profile. Length of muzzle to whole head and face as 1 to 3. Circumference of muzzle (measured mid-way between the eyes and nose) to that of the head (measured before the ears) as 3 to 5.

Eyes
Small, wide apart, divided by at least the space of two eyes. The stop between the eyes well marked but not too abrupt. Color hazel brown, the darker the better, showing no haw.

Ears
Small, thin to the touch, wide apart, set on at the highest points of the sides of the skull, so as to continue the outline across the summit, and lying flat and close to the cheeks when in repose.

Mouth
Canine teeth healthy; powerful and wide apart; incisors level, or the lower projecting beyond the upper but never so much as to become visible when the mouth is closed.

Neck
Slightly arched, moderately long, very muscular, and measuring in circumference about one or two inches less than the skull before the ears.

Forequarters
Shoulder and arm slightly sloping, heavy and muscular. Legs straight, strong, and set wide apart; bones being large. Elbows square. Pasterns upright.

Body
Chest wide, deep and well let down between the forelegs. Ribs arched and well rounded. False ribs deep and well set back to the hips. Girth should be one-third more than the height at the shoulder. Back and loins wide and muscular; flat and very wide in a bitch, slightly arched in a dog. Great depth of flanks.

Hindquarters

Broad, wide and muscular, with well-developed second thighs, hocks bent, wide apart, and quite squarely set when standing or walking.

Feet

Large and round. Toes well arched up. Nails black.

Tail

Put on high up, and reaching to the hocks, or a little below them, wide at its root and tapering to the end, hanging straight in repose, but forming a curve with the end pointing upwards, but not over the back, when the dog is excited.

Coat

Short and close-lying, but not too fine over the shoulders, neck and back.

Color

Apricot or silver, fawn, or dark fawn-brindle. In any case, muzzle, ears and nose should be black with black round orbits, and extending upwards between them.

Note: Male animals should have two apparently normal testicles fully descended into the scrotum.

The United States of America   *Patricia B. Hoffman*

Careful study will show that the British and American Standards differ very little. However, the U.S. Standard includes a section on GAIT, which was added in 1982 after much consideration. It was generally felt that following the Standard as read, would lead to unsound dogs being winners; therefore the section on movement was added.

Basically, the two Standards are much the same, but a few minor differences may be seen. The English describe, the head as being of "square appearance"; the American as "massive appearance when viewed from any angle". The English also ask for breadth, but include a ratio of 2:3 for breadth in relation to head length.

Another point of difference, and perhaps a major one, is the question of wrinkle. The British Standard states: "Forehead flat, but wrinkled when attention is excited." The Americans ask for: "Forehead slightly curved, showing marked wrinkles which are particularly distinctive when at attention." Regardless of the variation, when one looks at head studies of English and American Mastiffs, there is little difference in the actual amount of wrinkle.

The desired coat here is "moderately coarse", and probably is given more consideration than it is in the U.K.. Wavy or very soft coats are not desired. We also ask for a "medium" eye (British—"small").

It would be possible to go through the two Standards point by point, showing the differences, but basically the same dog is being described.

The principal difference is that the American Standard includes a height requirement: 30 inches minimum for dogs, 27½ inches minimum for bitches. Failure to meet size is not, however a disqualification. In a way, this size requirement is unfortunate. Far too often one hears "But, he/she meets the Standard", referring only to height. True, but the vital words at the beginning of the Standard, *"large, massive, symmetrical and well knit frame"* (italics mine) are ignored. The British Standard has the same statement, phrased a bit differently, with "powerful" added. This is what we must follow, not aiming solely for those magic 30 and 27½ inch heights.

I would also like to emphasize character. As my English co-author states, Mastiffs are not a breed to be consigned to a kennel. A Mastiff is a companion—faithful, loyal and loving. It must be part of the family to be at its wonderful best. Once you've owned (or been owned by) a Mastiff, no other dog will satisfy you.

In conclusion, either Standard, in spite of slight variations, must be carefully studied, and meticulously followed, if we are ever to attain Mastiffs of uniform type, quality, and disposition.

Official American Kennel Club Standard for the Mastiff
(December 31, 1991)

General Appearance
The Mastiff is a large, massive, symmetrical dog with a well-knit frame. The impression is one of grandeur and dignity. Dogs are more massive throughout. Bitches should not be faulted for being somewhat smaller in all dimensions while maintaining a proportionally powerful structure. A good evaluation considers positive qualities of type and soundness with equal weight.

Size, Proportion, Substance

Size - Dogs, minimum, 30 inches at the shoulder. Bitches, minimum, 27-1/2 inches at the shoulder. Fault-Dogs or bitches below the minimum standard. The farther below standard, the greater the fault.

Proportion - Rectangular, the length of the dog from forechest to rump is somewhat longer than the height at the withers. The height of the dog should come from depth of body rather than from length of leg.

Substance - Massive, heavy boned, with a powerful muscle structure. Great depth and breadth desirable. Fault-Lack of substance or slab sided.

Head

In general outline giving a massive appearance when viewed from any angle. Breadth greatly desired.

Eyes - set wide apart, medium in size, never too prominent. Expression alert but kindly. Color of eyes brown, the darker the better, and showing no haw. Light eyes or a predatory expression is undesirable.

Ears - small in proportion to the skull, V-shaped, rounded at the tips. Leather moderately thin, set widely apart at the highest points on the sides of the skull continuing the outline across the summit. They should lie close to the cheeks when in repose. Ears dark in color, the blacker the better, conforming to the color of the muzzle.

Skull - broad and somewhat flattened between the ears, forehead slightly curved, showing marked wrinkles which are particularly distinctive when at attention. Brows (superciliary ridges) moderately raised. Muscles of the temples well developed, those of the cheeks extremely powerful. Arch across the skull a flattened curve with a furrow up the center of the forehead. This extends from between the eyes to halfway up the skull. The stop between the eyes well marked but not too abrupt. Muzzle should be half the length of the skull, thus dividing the head into three parts-one for the foreface and two for the skull. In other words, the distance from the tip of the nose to stop is equal to one-half the distance between the stop and the occiput. Circumference of the muzzle (measured midway between the eyes and nose) to that of the head (measured before the ears) is 3:5.

Muzzle - short, broad under the eyes and running nearly equal in width to the end of the nose. Truncated, i.e. blunt and cut off square, thus forming a right angle with the upper line of the face. Of great depth from the point of the nose to the underjaw. Underjaw broad to the end and slightly rounded. Muzzle dark in color, the blacker the better. Fault-snipiness of the muzzle.

Nose - broad and always dark in color, the blacker the better, with spread flat nostrils (not pointed or turned up) in profile.

Lips - diverging at obtuse angles with the septum and sufficiently pendulous so as to show a modified square profile.

Canine Teeth - healthy and wide apart. Jaws powerful. Scissors bite preferred, but a moderately undershot jaw should not be faulted providing the teeth are not visible when the mouth is closed.

Neck, Topline, Body

Neck - powerful, very muscular, slightly arched, and of medium length. The neck gradually increases in circumference as it approaches the shoulder. Neck moderately "dry" (not showing an excess of loose skin).

Topline - in profile the topline should be straight, level, and firm, not swaybacked, roached, or dropping off sharply behind the high point of the rump.

Chest - wide, deep, rounded, and well let down between the forelegs, extending at least to the elbow. Forechest should be deep and well defined with the breastbone extending in front of the foremost point of the shoulders. Ribs well rounded. False ribs deep and well set back.

Underline - there should be a reasonable, but not exaggerated, tuck-up.

Back - muscular, powerful, and straight. When viewed from the rear, there should be a slight rounding over the rump.

Loins - wide and muscular.

Tail - set on moderately high and reaching to the hocks or a little below. Wide at the root, tapering to the end, hanging straight in repose, forming a slight curve, but never over the back when the dog is in motion.

Forequarters

Shoulders - moderately sloping, powerful and muscular, with no tendency to looseness. Degree of front angulation to match correct rear angulation.

Legs - straight, strong and set wide apart, heavy boned.

Elbows - parallel to body.

Pasterns - strong and bent only slightly.

Feet - large, round, and compact with well arched toes. Black nails.

Hindquarters

Hindquarters - broad, wide and muscular.

Second thighs - well developed, leading to a strong hock joint.

Stifle joint - is moderately angulated matching the front.

Rear legs - are wide apart and parallel when viewed from the rear. When the portion of the leg below the hock is correctly "set back" and stands perpendicular to the ground, a plumb line dropped from the rearmost point of the hindquarters will pass in front of the foot. This rules out straight hocks, and since stifle angulation varies with hock angulation, it also rules out insufficiently angulated stifles. Fault-Straight stifles.

Coat

Outer coat straight, coarse, and of moderately short length. Undercoat dense, short, and close lying. Coat should not be so long as to produce "fringe" on the belly, tail, or hind legs. Fault-Long or wavy coat.

Color

Fawn, apricot, or brindle. Brindle should have fawn or apricot as a background color which should be completely covered with very dark stripes. Muzzle, ears, and nose must be dark in color, the blacker the better, with similar color tone around the eye orbits and extending upward between them. A small patch of white on the chest is permitted. Faults-Excessive white on the chest or white on any other part of the body. Mask, ears, or nose lacking dark pigment.

Gait

The gait denotes power and strength. The rear legs should have drive, while the forelegs should track smoothly with good reach. In motion, the legs move straight forward; as the dog's speed increases from a walk to a trot, the feet move in toward the center line of the body to maintain balance.

Temperament

A combination of grandeur and good nature, courage and docility. Dignity, rather than gaiety, is the Mastiff's correct demeanor. Judges should not condone shyness or viciousness. Conversely, judges should also beware of putting a premium on showiness.

Chapter 12
Mating and Breeding *

The United Kingdom   *Elizabeth J. Baxter*

Turn to any dog book and the prospective Mastiff breeder will read that a bitch comes into season about every six months; that they should be mated about the 10th and 13th day of their season and that puppies will then be born in about 63 days—no trouble, no fuss, everything straightforward and aboveboard.

I am afraid that with this is often very far from the truth and although I will try to explain the actual mechanics of reproduction in the canine, I will also be pointing out the many pitfalls that can be expected when one decides to let a beloved Mastiff bitch have a litter.

Let me say here and now that if a bitch is bought as a pet, then do not fall into the old error of "letting her have a litter for the good of her health". I think this was a ploy thought up by hopeful stud dog owners thinking of stud fees. A bitch, of any breed, is as likely to live a long and as happy a life in a virginal state as any matron.

Let us suppose that you want to breed from your Mastiff bitch, always assuming that she is not too young (not before her second birthday), not too old (personally I would not dream of breeding from a Mastiff bitch over the age of six years), that she is healthy and a good specimen of the breed. The first thing you must do is find a good stud dog, with bloodlines that are complementary to and compatible with your lady's. Here, if you are a comparative novice, you should ask advice from some trustworthy and reputable breeder. When a suitable stud is found, and this may well be hundreds of miles away, then book the service in advance and let the stud dog owner know as soon as the bitch comes into season. Do not ring up late at night and say that you want to bring the bitch for mating the next day.

*This is not meant to be a complete discussion of mating and breeding.

A Mastiff bitch comes into season, or into heat, for the first time usually about 10 -11 months of age though I have known some who have not done so until almost two years of age. Please do not contemplate mating a specimen of a giant breed until the bitch has finished her own growth, and the first season after the age of two is the best. The signs to look for are the swelling of the vulva itself and the area just above this; the bitch may start to wash herself more frequently and traces of blood will appear. A heavyish discharge is usually normal for about ten days or so and gradually the bright red will turn more pinkish. If you tickle the inside of the bitch's thigh, she will most probably press against you and turn her tail to one side; this is a sign that she is ready for mating.

Here we come up against the first difficulty among many. A lot of Mastiffs have what is called a "silent heat"; instead of a discharge appearing early in the season it does not do so for several days and therefore when we think the bitch is on her l0th or 11th day, in reality she has reached the 15th or 16th and may well be too far gone to mate. The only really safe barometer as to whether or not she is ready is a male of the species. I well remember our old Alice who had been mated on what we thought was the correct date for all of her six years; she was mated when to all intents and purposes she was not even in season and thereafter had her one and only litter. Therefore I would suggest that the—to use a crude phrase—touching up process is embarked upon early on in the season to make sure she is not turning her tail and looking hopeful long before we feel she should be doing so.

The actual ovulation, or shedding of the eggs ready for fertilisation, seems to take place at different times with Mastiffs; there is no hard and fast rule here despite what books tell us; and of course, if a bitch is to conceive, she must have ovulated at about the time the mating takes place.

Whether you intend to mate your bitch or not, do keep a careful eye on her for all the time she is in season. You do not want her either to have an unwanted litter or to get mated to a dog that you did not choose. Even if you have a successful mating to the dog of your choice, this does not mean you can then relax—in fact, you must be even more vigilant until she is completely over her season; she may have decided that she approves of sex!

In contrast to the very early matings that some Mastiff bitches seem to enjoy, there are others who will not conceive unless mated about the 18th day of their season—a late ovulation occurs here, obviously. There is nothing cut and dried about nature as prospective breeders will find out to their cost. To be perfectly honest, although one takes a bitch that seems ready to an experienced and proven stud dog, and gets what seems to be a good mating, this is no guarantee of puppies. I have found that the best way of making sure is either to keep a dog yourself—not practicable in most cases—or to see if the bitch can be kept by the stud dog owner for about a week, so that she can be mated from almost the first day that she will accept the dog until she rejects him. Again, this is not always possible because the stud dog may have other bitches booked to him but I would advise the bitch's owner to enquire about this.

We now encounter the next difficulty that seems inherent in Mastiffs—their love of celibacy. She may have turned her tail for you; she may, have flirted unmercifully with the small Jack Russell in the park, but introduce her to a male of her own breed and the chances are she will either swoon, Victorian fashion, or turn into a raging virago. I honestly think that a lot of Mastiffs have a mental block about sex; they may be physically ready but that's all. Also, they do have marked likes and dislikes. Any stud dog owner will tell you of the bitch that fought like a fiend against the dog chosen for her but happily accepted another, brought out in desperation. So although you may well get a normal and cheerful mating with your bitch, be prepared for storms. Miss Bell of the Withybush Mastiffs, used to use a complicated pulley and rope system and when I first heard of this, I thought it very foolish. I soon found out to my cost that it was not, and many a time I have wished that I had something similar as four or five of us have struggled to hold a recalcitrant Mastiff bitch. In any case, it is always useful to have a bale of straw available when a mating is going to take place as often the bitch may be smaller than the dog and find it difficult to take his weight. Placed over a bale of straw, she has a comparatively soft support.

Let us now turn to the other partner, the stud dog. A dog used at stud must be a typical specimen of its breed and it should have a well-developed interest in the opposite sex. As my husband was always saying however, the majority of Mastiff dogs do not know that it's a "do it yourself" kit. There is nothing more embarrassing for a stud dog owner than to have a Mastiff bitch brought, a bitch actually eager and willing, and to have the stud dog sniff, yawn, and walk away. To a certain extent you can hold a bitch for mating; you cannot force a stud dog to work. If you have a keen and efficient stud dog; if you have a happy and willing bitch, then you have creatures that are above the price of rubies—cherish them!

I would not recommend that a pet Mastiff dog be used at stud. It's a case of what he hasn't had he won't miss and stud work is for the experienced dog and owner. A young Mastiff that is going to be used at stud should, ideally, have his first bitch brought to him when he is about 11 months of age, and she should be a friendly, co-operative matron who will show him what it's all about. Thereafter he can be used again at about 18 months, and after he is two years old he can be used as often as may be required. A Mastiff that is not introduced to stud work until he is two or three is often completely ignorant of what is expected of him, and cannot be induced to cooperate.

It is most important that a young stud dog becomes accustomed to being handled and helped during mating; it is infuriating when the dog who, needing assistance in actually penetrating the bitch, gets down and walks off if the handler goes to help him. That is why a dog's first bitch should be experienced, one who will not fight or fidget but who will flirt gently with the youngster and encourage him and take the presence of the stud dog owner for granted; if she does not mind the human presence, there to assist the young fellow, the chances are that the youngster will accept it as natural.

A dog that is going to be used at stud should not be chastised if he is a bit "sexy" with other animals during his adolescent period. This is reason why it is better not to use the beloved household pet at stud unless there is a special reason for doing so—such as the saving of a particular bloodline.

The dogs that we keep always seem to be good stud dogs and I think this is because all of the Mastiffs, males and females, run together, live together (mostly in the kitchen!) and grow up together. They have no inhibitions and are not checked for showing interest in the bitches while they, the dogs, are young. If they get too importunate the bitches tell them off, but they are not scolded by us. I think I can safely say that with this sort of upbringing you will end up with a keen stud dog who will not object to working under great difficulties, e.g., four strange people hanging on to a bucking, swearing, heaving bitch held over a bale of straw.

I may perhaps seem to be over-emphasising the difficulties inherent in breeding Mastiffs but I believe it to be a case of forewarned is forearmed. Perhaps your first experience will be different, as was mine. I took Diamond Lil to Ch. Balint in fear and trepidation. They took to each other at once, mated naturally within about ten minutes of being introduced, had just two matings both the same evening, and she produced a good litter with no trouble. I hope all my readers have the same experience—though I should perhaps say that things were never quite as easy again.

However, let us assume that your bitch seems to be ready for mating; you have forewarned the stud dog owner and you take your bitch over for mating. It is strange but in dogs, the female is always taken to the male, the exact opposite to the bovine or equine world. Even if you intend to leave the bitch at the stud dog's kennel for several days, you will of course hope to see a mating while you are present. Normally, the dog and bitch are introduced to each other, either with both on leads, or loose in an outside run.

Wherever the mating is to take place, it should be secluded and quiet, and the animals given time to get to know each other. Hopefully, the bitch is willing and after preliminary flirting and playing, stands for the dog to mount her. At this stage the owner should go to her head to steady and restrain her if necessary, the stud dog owner attends to the needs of his or her charge and a third person ought to be available to help support the bitch and hold her. Remember the stud dog may weigh over 200 lbs. and that's a lot of weight for the bitch to support.

If the stud dog finds it difficult to locate the bitch's vulva, then usually the stud dog owner, kneeling by the side of the bitch, will put his or her hand under the bitch's belly, bringing the hand out behind the hind legs, and put a finger on each side of her vulva, attempting to drop the vulva on to the dog's penis rather than try and take the dog's penis and insert it into the vulva: the latter method will often cause a premature ejaculation. This is where a good stud dog is invaluable; the over-keen thruster will, if my readers will excuse the expression, bash away like a bull at a gate and overtire himself, sometimes either ejaculating prematurely (which means a retirement and rest until ready to try again), or otherwise he just runs out of puff and gets too tired to proceed. Added to which, an inept and clumsy dog can hurt the bitch and even the most patient can lose her temper in such a case. The experienced stud, although eager, thrusts fairly slowly to start with and makes sure that he finds the vulva before the heavy thrust that is used to penetrate. Once he has penetrated, the gland at the base of the penis will swell, inside the bitch, thus effecting what is known as the "tie" and the dog cannot withdraw. It is at this stage that care must be taken to hold the bitch tightly as although the actual penetration is not painful, the size of the swollen gland is, and the bitch especially if a maiden, may cry out and struggle to get free. This is one of the reasons it is extremely important that large dogs are never, ever, left alone to mate—a bitch struggling desperately to free herself from the dog could cause him great damage if unrestrained and could ruin him as a stud dog for life.

The History and Management of the Mastiff

Some dogs, a little too excited too soon, will swell before penetrating far enough so that the gland swells outside the vulva and here of course the dog will just fall away from the bitch. Although some semen may have been deposited the dog should be taken away to retract and rest and another attempt take place in half an hour or so. Stud dog owners know, or should know, their charges and very often even though kneeling beside the bitch and holding her vulva with their right hand, they will deliver a hard and positive push at the base of their dog's tail at the moment of penetration, thus making sure that such penetration is complete and that the swelling takes place inside the vulva and a tie results.

After the mating has taken place, the dog will lie resting along the bitch's back for a few moments and will then very likely try to turn. Some have a preference for turning to one particular side; whichever this is, take one of the front legs and pass it over the bitch's back so that the dog now has both front feet on the ground, but one of his hind legs still on the opposite side. With the bitch being firmly held, lift the hind leg and pass it gently across the bitch's back so that the animals are standing back to back, hopefully both quietly. Now is the time to straighten up, rub one's bruises and hope for puppies. The tie may last from five minutes to over an hour but 25 minutes is about normal. If you place your hand on the bitches abdomen you will feel her muscles pulling and retracting and watching the base of the tail on the dog, you will see a "pumping" action taking place.

After the animals part, separate them and put both into quiet places to rest. Do not put a stud dog back, immediately, with another male; it could result in a fight. If you are taking the bitch home again then wait a while before setting off on the return journey. Always make sure before the mating, what is to be done as far as a stud fee is concerned. Normally, the stud fee is payable at the time of mating and, roughly speaking, a stud fee is the price of a puppy. With Mastiffs this is not always the case and because of the difficulty in breeding them, many stud dog owners take a gamble and say that they will accept a puppy instead of a stud fee. Find out before the mating takes place, though, as arguments and ill-feeling can result from misunderstanding. If a puppy is to be taken in place of a stud fee, it is most important that this is set down in writing, saying whether the puppy is to be the pick of litter, the second pick of litter, what happens if there is only one puppy, etc. Personally I ask for pick of litter if three or more puppies are born and reared; less than that number and I ask for a stud fee. This may seem greedy but bearing in mind that in actual fact, in Mastiffs, the stud fee is far less than the price of a puppy, I think it is fair. Whatever is decided, do get it all down in writing, and signed by both partners. If a stud fee is to be paid then this is paid at the time of the mating and although not obligatory, most stud dog owners will give a "free service" should the bitch not conceive. There seems to be a misconception on the part of many bitch owners that the stud fee is payable only if there are puppies—this is not so. The stud fee is for the actual service.

I should emphasise that all the above, about stud fees, is applicable only to the United Kingdom, and that America does not necessarily follow the same procedure.

The mated lady either now (or in a few days time if she is left at the kennels for one or more repeat matings) can be taken home and great care taken for another week or so that she does not sneak off and find herself another husband. This would upset all carefully laid plans. There is no need to change her régime or diet for the first few weeks of pregnancy, indeed there will be no signs of change for some time although some bitches do suffer from morning sickness at about three weeks of the nine weeks gestation period. From four weeks onwards some bitches seem to undergo a slight character change, becoming especially loving and clinging and following their owners about the house. At five weeks, if one is lucky, a slight thickening round the loins is discernible accompanied by a general air of contented well-being and plans can now be put in hand for the actual confinement. However, as emphasised elsewhere in this chapter, please do not be too disappointed if despite all efforts, there are no puppies. One of the little tricks commonly used by Mastiff bitches, is re-absorbtion and this normally takes place between five and seven weeks, just when one is most hopeful. A prospective Mastiff breeder must be prepared to try and try again—perhaps mating at a slightly different period of the heat—perhaps trying another dog or even getting veterinary help if re-absorbtion seems to be the problem. Do not give up hope; remember our Alice had her first litter at the age of six when we thought we would never, ever, get her in whelp.

The United States of America   *Patricia B. Hoffman*

My coauthor has gone into detail on the actual mating and breeding, therefore my remarks will be general.

If you are considering breeding your Mastiff, stop and think. What are your reasons? Do you want to improve the breed? Is your dog (dog refers to both sexes) a good example of the breed, healthy and free of genetic defects?

Or do you think you will make money? This is the worst possible reason. Given the high price of Mastiff puppies, plus the cost of stud fees, many unwary people believe that raising a litter would be profitable. Not so. Consider all the problems that are involved. For your bitch, you must find a suitable stud. A reliable breeder will insist on complete information: pedigree, genetic faults, general health and temperament. Secondly, your expenses will be great. In addition to the stud fee (which may be non-refundable should the breeding fail), you must add in cost of veterinary care for dam and pups. Third: You may not be able to sell your puppies. Would you be able to keep them, possibly until they are full grown?

Given that you are sure your Mastiff bitch is worthy of producing a litter, your first step is to locate a suitable stud. Careful study of suitable males is a must, considering pedigree, offspring already produced and health. Don't wait until the last minute to call the dog's owner to tell him/her that your bitch is ready to be bred. You may not be able to distinguish the precise time of breeding. Females are notoriously tricky, and the correct date may vary from ten days to two weeks. Normally, when a bitch comes in season and begins to "show color", which means the vulva swells and bleeds slightly, she is in proestrus. When this ceases, in theory, this is the time for the actual mating. Not always! She may go out of season or even come into season without the owner realizing it. This is known as a "silent heat".

As a rule, the bitch is sent to the male, which may involve some careful arrangements. Let us assume that your female is ready, the stud dog is present, and the pair is introduced. If all goes well, the male, after a certain amount of investigation, will mount the female. A "tie" may or may not take place. Inexperienced partners may require "help" in such cases expert assistance is needed. After mating, let both animals rest. It may be that you will try the breeding on two or three days, depending on the bitch's willingness.

It is also possible to use artificial insemination. Frozen semen is available and resulting litters are now registerable with the AKC. Owners of many stud dogs will advise you if they offer this option. Thus it is possible to mate a bitch located in California with a male in New York without the worry of shipping and timing.

Chapter 13
Whelping, Weaning, and Rearing *

The United Kingdom   *Elizabeth J. Baxter*

This chapter covers a rather emotive subject and what I write here is our (my late husband and my own) opinion. I will set out what we have found to be best for our dogs, what we do and why we do it. I am sure there will be some who disagree and to them I say do things the way that suits you. There are few hard and fast rules in animal husbandry.

As indicated in the previous chapter, because a bitch is mated it does not necessary follow that she is in whelp. Often it is impossible to be absolutely sure until the 63 days of pregnancy are almost finished. It is even more difficult to tell if the bitch tends to be overweight; but very often a change will take place in the bitch's demeanour and character at about the fourth or fifth week of pregnancy.

Do make sure that the whelping box is prepared well in advance and get her used to sleeping in it. Place the box in a quiet, warm and secluded place and once whelping starts make sure she stays there. My old Great Dane's favourite whelping place was a steaming compost heap at the bottom of the garden.

Warmth is essential for young puppies and so many pups of all breeds are lost simply through chill. We have a heat lamp, positioned above the box but not so low as to be too hot for the bitch, though many people prefer underbedding heat pads. Whatever you use, make sure it is safe and effective. For bedding we use the "Snug Rug" type of bedding which is warm and soft and can be washed easily. Newspapers underneath the bedding absorb urine and moisture and should be changed frequently, the bedding as a whole being kept warm and dry.

Things which should be close at hand in the whelping room are plenty of dry fairly rough towels; blunt scissors; plastic bag for rubbish; scales for weighing the babies and an easy chair for you to sit in.

*This is not meant to be a complete discussion of whelping, weaning and rearing.

Some Mastiff bitches whelp normally, others do not. I have found very often, unlike other breeds, that a Mastiff cannot be seen to strain and the only indication that whelping is actually taking place is an arching of the tail away from the body. When the birth is imminent, the area between the vulva and the anus will become hard and enlarged, and the puppy can be felt there awaiting delivery. Sometimes a maiden bitch will not know what to do and you may have to assist, perhaps easing the whelp out of the bitch, pulling downwards gently with a towel as the bitch strains. Do not tug or pull upwards, work in conjunction with the mother. Normally, unless she is not pushing, the puppy will come away naturally. If the bitch looks in amazement at this small object and obviously knows nothing of what to do next, it is up to you to break the sac in which the puppy arrives and do it quickly, making sure that priority is given to getting the head clear of the membrane and liquid. If the bitch does not herself bite through the cord attaching the pup to the placenta, then you must do this too, shredding the cord with finger and thumb or shredding it well away from the body with the blunt scissors. Do not cut cleanly and do not cut near to the puppy's body as bleeding will result.

When the pup is free from the placenta (which may come away immediately or a little later) if the newborn one is limp or not breathing, rub—and rub vigorously—with a warm dry towel. A puppy that shows no sign of life can be revived with persistence—do not give up. So many people are afraid of hurting a puppy by rubbing too roughly. Do not be afraid, pups are tougher than you think and comparatively rough rubbing is often called for. As soon as the puppy is moving strongly, put it to the mother and try to get it to suckle straight away as the milk the mother produces shortly after birth contains colostrum, a substance of great importance to a newborn puppy as it contains ingredients which give the pups resistance to infections.

Do not let a bitch go too long between puppies without getting veterinary advice, especially if she is straining. Mastiffs do tend to suffer from uterine inertia and you may have to get your vet to give assistance. Let him know in advance that your bitch is due to whelp; as I always say to mine "Hold yourself in readiness!" It is essential that you have a really good relationship with your veterinary surgeon.

We have found, over the years, that if a Caesarean operation is necessary, it must be done quickly. Other breeds seem to be able to go over the date of birth by several days. If a Mastiff has not whelped within 24 hours of the due date I get very worried. I expect this statement will be challenged and repeat that I can only talk about what we have found over the years; but it does seem that in unborn Mastiff pups, if birth does not take place naturally, the placenta separates from the whelp's body very quickly and no nourishment gets through. The placenta is the life support system, and once separated from it, the unborn pup simply dies. So often a Caesarean operation is performed which produces perfectly formed and normal pups, all dead, because the operation was delayed. This sort of situation can only be handled in a satisfactory manner by having a trusting relationship with your veterinary surgeon. I well remember a friend of ours, himself a vet, who pooh-poohed this argument, left his own Mastiff bitch to "whelp naturally" and lost the entire, perfect, litter. Since then he has Caesared a little more quickly. I am not advocating Caesarean birth as a matter of routine, far from it, but what I am saying is that we have found if a Caesarean becomes necessary, do it quickly if you want live puppies. Also, try to attend the operation itself, to see to the puppies. In a smallish practice the vet and his assistant will be so busy attending to the mother during the operation, that the puppies tend to be put aside to be seen to later because there are not enough hands to do all that is necessary. If you can get permission from your veterinarian to be there, he will hand the puppies to you as they are taken from the bitch and you can make sure that they live by stimulating, rubbing, and doing all the necessary. So often this makes all the difference between a live litter and a dead one.

If your bitch does need a Caesarean, she will probably be very dozy for the first 24 hours after delivery and care must be taken that she does not squash her babies, especially if it is her first litter. She will come round from the anaesthetic and wonder what on earth these little things can be. You must stay with her, keep the pups in a box on a well wrapped up hot-water bottle, and put them to her to nurse or feed them on a bottle until she is able to nurse them herself. The shock of the operation sometimes delays the production of milk.

If you have to feed the puppies, or to supplement the feeding, there are excellent milk substitutes that you can obtain from your vet. Again, make sure he knows in advance that you may need this so that he has it in stock. A baby's bottle, perhaps with the hole in the teat enlarged, is also needed. If you have to handraise a litter they should be fed every two or three hours to start with and, after feeding, you must stimulate bowel and bladder functions by wiping gently with warm damp cotton wool, to take the place of the bitch's tongue. Dry with more cotton wool and put back on the hot-water bottle.

The chances are, however, that your bitch will whelp normally and give you a good strong healthy litter. Again, care must be taken during the first few days as some Mastiffs are clumsy mothers and the babies can get squashed so easily. We stay with our Mastiff litters, night and day, for the first two to three weeks. It is tiring, but worth it.

Something to watch for in the bitch during the early days is mastitis. Feel the udders every day to make sure none are hard and swollen and sore. If they are, get your vet to attend to this, as it causes the bitch pain and can stop the supply of milk. Also as a matter of course, get your vet to check her after whelping to make sure there are no retained whelps or placentas, which could cause serious complications.

If your bitch is an easy whelper and a good mother, you have a paragon—cherish her and don't overwork her. Conversely, I have found that it is better not to let a Mastiff go too long between litters because they seem to get out of practice. If a Mastiff bitch is strong and healthy and a good brood, I tend to let her have two litters consecutively and then rest her for a year.

The puppies' eyes start to open at about 10 to 14 days of age and you will find all your trouble, toil and tiredness have been worth it when you look at your litter of fat contented babies. Don't forget to feed the mother really well, plenty of good food and as much as she can eat, as she has a very heavy demand upon her system.

Over the first three weeks, the pups, if all is well, need little additional care from you; but at three weeks of age, I find it best to start to wean them. Everybody has their own method and I will simply tell you ours. Supposing that the bitch has milk and the pups doing well, at about three-and-a-half weeks of age I introduce the pups to a tiny morsel of prime minced raw beef. Each pup is fed by hand, individually, a piece of the mince about the size of an almond. This continues for the next three or four days with meals of the mince being stepped up from once or twice a day to three or four times a day. At four weeks of age we introduce a really good all-in-one expanded puppy food, high in protein. This is soaked in boiling water and left to cool. When soft and crumbly it is given to the pups in a flat dish. At first they will wade all through it and get in a lovely mess but gradually, over the next few days, they will learn to put their heads down to the dish instead of lifting them up to seek a nipple or your hand with the mince.

As my co-author says, weaning is really very simple. It is a case of doing it gradually—gradually increasing the amounts and gradually increasing the frequency of the meals. As they go on to solid foods the mother will stop cleaning up after them and will leave them for longer and longer periods. By five weeks of age our pups are normally completely weaned and sleeping alone even during the night. At that age they are on five small meals a day, a mixture of the complete puppy food either given alone, or with milk or with the raw beef mince mixed with it. If you want to give milk alone then do not give cow's milk; give a first class milk supplement powder or, if possible, goat's milk as this is excellent. As a rule I do not give a great deal of milk preferring to go direct on to the solid food which puppies seem to be able to eat more easily. Some reputable breeders swear by honey—which puppies love and which is a wonderful food—and home produced and prepared meals. Eggs, if given, I find should be cooked first and not given raw, but all weaning is a matter of personal preference and as long as you use commonsense and keep the puppies' health and needs paramount, weaning can proceed in several different fashions.

From the five meals a day at five weeks bring down to four meals a day at seven or eight weeks, gradually increasing the amounts at each meal. It is difficult to give exact weights and quantities as we feed to appetite but do remember that with puppies that grow as fast as Mastiffs, it is essential that good nourishing food, and plenty of it, is given during the growing period.

We worm our puppies just after three weeks of age, obtaining special pills from the vet, and then continue to worm every two weeks. If sold, instructions are given to the buyers to continue this regime until the puppies are over three months of age. After this we recommend worming at least once a month until six months of age, and thereafter twice a year. What must be remembered with worms, and more especially with tape worms, is that however thoroughly an animal is wormed it is essential that external parasites such as fleas are also eliminated. Many people do not realise that the flea is the intermediate host, and a dog having been wormed satisfactorily, has only to swallow a flea while grooming itself, for the whole cycle to start all over again.

As for food, the amount a puppy will eat will vary. Let a youngster eat to appetite but guard against overweight in the older animals. A diet sheet must be given to puppy purchasers. If the pup is retained by us, we cut down the frequency of the meals to three a day at four months, and at about seven months of age our dogs go on to two meals a day, morning and late afternoon. They stay on this régime for the rest of their lives. Personally I do not like to feed a large dog last thing at night. Big breeds are subject to distension (or bloat), a condition for which there is still no hard and fast explanation. This is where, in layman's language, the stomach "swings over" like a hammock, so that both ends are blocked.

The History and Management of the Mastiff

Gases then swell inside the stomach and death occurs unless veterinary assistance is called immediately. Unfortunately, this condition is common in all giant breeds and seems to occur most frequently about 1 or two hours after feeding. Therefore, do not exercise after feeding and do not feed late at night because if a dog is fed late at night and put to bed, distension could take place without the owner being there to see the dog, and realise what was happening.

Some Mastiffs are fussy feeders, others the exact opposite. If you have a Mastiff that will not eat, a good tip is to look down their throat for enlarged, red tonsils, as funnily enough Mastiffs seem to suffer from tonsilitis. If they have this, then it hurts to swallow so they do not eat. A simple course of antibiotic cures this condition quickly but sometimes an injection of vitamin B-12 will stimulate the appetite.

One subject which I have not mentioned is inoculations. Mastiffs, or any puppies, which are sold at about eight weeks of age, are normally too young to have had their permanent inoculations. Some vets will give them their "shots" at eight weeks, others not until they are twelve weeks of age. The best advice I can give prospective puppy purchasers here is, ask the breeder what, if any, injections they have had, and take the puppy straight to your own vet and follow his advice. Inoculations should be given against distemper, hardpad, hepatitis, leptospirosis and of course parvo-virus. Nowadays, most of these are given in a single "jab" followed by a second one two or three weeks later. Parvo-virus is an especially deadly killer and puppies need special protection. Again, we recommend another inoculation against this disease at about six months of age. Discuss the question of annual boosters with your vet and/or the puppy's breeder. Some people think annual boosters are necessary, others do not.

See the next chapter for more information on living with a young Mastiff.

The United States of America   *Patricia B. Hoffman*

Once safely bred, with puppies assured, pregnancy as a rule progresses uneventfully. The bitch should be allowed normal exercise until a few days before the whelping, and she will usually slow down by herself. If her appetite increases greatly, increase her food intake, but it is imperative that you do not allow her to become fat. Some breeders give supplements during pregnancy, but this is really not necessary.

As the date of the puppies' arrival nears, have the whelping box ready, and notify your vet of the event. Chances are that your bitch will ignore the place prepared for her to give birth, and may wander off and whelp in the most inconvenient spot she can find—under a porch outdoors, or in a closet indoors.

First signs of whelping are restlessness, panting, and licking at the rear end. Much has been made of a drop in the bitch's temperature, but this is a highly unreliable indicator. Lead the future mother to the box, and stay with her. Tell your veterinarian that the birth is under way. Do not try to help unless the bitch is in obvious distress. Watch carefully—if straining continues for any length of time, or there is a very long interval (over an hour is a good rule of thumb) get help at once.

If matters proceed normally, check to be sure the dam licks the puppy, removing the sac in which it has arrived (she will eat the sac and placenta, a perfectly normal procedure). If she doesn't clean the puppy, take a clean, rough towel and wipe it off. For a pup that isn't breathing, wrap it in a warm towel, hold it head down and shake it gently to remove fluid from the lungs. This normally will make it gasp, and start respiring. In severe cases, try mouth-to-mouth emergency measures!

As each puppy arrives, weigh it and check for severe defects (cleft palate, etc.). If normal, return it gently to the mother, being sure it nurses immediately. Chances are that the bitch is too busy with the next arrival to pay much attention to you, if you move quietly and slowly.

When you think the whelping is over, take the dam for a walk, but on a leash. The reason? She may be harbouring one more whelp, and may try to hide and deliver. I once retrieved a newborn puppy from underneath a bush, where the mother had bolted. Returned to the nest, the little one did very well.

Mastiffs all too frequently suffer from uterine inertia, which means that the puppies are slow to arrive, as the dam does not have strong contractions to force the puppy out. At such a time it is vital to use a stimulant, such as oxytocin, which should be given by your vet. If the worst comes to worst, a Caesarean section may be called for.

There is no way to predict the size of the litter. A bitch might present you with seven or eight puppies—or only one. A litter of sixteen has been recorded, but that was a phenomenon. Six would seem to be average.

Watch for feeble puppies—the ones that lie limply and don't seem to nurse, or else whimper plaintively. A good way to test is to take a fold of skin at the nape of the neck and pinch it gently (the puppy won't feel this). If the skin doesn't return to its natural folds, or feels dry, you have trouble. Supplemental feeding may be essential, or, with a big litter, rotating the nursing. If you are lucky, you may find a foster mother. I know of a Beagle that raised some Mastiffs with her own puppies and made no distinction between the different nurslings.

If you do have to take over the care of the puppies, there are substitutes for bitch's milk available. Some breeders use bottles for feeding, others tube-feed. This last is a rather tricky process, and your vet can show you how to do it.

Until the litter is weaned, the mother keeps the pups clean, licking them to make them defecate, and eating the droppings. Frequent changes of the whelping box lining are necessary, as the puppies wet and the dam often has a considerable discharge for a few days after the birth. Newspapers are preferable to fabric as they may be changed frequently.

If you can find a source, shredded computer paper makes excellent bedding for puppies, as it does not pack down nor can the puppies smother. In addition, it doesn't become sodden and smelly like newspaper.

Most Mastiff mothers are quite agreeable and will allow you to handle the puppies, but will resent a lot of interference. You must, of course, keep the box warm for the first week, and a heat lamp such as used for baby pigs is useful. Be sure to have a thermometer to keep a check on the temperature, about 80° to 85°F. is ideal.

Keep a strict watch for the first twelve days or so, or until the puppies' eyes open. Mastiff dams can be very clumsy and have been known to squash a puppy without realizing it. The best type of whelping box has an inner ledge, or shelf, under which the little ones can crawl for safety.

Having got the litter through the first admittedly exhausting days, it is fun to watch them open their eyes, start to stagger around the box, give puppy yelps and begin play. The pups should be weighed daily and charts kept on their progress.

Weaning will depend somewhat on the bitch. At about four weeks, you may put a little solid food, such as puppy food well soaked in water, in a flat dish, and let the little creatures try it. As the milk supply lessens, add more of one of the proprietary puppy foods until the whelps no longer nurse. Weaning is really a very simple process. Toward the end of the period, your bitch will want to leave the puppies and will stop cleaning them.

Once on solid food, four feeds a day will be necessary. At five to six weeks, "puppy shots" should be given, and probably worming will be necessary. It has been established that virtually all bitches carry worm cysts (both round and hook), and these are transmitted to the puppies both through the placenta and the milk.

As to feeding, each breeder has his own method. Some rely completely on commercial products, others go to great pains to prepare their own food. My own feeling is that, once the pups are on solid diet, kibble of some kind (that formulated for puppies for the first year) that contains no soybean meal, plus meat, is the best way to feed. Supplements should be avoided, especially calcium. Many novices believe that since Mastiffs grow so rapidly and are so heavy-boned, that calcium and minerals should be added to the diet. This is wrong! Calcium causes severe problems, and its use may have the opposite effect to which it is intended, and cause fragile, weak bones.

Most important throughout the Mastiff's life is keeping the him fit and not over weight. Fat is not beautiful. Too many owners equate extra pounds with massiveness! A chubby puppy may be appealing, but that extra weight puts extra stress on growing bones and muscles.

As the puppy grows, you will need to adjust the amount of food and the number of feedings a day. Do not give any extra vitamins or supplements unless prescribed by your veterinarian. A puppy should always have exercise, but beware of rough play and over exertion. These may cause lameness or potential structural problems (common to all large breeds).

House training is a major concern with many owners. Luckily, Mastiffs are easy to house train, being essentially clean dogs. Of course, the first few weeks after weaning can be difficult. Bear in mind that the young dog does not have complete control of bladder and bowels for some weeks.

You should set up a schedule and follow it closely. Feed, take puppy out, and praise it when it performs. It will need to go out when it wakes from a nap, after playing and when it seems restless. If you don't get out in time, do not, repeat, <u>do</u> <u>not</u> punish it.

You will want to get puppy accustomed to a collar. Use a lightweight rolled leather type and let the dog become used to it. Then try using a leash—even a very young Mastiff can be taught to walk on lead. Don't force the issue. Do it gradually and the puppy will enjoy it. If you can find a "puppy kindergarten," or early training class, by all means take your pet. It will provide excellent training, as well as the all-important socialization.

It cannot be too strongly emphasized that a young Mastiff must be socialized! This means taking it with you to all kinds of situations: meeting other people and dogs; seeing cars, trucks and traffic; walking in crowded areas and similar places. For some reason Mastiffs need contact with various people and situations at an early age, or timidity may be a problem in an older dog.

Chapter 14

Advice on Buying and Rearing a Puppy

The United Kingdom   *Elizabeth J. Baxter*

Because Mastiffs are comparatively rare, it is unlikely that the purchase of a puppy will be an impulsive buy. It is more likely that a person wanting a Mastiff will have to put his name down with a breeder and wait, for anything up to a year. This is because it seems that the number of Mastiff puppies born during any twelve-month period varies enormously. I have known some years when no puppies were born at all, others when several litters have been bred.

Advice to those contemplating the purchase of a dog such as a Mastiff is to try and see as many of the breed as possible, before buying. Go to dog shows and see the animals; talk to the breeders; decide which dogs you like and which breeders you find most helpful; get a copy of the breed Standard from the Kennel Club and read it and try to understand it in relation to the Mastiffs that you see at shows. If any of the breeders have puppies, go and see them; if not, put down your name and wait patiently.

I think it very important that when the time comes for you to go and see a litter of puppies with a view to choosing one for yourself that at least the mother, and if possible both parents, are seen and touched. Make sure that you like both their looks and their characters; also make sure that the puppy you choose is sound mentally and physically and a good specimen of its breed. Speaking from personal experience, I find that the difference in price between a pet and a show puppy is not very great unless there is something that actually debars the dog from the show ring, such as a really long coat.

I have mentioned in the chapter on the breed Standard how so many Mastiffs appear to be nervous; nine times out of ten this is due to environment, but of course heredity does play a part. As there is nothing more miserable to own than a really nervous big dog, do be careful that the puppy you choose is bright and friendly, and that the parents are not animals that cringe away in fear—remembering at the same time that many Mastiffs are quite stand-offish, and not hail-fellow-well-met with one and all.

When you have decided on your puppy, you will probably be asked to collect it at eight weeks of age. Be sure to get from the breeder a diet sheet, a pedigree (the official registration papers from the Kennel Club may well take a month or two to materialise) and a list of what inoculations and wormings it has had. My own thoughts on these last two subjects are set out at some length in the previous chapter on Weaning and Rearing so need not be gone into again here.

When you have your puppy and once its inoculations are completed, a good plan is to go to the village square to sit and meet the public. Go to the railway station and sit on the platform and watch the trains; to the local pub; anywhere where your pup can see people and traffic and hear noises. It is an excellent idea to take it to the local Obedience or Ring Training class—not necessarily to take part but just to sit and watch, to be admired and petted.

Having said that, it must also be stressed that a young Mastiff puppy MU.S.T NOT be taken out for "walks" as such, as the animal is heavy and the bone very soft. Real walks should not start until the bone has finished forming, i.e., until the "puppy knees" those knobs of bore on the front legs, from which he does the growing, have disappeared. After about ten months he can start going on longer walks until by the time he is two years, he can follow behind a horse all day if that is your desire! (Work up to anything like that gradually, of course.) Most Mastiffs love the car and are good travelers so get the puppy used to a car early in life.

To house train, put out first thing in the morning, last thing at night and after every sleep and every meal. If necessary stay outside with the puppy until it has "performed" and then give plenty of praise. Mastiffs are normally very clean and learn quickly.

It is important that clean fresh water is *always* available, especially if the diet consists, even in part, of complete expanded food. The question of giving bones to Mastiffs is a difficult one. It used to be stressed that bones should never be given, but nowadays what is called a raw, natural diet is much more popular, and indeed a well known Australian Veterinarian, Dr. Ian Billinghurst, insists that it is perfectly acceptable, indeed beneficial. I now do give my dogs bones, lamb, veal and small beef ones, which they love, but of course you must never ever give cooked bones as they splinter. Again, if you are unsure, consult your vet. I would say here, however, and this is something that contradicts what I wrote in the first edition of this book, that I have found that the big rawhide chews can also be quite dangerous, as the strong jaws of a Mastiff can unravel them, and then they try to swallow them whole which can cause choking. So, it is a personal decision, but whichever type you give, just keep an eye on your dog.

My views on the necessity of vitamins and supplements are at odds with those of my co-author, as I believe these are necessary whereas she does not. I feel that a general all-around supplement can do nothing but good, but would suggest that you talk to your veterinary surgeon about this and take his advice on the matter. Remember that this is a breed which very often grows upwards before filling out and a young Mastiff can, at a year or two years, look like a lanky Great Dane. They often do not start to fill out until well over two, and sometimes not until they are over three. I feel it is better that they do the growing upwards first, as this means that the puppy will be both tall and massive by the time it finishes growing—and a Mastiff does not stop growing as early as other breeds.

I would advise the buyer of any puppy to insure him or her; even if you do not insure the animal itself, take out a third party liability policy. This costs very little and if he should accidentally knock down a neighbour's child, or cannon into an elderly person, it is comforting to know that all claims for compensation are covered.

Mastiffs are wonderful family dogs; I have said elsewhere and cannot emphasise too strongly, that they are not kennel dogs. They crave human companionship. They are superb guards and seem to know by instinct when it necessary for them to assume this role. They are wonderful with children whom they will protect and cherish; they are not natural hunters or "chasers" and provided they are introduced to stock and taught that these animals are not to be touched, they can be trusted with other livestock whether it be ducks or horses. Other dogs are normally ignored, though some Mastiff bitches do have, it must be confessed, a weakness for small dogs such as Yorkies or Chihuahuas! But once they have had the error of their ways pointed out to them, and properly scolded, they will ignore even these small yapping creatures. They are not fighters, indeed an adult Mastiff is so self-assured that it has no need to fight and no desire to do so. If provoked beyond endurance by either canine or human, the Mastiff's reaction is merely to knock down—and probably sit on the provoker.

Mastiffs were originally bred as guards of the manor house and grounds and outlying property. They are therefore not wanderers but tend to take their duties as guardians very seriously. They will stay around the house, friendly but watchful. Because of their enormous size they are not always very quick or agile, though they can move with surprising speed when the need arises. A Mastiff, well reared and loved, will prove to be a friend and companion who can be utterly trusted with anything or anybody. An unwelcome intruder, having entered unchallenged, will find that it is impossible to leave. The Mastiff trait is to allow in, but not to allow out. And if a Mastiff is determined that you are not going past him or her, then you are not going to do so. If you persist, then an arm will be taken firmly in the animal's mouth and it is then impossible to move, although afterwards there will probably be not a mark to be seen on the skin. The size and strength of the animal is so great that it is only rarely that it has to be demonstrated and I can tell you from experience that when a Mastiff is really roused, there is no more frightening sight.

It therefore follows, that with a dog that may well end up over 200 lbs. in weight, it will be impossible to force him to be obedient when fully grown. Try pushing or pulling an unwilling Mastiff and it is like trying to shift a tank. They have an infuriating habit of going completely limp and helpless when pushed and when a Mastiff rolls on its back, shuts its eyes and pretends to be deaf there is nothing much a mere human can do. The secret is to brainwash the puppy while it is still young enough to be made (gently, of course) to do what it is told to do. A Mastiff must have firm but kind training while young to reach its full potential. Patience, kindness, but determination on the owners' part is essential, although it must also be said that most Mastiffs want to please and love praise and attention. A saying that I used to declaim when taking training classes, and which I think equally relevant to the training of any dog is: "If it knows what you want and is physically capable of doing it without hurt or harm to itself, then, if told to do something it must do what it is told." A corollary to this, of course, is that if the owner does not feel physically capable of following the command through, then it is wiser not to give it in the first place, as a command that is not obeyed is a victory to the dog. A Mastiff is basically gentle and is not likely, fortunately, to try and challenge his owner and to take over as "pack leader"; as some of the other guard dog breeds might. Even so, it is wiser for the owner to remain in charge and not get into a situation where the animal ignores a command that cannot be enforced.

There is one other aspect of buying a Mastiff which I think should be made known, although probably many people will not agree with me, and that is the question of hip dysplasia. In layman's terms, a dysplastic dog is one where the ball of the hip joint does not fit snugly into the socket. According to the degree of dysplasticity (or "bad fit") you will, or may, get pain and lameness in later life because arthritic changes take place in the hip. This is a condition that affects many giant breeds and it is a serious one. Hip dysplasia is almost certainly hereditary, although it is also thought that upbringing has some part to play, and big puppies who put on enormous amounts of bone and are therefore very heavy on their legs too soon, tend to be more at risk.

The only way to eradicate hip dysplasia is not to breed from affected animals, and breeds such as German Shepherds, etc., have strict screening of breeding stock and do not breed from affected animals. People buying a Mastiff puppy are all too often told nothing about this condition and when their puppy is shown in later life to be suffering from a certain degree of dysplacity they blame the breeder. The breeder is indeed to blame inasmuch as he or she made no mention of the condition to the puppy buyer. A dog can be dysplastic and still lead a perfectly normal and happy life, in fact, many dogs that are dysplastic show no signs whatsoever, and the condition can only be diagnosed by X-ray. Animals in other breeds, or rather breeding stock in other breeds, are X-rayed as a matter of routine, but Mastiffs in the U.K. are hardly ever X-rayed in this way—perhaps because so many of them do not take kindly to anaesthetic.

What I am trying to tell my readers is this; if you want a breed where you can guarantee that your puppy is not going to suffer from hip dysplasia, or throw puppies that might suffer from it, do not buy a Mastiff, because it is impossible to give such a guarantee. As I have shown, after the war only seven dogs were responsible for the revival of the breed; hip dysplasia obviously was present in one or several of these and is therefore endemic in the breed as a result of the extreme inbreeding which took place. This happened approximately 55 years ago now, but hip dysplasia once in a breed, remains, and there is nothing that can be done about it except breed from animals that are sound. This indeed nearly all Mastiff breeders do, but this condition can skip several generations and reappear. Just because you breed two "clear" animals does not mean that the puppies will be unaffected, although it is more likely. It is most important that lame animals are not used for breeding, but two animals showing no sign of lameness can produce a puppy or puppies that eventually will do so. X-raying cannot take place until the animal is over a year old so it is impossible to X-ray a puppy before purchase.

The incidence of hip dysplasia is less now than it was 15 years ago—the breeding only of animals that move soundly is paying off—but there is always a good chance that any Mastiff in the country is capable of producing dysplastic puppies, even if it is completely sound itself. There is, I think, no absolute answer to this problem because the only solution would be to find a line that was completely "clear" and to breed only to this line, but this is impossible because it must be realised that, with Mastiffs, there is no fresh blood, anywhere, in the whole world. America has the same problem because the blood is the same there as here.

When buying your puppy, therefore, bear all this in mind. Make sure that both parents are good, sound movers as well as being good breed types. Ask if they have been X-rayed, but always keep the realisation that there is not a Mastiff in the world today who is not capable of producing a dysplastic puppy. The chances are that you will be lucky and your puppy will not know the meaning of the words hip dysplasia, but if you should not be so lucky, please do not merely blame the breeder; they will probably be even more upset than you, especially if both the parents give every appearance of being completely sound.

Some people have said quite strongly that I should not mention the incidence of hip dysplasia in the breed, but I think it only right that a prospective buyer is acquainted with all the facts. To pretend that no Mastiff is adversely affected by hip dysplasia would be quite wrong, and people who have purchased a Mastiff without being warned of the possibility of them having this condition, have every right to feel extremely badly treated.

Do not worry unduly however. Buy a strong and healthy puppy from strong and healthy parents and all should be well and even if it turns out that your puppy is dysplastic, most animals live with the condition with no ill effects until well on into later life, when arthritis can cause pain and means that medication has to be taken for this.

Another condition which needs intensive study and against which we should be on our guard is "Wobblers" or Hereditary Cervical Spondyolpahty. I have gone into this in Chapter 8. It is the word "Hereditary" that should cause concern. Work is being done and hopefully knowledge will become more widespread.

One other point to watch is a Mastiff's propensity to injure its legs, especially if playing roughly with other puppies. They are so heavy and so big, that a sudden twist or turn can result in a wrenched ligament or sprained leg; a puppy going out to play in the garden can come back in on three legs and a nasty wrench or sprain can take weeks to mend. So be warned, and keep a watch for too boisterous play.

I do not think there is much more advice that can be given with regard to the actual purchase of a Mastiff puppy. Most of what I have said with regard to choosing a bold, happy, sound, typey puppy from parents with similar attributes, is self obvious.

So all that remains to be said is that I hope you find the puppy you want and spend many happy years together. The only sad thing, and it is a very sad aspect of dog ownership, is the fact that a Mastiff, in common with all giant breeds, has a short life span, ten years being about the average.

The United States of America *Patricia B. Hoffman*

First and foremost: buy your Mastiff puppy from a reliable breeder! This is a point that cannot be too strongly emphasised: there are dealers, "middle-men" and pet-shops. Avoid them! And how do you tell a reliable breeder? Look at the puppy's parents, check the surroundings, and if the kennel is dirty (aside from the usual puppy chaos) and the sire and dam ill kept or untypical, leave.

When you have found a breeder whose stock you like, look at the puppies with as much detachment as possible. This is difficult, as all Mastiff puppies are delightful, awkward little bundles. There are some points to be noted immediately: does the puppy come to you, or does it back off and mope in a corner? There is, unfortunately, a strain of shyness in the breed, which should be avoided. Is the puppy sturdy and heavy-boned, without excess fat? A chubby one may be attractive, but too much weight can cause structural problems as the animal matures. Check markings: nice black mask and ears? Check the bite. The Standard allows moderate underbite (for the novice, this means that the lower teeth protrude beyond the upper). The scissors bite is preferred, but not too often found. Puppies are terribly awkward and trip and fall over their own big feet, but try to see if it moves nicely, without lameness or looseness.

The owner will help you. You will have decided whether you want a male or a female; if you are interested in future showing; or to have the dog as a pet. "Pet quality" does not imply a poor animal. The puppy may have some minor defect or lack of type that might make it unsuitable for the show ring. And frequently such a young one may turn out to be surprisingly good. It is almost impossible to tell which puppy is best in the litter. If a breeder tells you that all are "show quality", beware. There is absolutely no guarantee that all are "championship" prospects, or that the puppy that looks best at a few weeks of age won't grow up to be less than excellent.

Once you have spent some time studying the litter and observing behavior, one puppy should appeal to you, and you've made your choice. The breeder will give you detailed instructions on care and feeding, as well as a complete record of immunizations and worming. You will also receive a four-generation pedigree, and a registration form to be sent on to the AKC.

At this point, a quotation from the noted American breeder, Marie Moore, should be read carefully:

MARIE MOORE ON SELECTING A PUPPY

When I was raising Mastiffs, I liked to keep them until they were three or four months of age. It was my experience that the temperament factor became evident at that age and if they were going to be shy, they would begin to withdraw from personal contacts at that time. Of course, a very shy puppy would display this unsoundness at a much earlier age.

In purchasing a puppy, I like to see the sire and dam. I would try to select one that was very "outgoing" in temperament. Full of mischief, very active and playful. I would try to select a puppy with good bone, a heavy square body, a level (if possible) bite, because he would be inclined to become undershot as he matures. A good, clear coat color and a very dark mask and ears.

Actually, in my opinion, I don't think anyone can really tell at this age if the puppy will develop a "decent top-line, a good rear and a pleasing head". It was my experience that Mastiffs do not breed "true". By that I mean you can never really tell what the end result will be from a certain mating. Only the breed, be it soundness, size, head or temperament, can a definite line be established that can be counted on to carry from generation to generation. This takes years to do. *Midwest Mastiff Fancier's News*, March 1972

There are many excellent books on puppy training to help in rearing your Mastiff. Raising it will have its maddening and frustrating moments, but basically it's fun. All the wear and tear of time-consuming cleaning up and naughty puppy behavior will be forgotten and forgiven as your well-trained Mastiff lies at your feet (or on them) and looks up at you with those melting brown eyes.

A Mastiff is slow to mature, and normally is not fully-grown before two years of age. After the charming puppy stage comes the gawky age. At this point, paws and ears are too big for the rest of the body, joints look enormous, and probably the rear end will be higher than the front, or vice versa. Do not despair—the "teenage" period is relatively short.

There will be temperament changes, too. At about four months almost all dogs go through a state of withdrawal and a certain amount of timidity. Don't force issues then, but don't "baby" your adolescent. Keep calm and it will pass. Also, at some point, your dog may challenge you, and then you must show it that you are its superior. A firm hand is needed—which does not mean striking or punishing the puppy! If you must discipline, a severe "no" and possibly shaking the dog will be enough. To repeat, never hit your dog in any circumstances!

Socializing must continue. This is an ongoing process, and will result in a Mastiff that you can take anywhere, and one that will be agreeable with other dogs, pets, and people. Surprisingly, this will not affect its inherent instinct to protect and guard its owner and home.

The Mastiff is an easy dog to care for. Its short, smooth coat requires no grooming other than regular brushing. Yes, shedding will occur, about twice a year. Ears should be checked and wiped out with a soft tissue, as some dogs have considerable waxy discharge. Nails must be regularly trimmed, and will be more easily done if you start the job with the puppy. Dark nails are a bit tricky, but if you do happen to cut back too much, don't be alarmed, as bleeding can be stopped with a styptic pencil. Buy the very best nail clippers available, and keep them sharp.

The general opinion is that adult Mastiffs should be fed twice a day, morning and evening. Use only top quality food, never cheap or "generic."

Of course you will have the normal immunizations: rabies, leptospirosis and so on, as well as periodic checks for parasites (worms, fleas and so on). Heartworm is now a nationwide problem, so your dog should be tested annually, and put on preventative medicine during the mosquito season, as that insect is the carrier of the disease.

Another problem that is becoming widespread is that of Lyme disease. This is tick borne, and affects both canines and humans. There is now a vaccine for it, and also a special collar to repel ticks. This last does not kill fleas, and the usual flea collar may cause skin irritation with some dogs. Preventative methods against common canine ailments are constantly being improved, so check with your veterinarian for the latest advances.

Since this is not a treatise on veterinary medicine, we will mention only two major problems that affect the breed. These are hip dysplasia and bloat.

Hip dysplasia is a major concern in the breed. It is a condition where the hips are actually malformed. Normally, the end of the femur (thigh bone) fits snugly into the acetabulum of the pelvis. The acetabulum is a cup-like hollow, and when the femur is not firmly seated, joint looseness occurs.

A dog can very well be dysplastic and show no symptoms, such as lameness or difficulty in moving. There are various degrees of severity. The only way to determine the problem is by X-ray. The Orthopedic Foundation of America (OFA) is the preferred body to evaluate the dog. A permanent listing in its registry will not be given until the Mastiff is two years old. However, a preliminary rating can be given earlier.

A dysplastic Mastiff should never be used in a breeding program! Hip dysplasia is considered to be largely hereditary, so all breeding stock should be screened. More and more breeders are having their dogs evaluated.

The OFA also maintains a registry for elbow dysplasia, a degenerative disease of the elbow joint, again largely inherited.

It should be noted that even if a dog is diagnosed as dysplastic, there are methods to alleviate severe cases. Many dogs show no symptoms, and can lead a normal life.

The most dangerous and dramatic ailment that occurs in Mastiffs is bloat. This is also known as gastric dilatation volvulus (GDV), gastric rotation, or gastric distention. Its cause is as yet unknown. To simplify: a large amount of gas accumulates in the stomach, making it swell, and causing extreme pain and shock. The stomach actually turns, pressing on the large veins of the abdomen, cutting off blood flow to the heart. Unless treatment is immediate, the dog will die.

Symptoms are unmistakable. The dog becomes restless, paces and is uneasy. Its head is turned, looking back at the swollen abdomen. Breathing is rapid and the dog may try to vomit, but brings up nothing. It may collapse.

If your Mastiff shows any of these signs, do not wait. Go immediately to your veterinarian. Even with rapid intervention, many dogs die. Treatments vary, and improvements are constantly being made, but bloat is still a major concern in the breed.

Some guidelines have been set to help prevent the onset of bloat. Feeding two or three small meals a day and keeping the dog quiet before and after feeding for an hour or two may help. Also, moistening food and preventing the dog from drinking large amounts of water with meals may possibly be a preventative. Once a dog has bloated the problem may recur.

As the dog ages, the owner must be alert for any symptoms of discomfort, lameness or loss of hearing and impaired eyesight. Food may have to be adjusted—there are special diets for old and ailing dogs. Your veterinarian can prescribe them. Some dogs develop fatty skin cysts, which are normally not serious, but odd growths and tumors should be attended to promptly.

One of the saddest things about owning a Mastiff is that the breed is relatively short lived. To see a healthy specimen of the breed more than nine or ten years old is rare. One always hopes the dog will live a long and healthy life, but there may be a time when an owner will have to make the heart-wrenching decision to euthanize the Mastiff. This is an extremely difficult and sensitive situation, but there are times when the dog is ill and in great pain and it is a kindness to end its suffering. The grief caused by a pet's death is severe, and there are now groups and organizations to help owners deal with this blow—one that is not readily grasped by people who are not animal lovers. So seek help. It's there.

Chapter 15

Mastiff Activities

The United Kingdom   *Elizabeth J. Baxter*

The English Obedience and Working Trials are very different from those in the United States and Canada. For the CD, UD and TD titles, the dog must go over a six-foot high jump, as well as a nine-foot broad jump. These two strict requirements effectively rule out all large massive breeds from competing in the U.K. In addition, draft work and carting are illegal. Mastiffs do, however, engage in therapy work.

The United States of America   *Patricia B. Hoffman*

The Mastiff used to be considered a large, lazy, not too intelligent dog. A Companion Dog title was thought to be a very unusual achievement and few owners bothered to work with their pets. The very first CD was awarded to the breed in 1944. Not until 1958 did Carol and David Cole's Caesar of Seattle become the second title holder.

But matters have changed. One of the more interesting developments of the last few years has been the rapid increase in various activities in which Mastiffs and their owners have been engaged.

First, of course, are the standard AKC Companion Dog, Companion Dog Excellent, and the advanced Utility Dog. Through 1998 four Mastiffs have won UD titles and 36 are CDX. And many more are CD certified.

The sport of tracking, another AKC recognized activity, has been tackled by a few owners. Here, again, the breed is not known for scenting ability, but four Mastiffs have gained the TD title. To win it, the dog must follow a standard course by scent.

Agile is not an adjective usually applied to Mastiffs. However, a number of dogs and owners are now engaged in the sport of Agility. This is basically an obstacle course for the dog—it must go through a tunnel, climb an A frame, walk on a see-saw and a number of other challenges.

The owner races with the dog, but can give only verbal commands. Speed, as well as accuracy is essential. Any animal competing must be absolutely sound, and the owner must be in good shape too!

Mastiffs seem to be particularly suited to therapy. Owners take their dogs to nursing homes, hospitals and hospices. The candidate for this job must be obedience trained, very stable in temperament and have appropriate health clearance. It must be familiar with wheel chairs, crutches, odd noises and sudden movements. There are a number of organizations that test and certify dogs, the best known are Pet Partners Program from the Delta Society, *www.deltasociety.org*, and Therapy Dogs International, *www.tdi-dog.com*. Many owners do therapy visits as a personal and very rewarding project.

Mastiffs also are taken to school groups, libraries, pet parades and other events to demonstrate the dogs' excellent temperament and abilities. The AKC has instituted the "Canine Good Citizen" award. This is won by being officially tested in various situations: behavior with strangers; sitting without the owner's presence; other simple but effective exercises. CGC means that the dog will behave properly in public.

Temperament testing is popular, too. Here again the dog's responses to various situations are evaluated by a certified examiner, and is granted a TT (temperament tested) certificate, *www.atts.org*

Mastiffs have even been used in search and rescue. One owner trained several for this work, a process that takes a year. The dog must learn to ride in various vehicles, including planes and boats. It's reported that a Mastiff can actually detect scent coming up through water, as well as that of a person buried in earth or snow.

In response to the enormous increase in owners who enjoy working with their Mastiffs, the parent club has set up a Working Dog program. After much planning and consideration, the first awards were made at the 1995 annual banquet and meeting. 20 Mastiffs were presented with the title, and one was awarded Working Dog Excellent.

To earn a WD, the Mastiff must win 100 points in four categories. Obedience, Temperament, Tracking and Specialty. This last includes conformation title, therapy, Canine Ambassador (visits to schools, parades, pet fairs and so on). The complete list of AKC Titles is listed in Appendix IV.

Mastiff Club of America Working Dog and Working Dog Excellent (WD, WDX) Certificate

This program was developed to encourage members to show the world that the Mastiff is still truly a working breed. The idea behind the title is to demonstrate the attributes of the breed which make it a truly noble working beast. Trainability, tractability and obedience are important characteristics of a working animal, as are good, sound and appropriate temperaments. Most certainly the dog should look like a Mastiff; it should be conformationally correct. And, within the breed there should be evidence of versatility: tracking, draft/carting, search and rescue, agility, therapy work, and canine ambassadorship are all examples of activities befitting of a noble breed. With these basic tenets in mind, the MCOA Working Dog Committee set out to develop the criteria for establishing the Working Dog and Working Dog Excellent titles. The process of developing and refining the title is dynamic as the Committee continues to search for new and better ways to showcase our breed.

For a dog to qualify for the WD title it must earn a minimum of 100 points, or for a WDX title a minimum of 200 points from at least three out of four categories. At this time, the categories and point schedule is as follows:

CATEGORY 1 - Obedience

Companion Dog (25 points), Companion Dog Excellent (25 points), and Utility Dog (50 points). These may be either AKC, U.K.C, or CKC titles, but only one kennel club's title will count towards the WD. For example, you can't count an AKC CD as 25 points, and a U.K.C or CKC CD title as another 25 points. However, the points for advanced titles are cumulative, i.e. a UD titled dog earns 100 points. A photocopy of your title certificate serves as documentation.

CATEGORY 2 - Temperament

Passing a certified Temperament Test or an AKC Canine Good Citizen Test is worth 25 points. Only 1 of these may be counted towards your WD title. A photocopy of your test certification serves as documentation.

CATEGORY 3 - Tracking

Tracking Dog (50 points) and Tracking Dog Excellent (50 points). As with obedience titles, a TDX dog would earn 100 points, and again, a photocopy of your title certificate serves as documentation. The point value of a TD title was recently raised to 50 from 25, since only three Mastiffs have ever earned tracking titles.

CATEGORY 4 - Specialty

This is the most diverse category, with a number of activities that can earn your dog WD points. An AKC or CKC Championship is worth 25 points. Passing a Drafting/Carting test (now held at the National) is also worth 25 points. Being certified in Search and Rescue is worth 25 points. An agility title (AKC or U.S.DAA) is counted as 25 points. A registered Therapy Dog, with a minimum of 10 witnessed visitations to a nursing home, hospice, hospital, home shut-in, etc. is worth 25 points. And any dog that has served as a Canine Ambassador for ten documented public outreach activities, such as parades, school programs, library demonstrations, pet week programs, breed fairs, etc., is worth 25 points. Documentation for these activities or titles should be supported by photocopies of the appropriate certificate, or by a completed Therapy Dog/Canine Ambassador Visitation Log, which is available from the WD Committee.

15.1 Carting. Ch. Acorn Hills Ethan. Breeder/owner M.L.Owens. USA

15.2 Agility: On the teeter-totter. Owner M.L. Owens. USA

15.3 School visit. Ch. Medallion Bo-no-Regard with kindergarten group. Breeders/owners Medallion Mastiffs. USA

The History and Management of the Mastiff

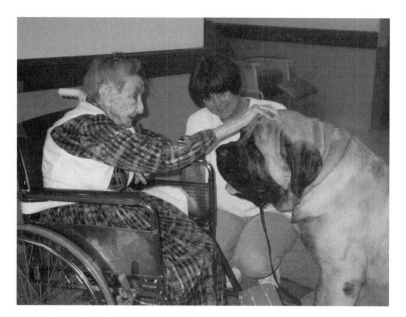

15.4 Nursing home visit. Ch. Acorn Hills Uther Pendragon and owner S. Krauser with centenarian patient. USA

15.5 Agility. Ch. Pendragon's Bailiff Farlough. Owners J. Tyrpak. Photo B. Faulstich. USA

Chapter 16

Cameo Portraits

The United Kingdom

It is difficult, given the number of worthy and noteworthy people in our breed, to single out a few for special attention. Most in fact have been mentioned frequently in the other chapters, notably people such as Mrs. Scheerboom, Miss Bell, Mr. and Mrs. Oliver and many others. I have therefore taken just half a dozen people who not only have been or who are dedicated to the breed and who may also have an interesting anecdote to relate about a Mastiff, or whose general background I think to be a little out of the usual.

Pam Day

First, there is Mrs. Pam Day, President of the Old English Mastiff Club from the death of Mrs. Scheerboom in 1982 until her own death on New Year's Day 1996. All Mastiff people know her through her Hollesley Mastiffs and realise that she had been breeding and showing successfully for many years. What the majority do not realise, because it was extremely difficult to get information out of a modest lady, is, that Mrs. Day had her first Mastiff in 1938. This was Hermit of Tiddicar, bred by Mr. Crook, and Hermit was with Mrs. Day throughout the war years. After this, Mrs. Day went to Canada, as she says "to find him a wife" but poor Hermit had never before been separated from his mistress and pined and died before she returned from Canada having obtained there Honey of Parkhurst. Thereafter Honey was mated to Valiant Diadem but as mentioned in an earlier chapter, their descendants seem to have died out. Mrs. Day then obtained Dawn of Havengore from Mrs. Scheerboom and the rest is history. Mrs. Day was one of the people who attended the "revival" meeting in 1946; she was on the OEMC committee from that time onwards becoming President in 1982 on the death of Mrs. Scheerboom. She said of herself that all she wanted to do was to "keep Mastiffs going" and her love of fawns with black masks was well known.

Flora Taylor

A person, one of the very few, to have been "in" Mastiffs even longer than Mrs. Day was Mrs. Flora Taylor who with her husband commenced breeding the Saxondale Mastiffs in the mid 1920's. Mrs. Taylor had a fund of information and knowledge; she was one of the people who attended the 50 year celebration function of the Old English Mastiff Club in 1933 and could tell fascinating stories about Mastiffs of the immediate post 1914-1918 period. She recalled how, long before that war, her husband saw two Mastiffs in a Wild Animal Show at Wakefield and determined to have one of his own. So in the early 1920's, when they were in a position to have a dog, they contacted a Mr. Moseley and got two bitch puppies. What they did not realise was that this was the renowned (notorious?) Bullmastiff breeder and the puppies were not pure bred Mastiffs. Not having the heart to return them, the pups were kept but later the Taylors acquired their main foundation bitch, Hilda of Hellingly, from the Olivers. Mastiffs were then bred by them up until the mid 1960's. I remember seeing her about 1965 with a big fawn dog called Beric the Briton, a son of Jason of Copenore. In 1984, she judged the breed for the first time at the age of nearly 79. "Florrie" Taylor as she was know was a person whose talent was wasted and who should have been used in this capacity many years ago. Florrie became the second President of the newly formed Mastiff Association, a position she held until her death in June 1990.

Barbara Blackstone

Miss Barbara Blackstone was someone to whom the adjective "lady" was truly applicable. Always polite, always so helpful, this was a person who, though devoted to the breed, had never to the best of my knowledge actually owned a Mastiff. The daughter of a doctor, she and her sister were good friends of Miss Ianthe Bell. In fact Miss Blackstone first met Miss Bell in 1925 and attended Crufts with her in 1926 where she saw that legendary breeder of Mastiffs, W. K. Taunton. Apparently, after the judging, Mr. Taunton came round to the Mastiff benches and all the dogs were brought forward for his assessment. Thereafter Miss Blackstone used to attend most of the shows with Miss Bell and this is how the story that she was Miss Bell's kennel maid came to be circulated! As previously mentioned, it was to her and her sister that Miss Bell left the terrible task of carrying out the instructions in her will that the dogs were to be put down.

Miss Blackstone was Secretary of the Mastiff club from 1964 to 1976 and was one of the Vice Presidents, a position she held until her death on the 28th December 1998 at the age of 98. She never missed a club show, be it Open or Championship, but was always there with her sister manning the Bring and Buy stall with the proceeds going to the Mastiff Rescue Fund.

Mrs. Maisie Lindley

Another person from whom it was difficult to get any personal information was Mrs. Lindley but through her good friend Mrs. Teversham—to whom as we have seen the Copenore prefix has been made over—she did tell me the story of Cleo of Saxondale, a bitch that she owned early in the sixties. Apparently Cleo had a litter of nine pups and occupied two separate kennels; one was for her and her pups and the other, opening off the first, was for her to use when she wanted a rest from her babies. Because of an electrical fault, fire broke out in the puppies kennel and nine times Cleo went between the two kennels through the smoke and flames, each time carrying one of her two-week-old puppies to safety in the second, unaffected, kennel. All were saved and the only injury was a slightly burnt tail on one of the pups. This puppy became Mrs. Teversham's first Mastiff and lived to within three weeks of his twelfth birthday. His weakness was whiskey and he enjoyed a small tot in the evening milk, to which Mrs. Teversham attributes his longevity! Mrs. Lindley gave up breeding and showing on the death of her husband in 1987, but once recalled how the famous Jason of Copenore once "sorted out" a gang of youths who were vandalising the tents at one of the Portsmouth dog shows. Mrs. Lindley was one of the Vice Presidents of the Club. She died in July 1992.

Mrs. Phil Greenwell

Mrs. Phil Greenwell was known best perhaps as the person who showed the renowned Ch. Hollesley Medicine Man. She always owned the Mastiffs with her friend, Mrs. Lloyd Jones and the first dog was a fawn, Ch. Baron of Moonsfield, bred by Mrs. Harrild. His sire was a son of the imported Canadian dog, Heatherbelle Bearhills Rajah, and she bought Baron when he was four months of age. As soon as he was brought to their home, a farm, much to everybody's astonishment he shot straight into the pen with a Jersey bull. The bull was so surprised that he accepted the dog and that is where Baron lived and slept, in the bull pen. He would never go into the house and would allow no stranger near the bull pen. When he was five years old, a new bull was installed

The History and Management of the Mastiff

and Baron was kept out of the pen. However, one day he got in and when the bull went to investigate the intruder, the dog, got him by the nose and thereafter was boss and once again took up residence with the bull.

The next Mastiff was Ch. Weatherhill Thor, a fawn dog I remember well as he always took Best of Breed against my Diamond Lil. Unfortunately he was only used at stud twice but one of his sons was Ch. Baron Spencer of Buckhall, the sire of Ch. Hollesley Macushlas's Sheba who produced that famous litter of champions, Dare Devil, Devil Dancer and Devil's Advocate, with Medicine Man being Devil Dancer's son. Mrs. Greenwell never kept more than three or four Mastiffs at a time because like me she was of the opinion that they are not kennel dogs.

Phil Greenwell has been on the committee of the OEMC since 1969, acting as chairman of Committee for some of that time and became President of the Old English Mastiff Club on the death of Mrs. Pam Day.

Mary Reardon

Lastly, we come to Mrs. Mary Reardon, who with her husband Gerry, owned the famous Buckhall Mastiffs. Major Reardon was one of the few people who had a full "master's" ticket for sailing ships--not yachts, but the tall ships, the clippers, and because of my husband's fascination with the same subject, we got to know them well. We spent quite a few nights at their lovely home talking, drinking, and playing cards and dice. Quite depraved we were--playing for our 5p stakes. It was always a matter of wonder to me how Mary, who went to bed with us at about 3 a.m., could be up at 6 a.m, apparently fresh as a daisy, to see to the boarding kennels. The kennels in which they kept their Mastiffs were superb, I think the best I have ever seen, and they were both dedicated to saving and improving the breed. They got their first Mastiff, "the cornerstone of the Buckhall Kennel" as Mary puts it, in 1954 and she arrived at Paddington Station in a laundry basket with a shinbone almost as large as she was herself. This was Guinevere of Sparry, by Faithful Gilliard of Sparry out of Semper Fidelis of Sparry and bred by Mr. and Mrs. Aberdeen, who lived in Cornwall.

Due to pressure of work on the farm, she was only shown locally. Her first litter was to Wey Acres Lincoln and apparently it was a never to be forgotten occasion to take "Jenny", as she was called, to Miss Bell's. There was always such a warm welcome with trophies and photos of Mastiffs everywhere. Mary says how saddened they were by meetings with passersby that would go thus: "What a beautiful dog, what breed is it?" "A Mastiff." "Oh, I thought they had died out." This kind of attitude made them all the more determined to try and help save the breed.

Mary well remembers the first time she showed at Crufts; only a few exhibitors with Mastiffs, but what a warm and friendly atmosphere. It was not a competition so much as a promotion of the breed to show the world that the Mastiff was by no means extinct. The Reardons set their sights high--physical soundness and good temperament allied to the standard set down by the Mastiff Club. Living a farm life, the aspect of physical soundness was a natural requirement and Jenny and Rufus used to double as sheep dogs and always went round the farm with Mary to check the flocks. In this day and age when everyone is so conscious of hip dysplasia and the necessity not to over exercise, it is probably amazing to consider the life those dogs led. Gates were never opened. Mary would vault over and the dogs jumped. Obedience in sitting and staying at the edge of the flocks came naturally from a Mastiff's desire to please rather than a shepherd's instinct, she thinks!

Silver of Havengore was an "outsider" obtained from Mrs. Scheerboom from whom they learned much Mastiff history. Another "import" was Buckhall Rillamill Cassandra obtained from Mrs. Taylor of Cornwall. In 1967, as already outlined, they obtained Threebees Friar of Copenore and his career is history. The Reardons became concerned about the declining number of brindles and managed to buy one of the Mrs. Creigh's, Hannah of Kisumu. This bitch became the mother of Ch. Buckhall Mr. Micawber of Overnoons.

Some years after the sudden death of her husband, Mary Reardon got another Mastiff, a fawn bitch, Bournewood Bluff Bustle of Buckhall, bred by Mrs. Denton, who obtained her foundation stock originally from the Reardons. I hope Mary Reardon continues with the same aims as before—physical soundness and good temperament being the main considerations; I am sure that she will do so.

United States of America

Eve Olsen-Fisher
Eve Olsen-Fisher and her late husband, Stuart Olsen, registered the name Willowledge in 1955. Prior to that date, the kennel prefix was Castle. Early imports were Ch. Beowulf of Havengore and Twinkle of Havengore, the foundation stock of a famous kennel that produced 66 champions. It ceased to exist in 1989.

One of the many records set by Willowledge was that of Ch. Willowledge Hero, who produced a litter of sixteen puppies, all of which survived, and many went on to become champions.

Mrs. Olsen-Fisher joined the Mastiff Club of America in 1945, and has served as President, as well as the Club's delegate to the AKC. She is now an Honorary Member, and wrote "One of the greatest honors for me is to be asked to judge our Mastiff Club of America Special in the year 2000."

In addition, she is licensed to judge all Working Breeds as well as Best in Show. She has judged in many countries: many times in Great Britain; New Zealand; Australia, Canada, Argentina, Germany—to name but a few.

Willowledge's importance and influence on the breed cannot be underestimated. Were it not for Eve Olsen-Fisher, the Mastiff in this country would not have become the established breed it is today.

Marie A. Moore

Marie Antoinette Moore was one of the most important figures in the breed. Mooreleigh Kennel began in 1952, when she acquired Peach Farm Michael from the Brills. Her kennel was active until the 70's, when she retired from breeding and devoted her time to judging.

In addition to the many champions from her own kennel, Mrs. Moore imported many dogs from England. Probably the most important were Rhinehart of Blackroc, 1963, and Falcon of Blackroc, both champions here and in England.

Mrs. Moore judged at many prestigious shows, including Westminster, Crufts and Richmond in England, as well as the specialty shows of both the American and English clubs.

Her book, *THE MASTIFF*, was published in 1978 and at the time was the only book on the breed. It has been reprinted, but the original edition with its many photos and extensive information on the Mastiff is difficult to find.

In addition to her interest in dogs, Mrs. Moore also maintained a racing stable. Her horses raced in England and Europe as well as this country.

She acquired an enormous collection of material on the breed she so loved. This ranged from bric-a-brac to noted paintings by such famous artists as Van Dyck and Landseer. The collection was donated to the AKC Museum of the Dog in St. Louis Missouri. One of her treasures, an antique merry-go-round figure, "Queenie" is now the Museum's mascot.

Always interested in animal welfare, Mrs. Moore singlehandedly operated a shelter. During the years she handled over 22,000 dogs, plus other animals including a herd of 20 neglected horses. When the Humane Society opened a shelter, hers closed.

Two years before her death, she endowed the Marie A. Moore Chair in Humane Ethics and Animal Welfare at the School of Veterinary Medicine at the University of Pennsylvania.

Patty and John Brill

Martha Fenn Brill, always known as Patty, and her husband John began their Peach Farm Kennel in 1935. Their first Mastiffs were acquired from Hobart Titus: Manthorne Mogul (Buddy x Milfold Lass) and Manthorne Matilda (Roxbury Boy x Goldhawk Elsie). Thus their foundation stock was basically English.

It can be truly said that the Mastiff would never have survived in this country had it not been for Peach Farm. It was the longest continuously operating kennel in this country, and its prefix is found in the pedigrees of many Mastiffs today.

It also played a part in the restoration of the breed in England. Although the Brills did not send any of their dogs, Peach Farm Priscilla was the dam of Wey Acres Lincoln, important in post-war history of the Mastiff.

John Brill died in 1975, and Patty Brill gave a permanent award in his honor. This is presented each year to a member of MCOA who has done the most for the club in the previous year.

Patty Brill died in 1982, marking the end of her historic kennel. Her dogs were a most important part of her life. She was most particular about matching a dog to a new owner, and would always take back a dog. If she could not find a home for one of her puppies, it was assured of a permanent home at Peach Farm.

Both the Brills served as President, and as Vice-President of MCOA, and held other offices during the years they supported the club and the breed. Their knowledge and willingness to help will be remembered by all who knew them.

Canada
Hyacinth Mellish

Hyacinth Mellish came to Canada in 1933. Heatherbelle Kennel was started the following year, with Scottish Terriers. In addition to breeding and showing, some were trained as a troupe of performing dogs. They did a little circus act, with such tricks as dancing, jumping through hoops and so on.

However, Mastiffs soon became Mrs. Mellish's main interest. She bought her first to protect her terriers, after an attempt to steal them. Later she acquired four more Mastiffs from different bloodlines, and began an active breeding program.

Probably her most important contribution to the breed was the export of several of her dogs to England, after World War II, when Mastiffs were almost extinct there. The Old English Mastiff Club had two; both registered to the Club and brought up by members. The pair were OEMC Heatherbelle Sterling Silver and OEMC Heatherbelle Portia of Goring, both sired by King Rufus of Parkhurst out of Canadian Ch. Heatherbelle Lady Hyacinth. Private owners imported several others from Mrs. Mellish. Among these were Heatherbelle Bearhill's Rajah and Heatherbelle Bearbill's Priscilla's Amelia. All these Mastiffs were invaluable contributions to the revival of the breed overseas.

In addition to her kennel, Mrs. Mellish operated the Heatherbelle Dog Training School in the 1950's. She was also an accomplished musician: a concert pianist who accompanied the local symphony and gave music lessons. Mrs. Mellish died in 1997.

Appendices

Appendix 1

Pedigree chart — **Miss Aglionby's Turk, whelped on the 6th of August, 1867. U.K.**

- **Field's KING**
  - Lukey's Rufus
    - Lukey's GOVERNER
      - Garner's LION
        - Garner's ADAM
        - Garner's EVE
      - Lukey's COUNTESS
        - Lukey's BRUCE II
        - Lukey's DUCHESS
    - Horn's JENNY
  - Field's NELL
    - Cautley's QUAKER
      - Thompson's SALADIN
        - Ackroyd's DAN
        - Thompson's VENU.S.
      - Thompson's DUCHESS
        - Sir George Armitage's TIGER
        - Thompson's COUNTESSs
    - Garrett's NELL
      - Lord Darnley's NELL
- **Agolionby's HILDA**
  - Nichol's QUAKER
    - Raymond's PRINCE
      - Cautley's QUAKER
        - Thompson's SALADIN
        - Thompson's DUCHESS
      - Garrett's NELL
        - Lord Darnley's NELL
    - Raymond's DUCHESS
      - George's LEO
  - Nickol's VENUS.
    - Sir Domville's OSCAR
    - DUCHESS
      - Ansell's LION
      - JUNO

Parkgate Duchess, whelped September 15th, 1913. U.K.

Parents	Grandparents	Great-Grandparents	Great-Great-Grandparents
Broderick Defender July 1910	Cleveland Leopold	Caractacus	Coeur de Lion - 1889
			Queen of Mary - 1896
		Princess Morton	Duke of Cleveland
			Lady Martan (Saint Bernard)
	Felicia	Adam	Black Prince
			Lady Curly
		Kitty Marton	Unregistered
			Unregistered
Leone August 1911	Brindled Prince	Murdered Monarch	Black Prince
			Princess - 1905
		Oscott Norah	Melinotte - 1897
			Queen Ernestine
	Lady Widmere	Ch. Ronald Widmere	Ch. Archie Hazelmere
			Lady Winifred
		Buenaventura	Unregistered
			Unregistered

Pedigree chart for Ch. Master Beowulf:

Beowulf 21.5.1912	Survivor 13.1.1909	Adam 3.10.1905	Black Prince 6.9.1901
			Lady Curley
		Oscott Nora 31.8.1905	Melnotte 29.9.1897
			Queen Ernestine 5.7.1898
	Berenice 11.12.1907	Ch. Ronald Widmere	Ch. Archie Hazelmere
			Lady Winifred 15.4.1902
		Buena Ventura Pedigree, Unknown	
Jessica 14.12.1917 Registered "Not for competition"	King of the North 10.9.1911	Survivor	Adam
			Oscott Nora
		Gyrlie Unregistered Unknown	
	Marwoods Pride 30.1.1912	Stapleford Pedro Unregistered Mastiff?	? Salisbury Mastiff
			? Pixton Pride Mastiff 8/06
		Connie Unregistered ? B.M.	TURK B.M.
			Roxie B.M.

Ch. Master Beowulf, whelped 31.3.1920. Bred by Miss E.H. Harbour. U.K.

The History and Management of the Mastiff

Ch. King Baldur	Ch. Young John Bull	Ch. Brompton Duke	Cleveland Leopold
			Felicia
		Galazora	Dick Marton
			Shy Portia
	Ch. Young Mary Bull	Ch. Brompton Duke	Cleveland Leopold
			Felicia
		Galazora	Dick Marton
			Shy Portia
Penkhull Lady Breeder Mr. H. Beasley Registered Cross Breed Bull Mastiff 29.2.1920	Stapleford Agrippa Cross Bred Bull Mastiff	Stapleford Pedro Unregistered ?Mastiff	? Salisbury - Mastiff
			? Pinxton Pride - Mastiff 8/06
		Stapleford Nance Bull Mastiff	Nottingham Bendingo - B.M.
			Stapleford Gyp - B.M.
	Helen Bull Mastiff	Ausworth Lion Bull Mastiff	Major II - B.M.
			Ilkeston Lady - B.M.
		Connie Unregistered	Turk - B.M.
			Roxie - B.M.

Shirebrook Lady, whelped 26.7.1921. Registered as Mastiff August 1922 and re-registered as Correction, Cross Breed-Bull Mastiff in Spetember 1922. Mother of Crescent Rowena, the Havengrove foundation bitch, and litter sister to Clayton Betty who is behind the 1920 exports to Canada, i.e., Thor. U.K.

		Cleveland Leopold 1904	Caratacus
			Princess Marton - 1.4.1897
	Brompton Duke 20.7.1910 Mastiff	Felicia 1907	Adam
			Kitty Marton - Unregistered
Poor Joe (Who also sired Bull Mastiff Sir Roger and Mastiff Poor Jerry)		Dick Marton	Nuneaton Lion
			Kitty Marton
	Galazora 10.5.1911 Mastiff	Shy Portia	Adam
			Peggy Marton - 1903
	Collyhurst Squire Born 1914 Registered 1921. Rich Apricot - Mastiff	Stapleford Pedro Unregistered ?Mastiff	? Salisbury - Mastiff
			? Pinxton Pride - Mastiff 8/06
Squire's Daughter of Wescroft		Minerva 21.5.1912 - Mastiff	Survivor
			Berenice - 11.12.1907
	Nell or Ryhll Unregistered, Unknown		

Ch. Woden, whelped 12.1.1924. Bred and owned by Miss Ianthe Bell of Withybush Mastiff. U.K.

Ch. Bill of Havegore pedigree

Ch. Bill of Havegore	Gen 2	Gen 3	Gen 4	Gen 5
Ch. Master Beowulf	Beowulf 21.5.1912	Survivor	Adam	Black Prince
				Lady Curly
			Oscott Nora	Melinotte
				Queen Ernestine
		Berenice	Ch. Ronald Widmere	Ch. Archie Hazlemere
				Lady Winifred
			Buena Ventura Pedigree Uknown	
	Jessica 14.12.1907 Registered as 'Not for Competition'	King of the North	Survivor	Adam
				Oscott Nora
			Girlie (Unregistered)	
		Marwood Pride 30.1.1912	Stapleford Pedro Unregistered ? Mastiff	? Salisbury - Mastiff
				? Pinxton Pride - Mastiff
			Connie Unregistered Believed to be B.M.	Turk - B.M.
				Roxie - B.M.
Crescent Rowena	Duke of Asshenhurst	Adamite	Count Willington	Duke of Heatherville
				Lusitania
			Adams Last	Adam
				Lady Godiva
		Tilly Dunn	Thunderbold 19.10.1911	Cleveland Leopold
				Goatham Daisy
			Jessie Marton	Clemison's Alfric
				Whinfield Rosie
	Shirebrook Lady 26.6.1921 Cross Breed Bull Mastiff	Ch. King Baldur	Ch. Young John Bull	Ch. Brompton Duke
				Galazora
			Ch. Young Mary Bull	Ch. Brompton Duke
				Galazora
		Penkhull Lady 26.6.1921 Cross Breed Bull Mastiff	Stapleford Agrippa Cross Breed Bull Mastiff	Stapleford Pedro - Unr. Mas.
				Stapleford Nance - B.M.
			Helen Bull Mastiff	Answorth Lion - B.M.
				Connie Unr. ? B.M.

Ch. Bill of Havegore, foundation dog of Havegore Kennels. Whelped 10.5.1925. Bred by Mrs. L. Scheerboom. U.K.

		Ina Pauls Ben of Lovecreek
	Lord Marcus of Kenacres	
		Sabrina of Windsor
Ch. The Devil from Wayside		
		Bowats Roar'n Rumble of Corgen
	Wayside Delilah	
		Willowledge Long Run Magda
		Ch. Weatherhill Thor
	Baron Spencer of Buckhall	
		Buckhall Rillamill Cassandra
Ch. Hollesleys Macushula's Sheba		
		Jason of Copenore
	Ch. Macushla of Hollesley	
		Ch. Dawn of Havengore

Ch. Dare Devil of Hollesley (owner Mrs. E. Degerdon), Ch. Devil Dancer of Hollesley (owner Mrs. P. Day), Ch. Devil's Advocate of Hollesley(owner/breeder) b. 20.4.1975. Breeder Mesdames Lloyd Jones and P. Greenwell. U.K.

Roxbury Boy	Ch. Ajax of Hellingly	Ch. Arolite or Ch. Joseph of Hellingly
		Lumbering Sheila of Hellingly
	Sweet Memory	Grimshaw's Pride
		Pinfold Beauty
Goldhawk Elsie	Sioux Chief	Ch. Cleveland Premier
		Goldhawk Jasmine
	Tess of Woodbrook	Ch. Dukle
		Bess of Bronygarth
Ch. Ajax of Hellingly	Ch. Arolite	Duke of Sadberge
		Countess of Sadberge
	Lumbering Sheila of Hellingly	Ch. Blaise of Westcroft
		Lady Lydia of Hardingham
Sweet Memory	Grimshaw's Pride	Ch. Cedric of Ashenhurst
		Gillian
	Pinfold Beauty	Country Squire
		Battle Queen

Woodstock Lass of Manthorne, born January 22, 1937, Apricot Fawn. AKC Registration No. A154653. Bred by Hobart Titus. USA

Shanno of Lyme Hall, born August 2, 1940. USA

Angeles Tristam	Brian of Roxbroom	Roxbury Boy
		Broomcourt Nell
	Goldhawk Elsie	Sioux Chief
		Tess of Woodbrook
Merle's Brunhilda of Lyme Hall	Roxbury Boy	Ajax os Hellingly
		Sweet Memory
	Buzzard Pride	Comet Menai
		Judy Hellingly

	Generation 2	Generation 3	Generation 4
Withybush Magnus	O.E.M.C Heatherbelle Sterling Silver	King Rufus of Parkhurst	Emblem of Parkhurst
			Joy of Parkhurst
		Heatherbelle Lady Hyacinth	Shanno of Lyme Hall
			Merle's Tanna
	O.E.M.C Prudence	Valiant Diadem	Hector of Knockrivoch
			Valiant Cythera
		Nydia of Frithend	Templecombe Taurus
			Sally of Coldblow
Peach Farm Priscilla	Austin of Chaseway	Angeles President	Angeles King
			Rolanda
		Gwendolyn of Altnacraig	Aldwin of Altnacraig
			Kathleen of Hellingly
	Peach Farm Belinda	Hector of Knockrivoch	Eric of Altnacraig
			Glyn of Hammercliff
		Peach Farm Rosita	Manthorne Mogul
			Peach Farm Hugenot

Puppies whelped November 13, 1952. AKC Litter Registration No. WL-95355. Bred by Mrs. F.L. Weyenberg. USA

Goff's Leo	Wey Acres Tars	Withybush Magnus
		Peach Farm Priscilla
	Merle's Princess	Heatherbelle Priscilla's Leo
		Wey Acres Winnie
Merle's Puella	Merle's Alvin	Wey Acres Tars
		Merle's Princess
	Fidelle de Fenelon	Xohor de Fenelon
		Erine de Fenelon

Duncan of Windsor, July 20, 1962, Silver and Fawn. AKC No. WA301727. Bred by Merle F. Campbell. USA

Ch. Gulph Mills Mulcher, born 1981. USA

- Ch. Gulph Mills Mugger
  - Ch. Alexander of Dahlseide
    - Master of the Woods
      - Ch. Reveille Juggernaut
        - Am/Eng. Ch. Rhinehart of Blackroc
        - Ch. Mooreleigh Joyce
      - Allison of Devershem
        - Withybush Prashna of Zimapan
        - Robin of Havengore
    - Ch. Dahlseide Dame Dickens
      - Am. Eng. Ch. Falcon of Blackroc
        - Ch. Drake of Havengore
        - Gipsy of Havengore
      - Helena of Rainbow Mt.
        - Henry of Havengore
        - Greco's Heather
  - Ch. Massalane's Dinah-Might
    - Ch. Nemo of Massalane
      - Douglas Little
        - Ch. Alexas of Avonwaters
        - Ch. Odette of Kisumu
      - Gasparilla Farms Margaret
        - Willowledge Albert
        - Werenhold Brunhilda
    - Ch. Bengali Tigress
      - Laurenlane's Eeyore
        - William Adams of Somerset
        - Greco's Heather
      - Copyline Elza Doolittle
        - Heatherbrook Keynes
        - Willowledge Velvet
- Ch. Greenbranch Macushla
  - Ch. Willowledge R. Eko-Jim Bill
    - Ch. Willowledge Knute
      - Ch. Paul of Conturo
        - Farrnaby Merrick
        - Saxondale Rebecca
      - Ch. Raven of Blackroc
        - Ch. Drake of Havengore
        - Gipsy of Havengore
    - Ch. Brookmoor's Taffy Jane
      - Ch. Nelson of Hollesley
        - Ch. Weatherhill Thor
        - Lenora of Hollesley
      - K.J. Havengore Candy
        - Bowat's Roar & Rumble of Corgeen
        - Frideswide Susan
  - Ch. Buckhall's Lady Macbeth
    - Buckhall Tarzan of Kismu
      - Ch. Threebees Friar of Copenore
        - Jason of Copenore
        - Cleopatra of Saxondale
      - Buckhalls Hannah of Kisumu
        - Beaucaris Marcus
        - Bracken of Kisumu
    - Priscilla of Buckhall
      - Master Winston of Buckhall
        - Ch. Threebees Friar of Copenore
        - Mistress Alice of Copenore
      - Mistress Helen of Buckhall
        - Threebees Beowulf Buckhall
        - Buckhall Rillamill Cassandra

Orlando of Wingfield	Weland 25.9.1919	Adamite	Count William
			Adams Lass
		Gascoigne Queen	Duke of Heatherville 1910
			Cleveland Belle
	Princess Mary	Priam of Wingfield 1915	Prince Lie A Bed
			Eva 1912
		Parkgate Duchess	Broderick Defender
			Leonsha 1911
Eanfleda of Wingfield	Weland	Adamite	Count William
			Adams Lass
		Gascoigne Queen	Duke of Heatherville
			Cleveland Belle
	Gwenf Ra of Wingfield	Priam of Wingfield 1915	Prince Lie a Bed
			Eva 1912
		Mary of Knollwood	Wodin the Saxon
			Princess Mary

Rightmost generation (great-great-grandparents):

- Count William → Duke of Heatherville / Lusitania
- Adams Lass → Adam / Lady Godiva
- Duke of Heatherville 1910 → Ch. Felix / Oscott Shielah
- Cleveland Belle → Duke of Heatherville / Dam Unknown
- Prince Lie A Bed → Bayardo / Minerva
- Eva 1912 → Brindled Prince / Ch. Brompton Duchess
- Broderick Defender → Cleveland Leopold / Felicia
- Leonsha 1911 → Brindled Prince / Lady Widmere
- Count William → Duke of Heatherville / Lusitania
- Adams Lass → Adam / Lady Godiva
- Duke of Heatherville → Ch. Felix / Oscott Shielah
- Cleveland Belle → Duke of Heatherville / Dam Unknown
- Prince Lie a Bed → Bayardo / Minerva
- Eva 1912 → Brindled Prince / Ch. Bromton Duchess
- Wodin the Saxon → Conrad of Wingfield / Boadicea of Wingfield
- Princess Mary → Priam of Wingfield / Parkgate Duchess

Betty-C, born 1929. Canada

Pedigree of **Fidelle De Fenelon, born July 18, 1956. France**

Generation 1	Generation 2	Generation 3	Generation 4	Generation 5
Xohor de Fenelon 28, April, 1949	V'Pach 24, October, 1947	Tim x	Bonzo de Bordeaux 30, May, 1932	Bordeaux IV, 28, May, 1929
				Beaute II x, 3, Oct, 1930
			Zaza II de Bordeaux	Diamant x, 5, May, 1925
				Poupee x, 25, June, 1923
		Urah x	Bonzo de Bordeaux 20, May, 1932	Bordeaux IV, 28, May, 1929
				Olga x
			Poupee II de Bordeaux 6, April, 1930	Sigur II x, 30, Sep, 1930
				Mina de Belsigur, 13, Jan, 1933
	Sara x 10, September, 1944	Negus D'Hauptoul 27, January, 1939	Kaid x 16, June, 1936	Hussard x, 4, Dec, 1933
				Gamine II x, 18, Apr, 1932
			Java x 28, April, 1935	
		Ora x 1937	Negus D'Hauptoul 27, January, 1939	Brutus x, 1, May, 1932
				Rosy x, 1934
			La Creole x 15, July, 1937	
Erine de Fenelon 3, September, 1955	Bouddha de Bethsaida 12, October, 1952	Viborg de La Fon de Ce 22, June, 1947	Sam Du Cerbere 6, June, 1944	Sultan de Bordeaux
				Quessy du Cerbere, 7, May, 1942
			Ste Judith du Cerbere 6, June, 1944	Sultan de Bordeaux
				Quessy du Cerbere, 7, May, 1942
		X'Venus Du Cap Maure 11, May, 1949	Volcan x 23, April, 1947	Urus x
				Una x
			Venus du Cerbere 11, August, 1957	Sam du Cerbere, 6, June, 1944
				Scarlette du Cerbere, 6, June, 1944
	Dolphye de Fenelon 25, August, 1954	Xohor de Fenelon 28, April, 1949	Tim x	Bonzo de Bordeaux
				Zaza II de Bordeaux
			Urah x	Bonzo de Bordeaux
				Poupee II de Bordeaux
		Wlan de Fenelon 28, October, 1948	Urson de Fenelon 31, December, 1946	Sam du Cerbere, 6, June, 1944
				Sara x, 10, September, 1944
			Ukase Utine de Fenelon 15, May, 1946	Oural x
				Sara x, 10, September, 1944

Appendix II

Kennel Names and Prefixes

The United Kingdom
Prior to 1940

It must be remembered that before the First World War very few prefixes (kennel names) were used because the dogs were being registered with a simple name. Exceptions were Cleveland (Mr. H. Cook, Senior), Haselmere (Mr. Robert Leadbetter) and Ilford.

After the First World War, many Mastiff breeders still did not have a registered prefix; Miss Bell, Mr. Illingworth, Mr. Guy Greenwood and Mr. F. Bowles, all well known and respected, are names that come to mind. Mr. Greenwood's dogs were sometimes called the Hillcrest Mastiffs, after his house, but the dogs themselves rejoiced in a variety of names.

Of these four people, Miss Bell and Mr. Bowles were both extremely active after the Second World War, and soon after the cessation of hostilities Miss Bell registered the prefix Withybush. Mr. Bowles took the name Mansatta, from the prefix of the two American dogs on which he founded his post-war kennel. He was one of the breeders who had exported his animals to America in the immediate pre-war period.

The names given below were those in use in the 1920-1940 period, but many Mastiffs were still being bred, as they had always been, without a specific registered kennel name.

Cleveland	Mr. H. Cook (son of the elder Cook)
Benton	Mr. H. C. Liddell
Westcroft	Mrs. C. Kennett
Delaval	Mrs. W. M. Edgar
Broomcourt	Mr. B. Bennett
Menai	Messrs R. Thomas and C. Oliver
Tiddicar	Mr. H. Crook
Saxondale	Mr. and Mrs. H. Taylor
Hellingly	Mrs. E. G. Oliver
Goldhawk	Mrs. F. J. Hawkins
Iledon	Mrs. Woods
Parcwood	Mrs. M. Hector
Goring	Mrs. N. Dickin
Trelyon	Mrs. J. H. Thomas
Havengore	Mr. L. Scheerboom

Kennel names that are no longer active - 1950 to present

I give below a list of those which are no longer active; some because of the death of their owners, others because they have left the breed. Many, such as Copenore, Blackroc, Withybush, Buckhall, Havengore, Hollesley, etc. were of great importance, others less so, but all played their part. The following covers the period 1950 to date, a period of over 50 years.

Alcama	Prosser
Andwell	Coan
Avonwaters	Pyke
Balclutha	Smith
Bannwater	Blackwell/Barham
Bardayle	Anderson
Belbeck	Easy
Bellabees	Ede
Blackrock	Hanson
Bonners	Williams
Bournewood	Denton
Buckhall	Reardon
Caemes	Phillips
Canonbury	Shorter
Celerity	Norfolk
Clochodrick	Jagielko
Coopell	Elsworthy
Copenore	Lindley
Cornhaye	Roberts
Craig Goch	Lewis
Damaria	Joynes
Dawnstar	Mantle
Devaro	Burton
Fanifold	Mayne
Forefoot	Cowe
Frideswide	Monostori
Glynpedr	Boatwright
Grangemoor	Degerdon
Havengore	Scheerboom
Hollesley	Day
Honeycroft	Atkinson
Hubbadane	Bulloch
Inniscorrig	Stamper

Jakote	Corbett
Jilgrajon	Hicks
Kisumu	Creigh
Lesdon	Baxter
Lisken	Brett
Mansatta	Bowles
Melrock	Furnival
Meps	Perrenoud
Moorgrove	Brett
Mountkora	Kerr
Nandina	Evans
Nantymynydd	Davies
OEMC	
Ormondstow	Critchley
Overnoons	How
Oxhaege	Cooper
Ragtime	Alcock
Rhossnessney	Mercer
Ritonshay	Parrott
Rousillon	Latta
Sallymass	Vobe
Shute	Harris
Sparry	Aberdeen
Sylvadown	Barton
Trevabyn	Sargeant
Weatherhill	Allison
Withybush	Bell
Zilgul	Curzon

Kennel names still active – 1950 to present

Ankerston	Anderson
Apolin	Richardson
Beezaville	Attfield and Taylor
Bournewood	Denton
Bredwardine	Thomas and Tugwell
Brookview	Seager
Bulliff	Say
Cadermist	Simister
Cedwalla	Chidwick
Chevelu	Duval
Cennenpedr	Davies

Coinmor	Chell
Darkling	Ridley
Delbeech	Beech
Domas	Griffin
Elisgrai	Higgs
Faerdorn	Harvey
Falmorehall	Windham
Farnaby	Baxter
Faynad	Zadeh
Fearnaught	Payne
Fitsam	Ledwards
Gildasan	Robson-Jones
Heffalump	Dodd
Helmlake	Le Mare
Jengren	Green
Kingrock	Thomas and Godfrey
Klanzmun	Knight
Kufema	Cooper
Kumormai	Knight
Leyfarm	Shaw
Marcolian	Golightly
Masnou	Sylvia Blaxter
Maskett	Kett
Massaluv	Collinson
Namous	David Blaxter
Penrichlar	Ratti
Quixhill	H. Sargeant
Prixcan	Manfredi
Saltcountry	Steele
Santmichal	Rischmiller
Terheath	Johnson
Tregambo	G. Sargeant

The United States of America
Kennel names prior to 1930

English kennel names were freely used: dogs descended from Ilford, for example, were given that prefix. Many breeders did not use a kennel name: Charles Bunn, Forest Martin, Herbert Mead, C. A. Lougest, William Wade. J. L. Winchell often used the prefix Beaufort but other breeders also used this prefix. The only way to find a breeder in most cases is by checking the pedigree.

Ashmont	J. Frank Perry, Massachusetts
Beech Grove	George Jackson, Indiana
Berkshire	P. Amidon, New Hampshire
Caumsett	Richard Derby, New York
Day	James Day, Connecticut
Elm Place	L. D. Ely, New York
Flower (Flour) City	James Whitney, New York
Gillivan	George Gillivan, Ohio
Heywood	J. B. Heywood, Indiana
Ingleside	George Glazier, Massachusetts
Kinnelon	Morris Kinney, New Jersey
Melrose	E. H. Moore, Massachusetts
Monmouth	Charles E. Wallack
Orleans	Septimus Villere, Louisiana
Richland	W. W. Bradley, North Dakota
Sans Souci	Sans Souci Farms, South Carolina
Wacouta	Wacouta Kennels, Minnesota and New York
Webster	George Webster, Wisconsin
Wingfield	C. W. Dickinson, Canada
Winlawn	W. P. Stevenson, New York

Kennel names 1930 - 1950

Many breeders did not use a kennel name. Wayne Alter, Indiana, seldom used "Alter's". Harry Peters, Ohio, never had a prefix.

Altnacraig	Jane and James Foster Clark, Connecticut
Angeles	Dr. Harry Veach, California
Baskerville	Mrs. G. A. Hedfors, New York
Chaseway	William W. Chase, New York
Donaghmore	Walter Gabler
Griffin	Edwin L. Griffin, Washington
Hampshire	Paul K. Hampshire
Hampden	Karl Bissell, Connecticut
Heatherbelle	Mr. and Mrs. H. W. Mellish, Canada
Knockrivoch	John H. Leitch, Pennsylvania
Mansatta	Mr. and Mrs. Walter Frick
Manthorne	Col. P. H. Titus, Massachusetts
Merle's	Merle Campbell, Oregon
Montrose	Robert G. Wahn
Peach Farm	Martha Brill, Delaware
Roxbury/Deleval	Charles Ackerman, California

| Valiant | Robert B. Burn, Connecticut |
| Wey Acres | Helen Weyenberg, Wisconsin |

Kennel names of the 1950's
Donaghmore	R. and G. Patch
Greco	Mrs. Frank Greco
Mooreleigh	Marie A. Moore
Willowledge	S. and E. Olsen

Kennel names of the 1960's
Ballyherugh	G. and J. Danaher
Bowat	R. E. and J. Parker
Carinthia	Mrs. J. F. Hoffman
Dahlseide	Lois Savage
Gar Star	P. and E. Gaar
Greenbrier	E. and B. Funk
Love Creek	R. and D. Lissner
Rainbow Mountain	H. L. Newbold
Reveille	Adelaide Bolté
Roco	D. and C. Cole
Titan	Zita Deviny
Werenhold	R. and M. Kross
Windsor	C. and R. Strong

Kennel names 1970 - 1980
The Abbey	E. Dickey
Acadian	E. Howard
Alpenhoff	E. and J. Poor
Arborcrest	S. and M. Dollin
Banyon	J. and M. Zellen
Berngarth	E. Mitchell (Canada)
Blackheath	B. Simmons
Blacknight	L. Knight
Caledonia	W. and P. Armstrong
Canterbury	J. Kessler
Chancelot	V. Head
Classic's	T. and A. Gomez
Deer Run	T. Jackson
Diablo	C. Medinas
Ganarew	D. Smith
Greenbranch	E. Gerace

Grenveldt	A. Tinsley
Gulph Mills	M. and D. Gensburger
Indian Raid	R. Castellane
Jopay	J. and P. Fromm
Kingsborough	J. Blackwell
Kon Hall	M. Benolken
Lazy Hill	V. Bregman
Le Mar	B. Fontaine
Lockhart	A. LaCorte
Lyndon	D. and L. Urban
Massalane	A. Ficarotta
Montrose	A. Jacobson
Nanjay	L. and N. Ogden
Navonod	W. Donovan
Oak Ridge	Mrs. W. Powers
Oranshire	M. DiBona
Palaceguard	W. Blair
Peersleigh	R. and J. Guy
Ramblewood	S. Martin
Ram's Gate	J. Nash
Renrock	W. Newman
Rumblin Eko	C. Fitzgerald
Sanobar	R. and S. Buntaine
Scarey Creek	S. Lyons
Shire	M. and K. Freeman
Stonehedge	A. Garutti
Tamarack	C. Knutson
Thunderhill	G. Wallace (Canada)
Traymatt	B. Steinberg
Verdune	D. Edwards
Walnut Creek	Mrs. F. Bushnell
Wayside	D. Thornsbrough
Willow Point	B. and M. Chapman
Windamohr	J. and R. Mohr
Winterwood/Bankhouse	P. Goold
Wodemore	T. and A. Grittinger
Wyldewood	S. McGarity
Yorkstone	E. Ferris

With the enormous growth of the breed, and the number of breeders that come and go, kennel names from 1980 on are not included.

APPENDIX III

Weights and Measures
Some weights recorded by Patricia Bennett Hoffman

Bitch puppy at			
	7 weeks	14 lb.	N/A
	13 weeks	45 lb.	height 19½ inches
	17 weeks	59 lb.	height 22 inches
	20 weeks	66 lb.	N/A
	22 weeks	75 lb.	height 24 inches
	At 11 months	135 lb.	height 27 inches

		male	female
Littermates at:	7 weeks	14 lb.	11 lb.
	10 weeks	19 lb.	16 lb.
	17 weeks	45 lb.	38 lb.

	Birth	1 week	2 weeks	4 weeks	11 weeks
M	1½ lb.	2½ lb.	4 lb.	8 ¼ lb.	33½ lb.
F	1½ lb.	2½ lb.	4 lb.	8 ¼ lb.	26½ lb.
F	1 ¾ lb.	3 lb.	4 lb.	8 ¼ lb.	26½ lb.
F	1½ lb.	1 ¾ lb.	3 ¼ lb.	6 ¼ lb.	25½ lb.

	Birth	1 week	2 weeks	6 weeks
F	1lb.	2 lb. 13 oz.	4½ lb.	13½ lb.
M	1 lb.	1 lb. 14 oz.	2 ¾ lb.	13½ lb.
F	8 oz.	*(died at 3 days)*		
F	15 oz.	2 lb. 4 oz.	3 ¾ lb.	13½ lb.
F	1 ¼ lb.	3 lb.	4½ lb.	13½ lb.
M	1 ¼ lb.	3 lb.	4½ lb.	12½ lb.

Gensburger Weight Chart

Birth order	1	2	3	4	5	6
Sex	male	male	male	female	male	male
Color	fawn	brindle	apricot	brindle	brindle	brindle
Birth wt/lbs	1	1.1	1.4	1.2	1.4	1.5
Week 1	2.2	2.3	2.2	2.5	2.6	2.8
Week 2	3.9	3.8	3.4	3.14	3.11	3.11
Week 3	4.10	4.12	4.10	5.10	5.2	5.1
Week 4	7.0	7.10	7.2	8.9	7.5	7.8
Week 6	12.15	13.8	13.5	14.14	14.2	13.4
Week 7	15.12	17.15	17.5	18.12	18.10	16.4
Week 8	20	22.3	Sold	23.1	22.4	19.12
Week 9	24.4	25.8		Sold	27.3	23.10
Week 10	29.5	30			32	29
Week 11	Sold	35			36	34
Week 12		Sold			40	Sold

Mr. Gensburger contributed the following composite of ten litters:

Average litter size: 8.5 puppies
Average birth weight: 1.6 pounds

Week 1	1.8	lbs.
Week 2	3.3	lbs.
Week 3	4.2	lbs.
Week 4	7.0	lbs.
Week 5	7.6	lbs.
Week 6	11.9	lbs.
Week 7	15.1	lbs.
Week 8	20.6	lbs.

Of the ten litters, the smallest was two puppies and the largest was 12.

Our most grateful thanks to Mike Gensburger of the Mastiff Club of America for permission to use the previous weight chart. Mr. Gensburger, however, emphasised that the size of the puppy has little relation to its size when mature as often the largest puppy in a litter will be the smallest adult, or vice versa. P.B.H.

I too would also like to thank Mike Gensburger for this chart. The only comment I would make is that I have found pups at birth normally to be between 1 1b. 8 oz. and 1 lb. 12 oz. but the weights they attain at 6, 8 and 12 weeks are almost identical to the weights shown for those ages on this chart. E.J.B.

For comparison, figures for important dogs in the 1880's

Weight   Height

		Weight	Height
"Sylvia III"	(2 years old)	136 lb.	29½ inches
"His Lordship"	(1 year 10 months)	180 lb.	23 inches
"Creole"	(4 years old)	120 lb.	29 inches
"Rupert"	(3½ years)	170 lb.	31½ inches
"Beaufort"	(No age given)	165 lb.	29½ inches
"Jack Thyr"	(No age given)	156 lb.	28½ inches
"Wodan"	(No age given)	160 lb.	30 inches
"Orlando"	(No age given)	172 lb.	29 inches
"Hotspur"	(No age given)	140 lb.	28 inches
"Lady Gladys"	(No age given)	128 lb.	26 inches
"Lady Isabel"	(No age given)	135 lb.	27 inches

(From ASH: Dogs, Their History and Development, Houghton Mifflin, Boston c. 1927)

APPENDIX IV

Titles awarded by the American Kennel Club (Only those applicable to Mastiffs are listed.)

Conformation
Ch.   Champion of Record
Obedience
C.D.   Companion Dog
C.D.X.   Companion Dog Excellent
U.D.   Utility Dog
U.D.X.   Utility Dog Excellent
OTCH   Obedience Trial Champion
Tracking
T.D.   Tracking Dog
T.D.X.   Tracking Dog Excellent
V.S.T.   Variable Surface Tracking
C.T.   Champion Tracker
                       (Must have TD, TDX, and VST)
Obedience/Tracking
(For dogs that have earned titles in both disciplines)
U.D.T.   Utility Dog Tracking Dog
U.D.T.X.   Utility Dog Tracking Dog Excellent
U.D.X.T.D.X   Utility Dog Excellent Tracking Dog Excellent
U.D.V.S.T.   Utility Dog Variable Surface Tracking
U.D.X.V.S.T   Utility Dog Excellent Variable Surface Tracking
Agility
N.A.   Novice Agility
O.A.   Open Agility
A.X.   Agility Excellent
M.X.   Master Agility Excellent
Miscellaneous
C.G.C.   Canine Good Citizen
Other Non-AKC Titles
T.T.   Temperament Tested
T.D.I   Therapy Dog International
W.D.   Working Dog
                       (Offered by the national breed club)

APPENDIX V
Resources and Bibliography

While books, magazines and other publications still provide Mastiff fanciers with breed information, the Internet is also becoming a very useful tool in that regard. If you are not among the "computer literate", think of the Internet as an electronic post office (for e-mail), as well as a vast collection of interconnected, cross-referenced, electronic libraries (websites), created and accessed by people from all over the world. If you have a personal computer with Internet access you can find information on just about anything with a few simple clicks of a "mouse".

Many Mastiff enthusiasts who have questions or comments about Mastiffs (or want to brag about the accomplishments of their own dogs) are taking part in Mastiff-related Internet mailing lists. These are basically electronic discussion groups. Once you subscribe to one of these mailing lists, you can "post" your remarks by sending e-mail to the mailing list address. Anyone else who has subscribed to the same mailing list can then read those remarks, and perhaps publicly comment on them by making "posts" of their own. A series of posts on the same topic is known as a "thread" – and some of the threads can get quite lengthy and heated!

Most of the websites you will find pertaining to Mastiffs are related to the promotion of individual kennels. A number of these websites are grouped together into "webrings". Once inside a webring, you can click "next" or "previous" to go to adjacent sites in the ring – eventually ending up where you started.

Other Mastiff websites are more general in nature. The Mastiff Club of America maintains its own website, where people can find out about various aspects of Mastiffs and the club. One of this website's many "links" is the MCOA FAQ. "FAQ" stands for "frequently-asked questions". MCOA's Internet FAQ provides answers to what breeders consider are the most frequently asked questions they receive from potential Mastiff owners. MCOA also maintains its own webring of Mastiff websites developed by MCOA members.

Another of the most well known Mastiff websites is the Mastiff Stud Dog Register Online, which was developed by MCOA member Deb Jones, the creator of the printed version of the Mastiff Stud Dog Register. Breeders are able to list their stud dogs and make litter announcements on this website, reaching a global audience. There are also links to numerous articles – primarily written by Mastiff breeders – on a variety of Mastiff related topics.

Ash, Edward, C., *Dogs—Their History and Development* (2 vols.), Houghton Mifflin Co., Boston and New York, 1927.

British Sportsman's Dictionary, 1792.

Caius, *Of Englishe Dogges.* Reprint of 1575 ed., Denlinger, Washington, D.C. (n.d.).

Compton, Herbert (ed.), *The Twentieth Century Dog (Non-Sporting),* Vol. I, Grant Richards, London, 1904.

Croxton-Smith, A., *British Dogs,* Collins, London, 1947.

Dakers, Andrew, *Dogs Since 1900,* London, 1950.

Dalziel, Hugh, *British Dogs* (2 vols.); L. Upcott Gill, London (n.d.).

Dickin, Norah, *The Mastiff,* 1935.

Dictionary of Middle English, Ann Arbor, Michigan.

Drury, W. D. (ed.), *British Dogs* (2 vols.), L. Upcott Gill, London, Third Edition (n.d.).

Hubbard, Clifford L. B., *Dogs in Britain,* Macmillan, London, 1948.

Hutchinson, Walter (ed.), *Hutchinson's Dog Encyclopedia,* 1937.

Idstone, *The Dog,* Cassell, Petter, Galpin, London, 1871.

Keller, Helen, *The Story of My Life,* Doubleday, New York, 1954.

Lee, Rawdon B., *Modern Dogs (Non-Sporting,* Horace Cox, London, 1894.

Leighton, Robert, *Cassell's New Book of the Dog* (4 vols.), Waverley Book Co., London, 1907).

Mason, Charles H., *Our Prize Dogs,* Forest and Stream Publishers, N.Y., 1888.

Moore, Marie Antoinette, *The Mastiff,* Denlinger, Fairfax, Virginia, 1978.

Oliver, E. G., *The Mastiff in the Eighteenth Century.* Reprinted from "The Kennel Gazette" June, 1936.

Shaw, Vero, *Book of the Dog,* Cassell, London,1879-81.

Shields, G. O. (ed.), *American Book of the Dog,* Rand, McNally, Chicago, Ill., 1891.

Stonehenge, *The Dogs of Great Britain, America and Other Countries,* O. Judd Co., New York, 1887.

Turner, J. Sidney (ed.), *Kennel Encyclopaedia* (4 vols.), London, 1910.

Vesey-Fitzgerald, Brian, *The Book of the Dog,* Nicholson and Watson, London, 1948.

Watson, James, *The Dog Book,* Doubleday, Page, New York, 1906,

Webb, Henry (ed.), *Dogs: Their Points, Whims, Instincts and Peculiarities,* Dean and Son, London 1875(?).

Wynn, M. B., *The History of the Mastiff,* William Loxley, Melton Mowbray, 1886.

PERIODICALS (U.K.)
Our Dogs, 1930 onwards.
The Kennel Club Breed Supplement.
The Kennel Club *Stud Book.*
OEMC Newsletters.
The Kennel Gazette.

PERIODICALS (USA)
American Kennel Club *Stud Book.*
American Kennel Club *Gazette.*
American Kennel Register.
Century Magazine.
Dog World (U.S.).
The American Field.
Harper's New Monthly Magazine.
Popular Dogs.
Mastiff Club of America Newsletter.
Midwest Mastiff Fanciers Newsletter.
Southern States, Mastiff Fanciers Newsletter.

About the Authors

Elizabeth J. Baxter of England is the owner of the well-known Farnaby Kennels. Betty's interest in the breed started with her grandfather, Norman Higgs, a well-known 19th century breeder, a founder of the Old English Mastiff Club and author. Since 1963 she has bred and shown many champions and Mastiffs from her kennel have won honours worldwide. She judges dogs internationally and is a frequent contributor to canine and breed periodicals.

Patricia Bennett Hoffman of the United States acquired her first Mastiff in 1961. Although she bred on a very limited scale, her Carinthia kennel name shows up in many pedigrees. Mrs. Hoffman has written extensively on dogs and for many years reviewed books for the AKC Gazette. She is also the co-author of a book on Border Terriers and is a free-lance writer.